Cultural Production and Participatory Politics

This book addresses the conceptual lapse in the literature regarding the relationship between cultural production and participatory politics by examining their connections in a range of national and political contexts.

Each chapter examines how youth engage cultural production as part of their political participation, and how political participation is sometimes central to, and expressed through, cultural production. The contributing authors provide examples of the intersections between youth cultural production and participatory politics and bring together a range of approaches to the examination of these intersections, providing illustrations of the complexities involved in these processes. Each of the chapters takes up different kinds of practices – from street art to video production, from online activism to installation work. They also examine a range of political contexts – from students striking at the University of Puerto Rico to activism in community arts centres and university classrooms. The book considers what becomes evident when close attention is paid to the intersection of cultural production and participatory politics: what does participatory politics help people to see about cultural production and how does cultural production expand how people understand participatory politics?

This book was originally published as a special issue of *Curriculum Inquiry*.

Rubén Gaztambide-Fernández is Professor at the Ontario Institute for Studies in Education, Canada, and Editor-in-chief of *Curriculum Inquiry*. He is Director of the Youth Research Lab and Principal Investigator of the Youth Solidarities Across Boundaries Project, a participatory action research project with Latinx and Indigenous youth in the city of Toronto, Canada. His theoretical work focuses on the relationship between creativity, decolonization, and solidarity.

Alexandra Arráiz Matute is Assistant Professor of Childhood and Youth Studies in the Institution for Interdisciplinary Studies at Carleton University, Canada. Her research and pedagogical interests lie at the intersections of identity, culture, race, migration, and (de)colonization. Her past research has focused on the importance of relationships in teaching and learning, as a site of healing and resistance for marginalized communities.

Cultural Production and Participatory Politics

Youth, Symbolic Creativity, and Activism

Edited by
Rubén Gaztambide-Fernández and
Alexandra Arráiz Matute

LONDON AND NEW YORK

First published 2020
by Routledge
2 Park Square, Milton Park, Abingdon, Oxon, OX14 4RN

and by Routledge
52 Vanderbilt Avenue, New York, NY 10017

Routledge is an imprint of the Taylor & Francis Group, an informa business

First issued in paperback 2021

Introduction, Chapters 2–7 © 2020 The Ontario Institute for Studies in Education

Chapter 1 © 2015 Mizuko Ito, Elisabeth Soep, Neta Kligler-Vilenchik, Sangita Shresthova, Liana Gamber-Thompson and Arely Zimmerman. Originally published as Open Access.

With the exception of Chapter 1, no part of this book may be reprinted or reproduced or utilised in any form or by any electronic, mechanical, or other means, now known or hereafter invented, including photocopying and recording, or in any information storage or retrieval system, without permission in writing from the publishers. For details on the rights for Chapter 1, please see the chapter's Open Access footnote.

Trademark notice: Product or corporate names may be trademarks or registered trademarks, and are used only for identification and explanation without intent to infringe.

British Library Cataloguing in Publication Data
A catalogue record for this book is available from the British Library

ISBN13: 978-0-367-26643-1 (hbk)
ISBN13: 978-1-03-209062-7 (pbk)

Typeset in Minion Pro
by Newgen Publishing UK

Publisher's Note
The publisher accepts responsibility for any inconsistencies that may have arisen during the conversion of this book from journal articles to book chapters, namely the inclusion of journal terminology.

Disclaimer
Every effort has been made to contact copyright holders for their permission to reprint material in this book. The publishers would be grateful to hear from any copyright holder who is not here acknowledged and will undertake to rectify any errors or omissions in future editions of this book.

Contents

Citation Information	vi
Notes on Contributors	viii

Introduction – Creation as participation/participation as creation:
Cultural production, participatory politics, and the intersecting lines
of identification and activism   1
Rubén Gaztambide-Fernández and Alexandra Arráiz Matute

1   Learning connected civics: Narratives, practices, infrastructures   10
*Mizuko Ito, Elisabeth Soep, Neta Kligler-Vilenchik, Sangita Shresthova,
Liana Gamber-Thompson and Arely Zimmerman*

2   New media literacies as social action: The centrality of pedagogy in the
politics of knowledge production   30
Korina M. Jocson

3   Public pedagogy in the creative strike: Destabilizing boundaries and
re-imagining resistance in the University of Puerto Rico   52
Melissa Rosario

4   Educating for cultural citizenship: Reframing the goals of arts education   69
Paul J. Kuttner

5   The art of youth rebellion   93
Nathalia E. Jaramillo

6   *Shooting back* in the occupied territories: An anti-colonial
participatory politics   109
Chandni Desai

7   Glyphing decolonial love through urban flash mobbing and *Walking
with our Sisters*   129
Karyn Recollet

Index   146

Citation Information

The chapters in this book were originally published in *Curriculum Inquiry*, volume 45, issue 1 (January 2015). When citing this material, please use the original page numbering for each article, as follows:

Editorial

Creation as participation/participation as creation: Cultural production, participatory politics, and the intersecting lines of identification and activism
Rubén Gaztambide-Fernández and Alexandra Arráiz Matute
Curriculum Inquiry, volume 45, issue 1 (January 2015) pp. 1–9

Chapter 1

Learning connected civics: Narratives, practices, infrastructures
Mizuko Ito, Elisabeth Soep, Neta Kligler-Vilenchik, Sangita Shresthova, Liana Gamber-Thompson and Arely Zimmerman
Curriculum Inquiry, volume 45, issue 1 (January 2015) pp. 10–29

Chapter 2

New media literacies as social action: The centrality of pedagogy in the politics of knowledge production
Korina M. Jocson
Curriculum Inquiry, volume 45, issue 1 (January 2015) pp. 30–51

Chapter 3

Public pedagogy in the creative strike: Destabilizing boundaries and re-imagining resistance in the University of Puerto Rico
Melissa Rosario
Curriculum Inquiry, volume 45, issue 1 (January 2015) pp. 52–68

Chapter 4

Educating for cultural citizenship: Reframing the goals of arts education
Paul J. Kuttner
Curriculum Inquiry, volume 45, issue 1 (January 2015) pp. 69–92

Chapter 5

The art of youth rebellion
Nathalia E. Jaramillo
Curriculum Inquiry, volume 45, issue 1 (January 2015) pp. 93–108

Chapter 6

Shooting back *in the occupied territories: An anti-colonial participatory politics*
Chandni Desai
Curriculum Inquiry, volume 45, issue 1 (January 2015) pp. 109–128

Chapter 7

Glyphing decolonial love through urban flash mobbing and Walking with our Sisters
Karyn Recollet
Curriculum Inquiry, volume 45, issue 1 (January 2015) pp. 129–145

For any permission-related enquiries please visit:
www.tandfonline.com/page/help/permissions

Notes on Contributors

Alexandra Arráiz Matute is Assistant Professor of Childhood and Youth Studies in the Institution for Interdisciplinary Studies at Carleton University, Canada. Her research and pedagogical interests lie at the intersections of identity, culture, race, migration, and (de)colonization. Her past research has focused on the importance of relationships in teaching and learning, as a site of healing and resistance for marginalized communities.

Chandni Desai is an Assistant Professor in the Equity Studies Program at the University of Toronto, Canada. Her areas of research and teaching include comparative settler colonialisms, capitalist imperialism, the politics of the Middle East, state violence (carceral politics, militarism, and war), cultural resistance, global liberation and revolution, anti-racism, feminism, youth activism, solidarity, and decolonization.

Liana Gamber-Thompson is a Postdoctoral Research Associate with the Media, Activism and Participatory Politics project at the University of Southern California, USA. Her fields of interest include popular culture, identity and authenticity, and gender and feminism.

Rubén Gaztambide-Fernández is Professor at the Ontario Institute for Studies in Education, Canada, and Editor-in-chief of *Curriculum Inquiry*. He is Director of the Youth Research Lab and Principal Investigator of the Youth Solidarities Across Boundaries Project, a participatory action research project with Latinx and Indigenous youth in the city of Toronto, Canada. His theoretical work focuses on the relationship between creativity, decolonization, and solidarity.

Mizuko Ito is Professor in Residence and MacArthur Foundation Chair in Digital Media in Learning at the University of California, Irvine, USA. She is a cultural anthropologist specializing in learning and new media, particularly among young people in Japan and the USA.

Nathalia E. Jaramillo is Professor of Interdisciplinary Studies and Deputy Chief Diversity Officer at Kennesaw State University, USA. She has written extensively in the fields of politics of education and decolonial thought.

Korina M. Jocson is an Associate Professor of Social Justice Education at the College of Education at the University of Massachusetts-Amherst, USA. Central to her work are arts-informed sociocultural approaches that examine youth literacies and issues of equity among historically marginalized youth.

Neta Kligler-Vilenchik is an Assistant Professor in the Department of Communication and Journalism at The Hebrew University of Jerusalem, Israel. Her research focuses on youth civic and political participation in the context of the changing media environment.

She was previously a Researcher with the Media, Activism and Participatory Politics project at the University of Southern California, USA.

Paul J. Kuttner is Associate Director at University Neighborhood Partners, University of Utah, where he builds community-university partnerships to advance educational equity and justice. As an engaged scholar, Paul's research focuses on culturally sustaining civic engagement and reimagining relationships between educational institutions and communities.

Karyn Recollet is an Assistant Professor in the Women and Gender Studies Institute at the University of Toronto, Canada. Her research explores Indigenous performance, youth studies, Indigenous hip hop feminism, and gender studies.

Melissa Rosario is a Postdoctoral Fellow in Anthropology and Latin American Studies at Bowdoin College, USA, and a Visiting Assistant Professor at Wesleyan University, USA. She is interested in embodied knowledge, public space, and the micropolitics of resistance.

Sangita Shresthova is the Director of Henry Jenkins' Media, Activism and Participatory Politics project at the University of Southern California, USA. Her work focuses on the intersection between popular culture, performance, new media, politics, and globalization.

Elisabeth Soep is Research Director and Senior Producer at Youth Radio (a national youth-driven production company in Oakland, California, USA), where she founded the Innovation Lab in partnership with Massachusetts Institute of Technology, and where she collaborates with young people on stories for broadcast and digital outlets including National Public Radio.

Arely Zimmerman is an Assistant Professor in the Department of Ethnic Studies at Mills College, USA. Her interests include politics of identity (race, ethnicity, gender, sexuality), immigrant civic engagement and political participation, social movements and protest politics, migration and transnationalism, and Latin American/Latino politics.

Dedication

This book is dedicated to the memory of our dear colleague Dr. Greg Dimitriadis (August 27, 1969 – December 29, 2014). Greg was an indefatigable advocate for youth and his intellectual work provided our cornerstone to the foundation of contemporary urban youth studies and cultural production. He will be remembered as a dedicated scholar and a remarkable friend and human being.

Introduction – Creation as participation/participation as creation
Cultural production, participatory politics, and the intersecting lines of identification and activism

Rubén Gaztambide-Fernández and Alexandra Arráiz Matute

We write this editorial on the heels of troubling juridical manifestations of pervasive institutional racism in the United States of America – the dismissal of charges against two White police officers, Darren Wilson and Daniel Pantaleo, for the separate murders of two unarmed Black men, Michael Brown, in Ferguson, Missouri, and Eric Garner, in New York City, respectively. Meanwhile, Israeli Prime Minister Benjamin Netanyahu introduced "Jewish nation-state" legislation that would effectively legalize discrimination against non-Jewish citizens by limiting their right to self-determination. In Canada, the murder and disappearance of Indigenous women continues to make news, even as the state refuses to recognize that the pattern is evidence of continued violence of the white supremacist settler colonial state.

While state officials like Prime Minister Stephen Harper may believe that such instances of violence should be viewed as individual crimes and not "as a sociological phenomenon" (Boutilier, 2014), people on the streets beg to differ. Indeed, if the growth and success of the Idle No More movement in Canada and abroad is any indication, there is widespread agreement, at least among Indigenous peoples and their allies, that the otherwise inexplicable murder rate of Indigenous women only makes sense as a symptom of the violence of a settler colonial project based on sexism and racist ideology (Smith, 2005; Simpson, 2014; Sium, 2013). The same is true if we are to make sense not only of the grand jury decisions in both the Brown and Garner murder cases, but of the innumerable instances of police brutality against Black men, who are killed by police at a disproportionate rate when compared to the general population (Johnson, Hoyer, & Heath, 2014; Chang, 2014; Gabrielson, Grochowski Jones, & Sagara, 2014). Racism and settler colonialism also intersect through daily violence in the nation building project of the Israeli state, where illegal settlements and military actions that have been widely sanctioned by the international community continue unabated.

To such forms of state-sponsored violence, people respond through a wide range of means, some passively and others more actively. The latter, active engagement in political participation, has been a primary concern for educators and education scholars for some time, particularly for educators committed to notions of citizenship and civic participation who suggest that by some accounts such participation appears to be declining, particularly among young people (Kahne & Westheimer, 2006; Macedo et al., 2005). And yet, if the public outcry in response to the examples listed above and other recent manifestations against state violence across the globe—from Hong Kong to Mexico, from Egypt to Chile — is any indication, political engagement is alive and well in today's globalized and digitally mediated world.

What is clear, however, is that how people participate in politics today looks very different from the days when voting and writing letters to parliament or congress seemed like a good enough way to influence public life. Today, corporations and wealthy elites yield an inordinate amount of influence on both electoral politics and public policy (Gilens & Page, 2014). This has the effect of undermining traditional forms of participation, by delaying and shifting accountability and allowing the state — literally and figuratively — to get away with murder. While marches and other forms of protest have strong historical precedent, the present conditions have also forced the various publics to find other means of expressing their opinions and attempting to shape the conditions that impact their own communities and families.

One way in which communities express their opinions as well as confront the violence of social and political oppression is by engaging different modes for producing and disseminating cultural artifacts and exchanging ideas through symbolic and expressive means. In response to the failure of the state to indict the police officers that killed Michael Brown and Eric Garner, for example, spoken word artist Daniel J. Watts collaborated with 100 theater professionals in New York City to produce a flash mob in front of an NYPD station in Times Square, titled "This is how we shoot back" (https://www.you tube.com/watch?v=FpfTos6NroM). And according to author Chandni Desai (in this issue), shooting back is precisely what Palestinian youth are doing with their video cameras when they produce documentation of the violence perpetrated by Israel in their villages as a way to "participate" through forms of resistance. Such resistance is also often a form of what Anishinaabe scholar Gerald Vizenor (2008) calls "survivance" as it is manifested through the many cultural practices that have been central to the Idle No More movement in Canada, from walking, to drumming, chanting, and forms of visual art that give substance and life to political participation (http://www.idlenomore.ca/).

Of course, expressive and symbolic modes that draw on cultural production practices are not new to political participation. The singing of spirituals, for example, was central to the U.S. civil rights movement from its very beginnings, and cultural resistance has been central to anti-colonial movements throughout the 20th century across the globe, from Palestine to Puerto Rico, from South Africa to Taiwan. Yet, the analysis of cultural production within the context of political protest and participation has often treated these modes of expression as vehicles for communicating ideas rather than as forms of political participation in their own right. As new technologies transform the ways in which people express themselves and communicate with each other, it is increasingly important to understand the relationship between participatory politics and cultural production. This is critical if we are to take seriously the question of how educational projects of various kinds and in various settings may promote and support new modes of political engagement through youth cultural production.

This lack of attention to the relationship between cultural production and participatory politics is particularly striking when we consider that at least since the 1970s cultural studies scholars have examined the significance of cultural production in daily life. The early focus on youth "resistance" framed cultural production primarily through the lens of antagonisms with dominant culture (Hall & Jefferson, 1976; Hebdige, 1979). This focus became more layered by the work of scholars who paid attention to dynamics of gender and race in particular (Gilroy, 1991; McRobie, 1993). Later, scholars like Paul Willis (1990, 2003) moved toward a more nuanced attention to daily practices and "grounded aesthetics." Even more recently, others have provided examinations of cultural negotiation (Dimitriadis, 2009), embodiment (Maira, 2000), and affect (Muñoz, 2000), paying attention to interactions between the local and the transnational (Maira & Soep, 2004). In all, these scholars have provided significant insight into the role of cultural production in processes of identification and subject formation and how youth negotiate the symbolic and material conditions that shape their lives. Based on this work, cultural production can be conceptualized as any form of creative and symbolic exchange that arranges and/or rearranges available materials through cultural practices in order to express, create, and recreate ideas, feelings, and various aspects of cultural life. For Gaztambide-Fernández (2013), cultural production refers "to the broader landscape of cultural practices, processes, and products that may or may not be included under the discursive banner of the arts as practices of symbolic creativity" (p. 215), but which nonetheless involve engaging in creative work that reflects the particularities of material and symbolic relations that shape people's lives.

Parallel to this work, in recent years there has been an increasing interest in various forms of youth political engagement. This work has mobilized concepts of citizenship and civic participation and has paid particular attention to education for democracy (e.g. Kahne & Westheimer, 2006). More recently, this work has been framed around the concept of participatory politics. Kahne, Middaugh, and Allen (2014) define participatory politics as "interactive, peer-based acts through which individuals and groups seek to exert both voice and influence on issues of public concern" (p. 3, see also Cohen & Kahne, 2012). Such a broad conceptualization of participatory politics has been key for taking serious account of how the internet and various forms of social media increasingly provide the mechanisms for new forms of participatory politics to develop. This work has extended how civic engagement is conceptualized by bringing into view a wider range of contexts and practices through which young people in particular express their ideas and participate in the political sphere.

Despite this shift in attention, cultural production has not been theorized extensively in relationship to such activities. While the work on civic engagement and participatory politics tends to be more concrete regarding contexts of participation and political aims, it also tends to romanticize cultural practices, often through the language of "the arts," and tends to focus on these practices as vehicles for, rather than definitional to, participation. The seven articles in this special issue of *Curriculum Inquiry* collectively address this conceptual lapse by examining the relationship between cultural production and participatory politics in a range of national and political contexts. Each article examines how youth engage cultural production as part of their political participation, and how political participation is sometimes central to and expressed through cultural production.

The authors in this issue provide examples of the intersections between youth cultural production and participatory politics and bring together a range of approaches to the examination of these intersections, providing illustrations of the complexities involved in these processes. Each of the articles takes up different kinds of practices — from street art (Jaramillo) to video production (Desai), from online activism (Ito et al.) to installation work (Recollet), and examine a range of political contexts — from students striking at the University of Puerto Rico (Rosario) to activism in community arts centres (Kuttner) and university classrooms (Jocson). As editors, we engaged the seven articles in this special issue by asking ourselves what becomes evident when we pay close attention to the intersection of cultural production and participatory politics: what does participatory politics help us see about cultural production and how does cultural production expand how we understand participatory politics? In the next section, we provide a summary of each article and highlight what emerges for us as the key insights regarding this intersection.

Creation as Participation/Participation as Creation

In the first article of the issue, titled "Learning Connected Civics," authors Mimi Ito, Elisabeth Soep, Neta Kligler-Vilenchik, Sangita Shresthova, Liana Gamber-Thompson, and Arely Zimmerman provide a meta-analysis of several research projects that examine how youth engage in participatory politics. They look across a range of studies in order to draw insights about the relationship between socially connected learning, cultural production, and participatory politics, particularly within online environments. From slam poets to Harry Potter fans, the authors trace the ways in which youth mobilize their cultural contexts and productions to pursue civic and political action. They focus specifically on the possibilities offered by today's "networked ecosystem" (p. 10), which provides a fast and accessible way for youth to communicate and engage with their peers in a variety of ways and across settings. The authors propose the term "connected civics" to refer to "a form of learning that mobilizes young people's deeply felt interests and identities in the service of achieving the kind of civic voice and influence that is characteristic of participatory politics" (p. 11). Their work seeks to understand the connection between youth expressive cultural practices and civic culture, as well as how youth make sense of aspects of their political life, even when they do not necessarily understand these practices as political.

While Ito and her colleagues provide a large picture of the wide range of practices through which young people engage in online activism, Korina Jocson brings us into her own classrooms, as she engages her students in political action through a broadened conception of multiliteracies. In her article, titled "New Media Literacies as Social Action: The Centrality of Pedagogy in the Politics of Knowledge Production," Jocson reflects on the ways in which university students in a new media literacies class use cultural production to engage with social change in their community. The study of new media literacies afforded the class the space to think about "new ways of embodying identity and community" (p. 32), while developing new patterns for organizing, producing, and disseminating their own multimedia creations. The importance of these developing identities is evident in the selection of topics that students made for their culminating social action projects, which Jocson notes were "purposefully connected and contingent upon other discourses in which students had participated" (p. 42). Through the process of media making, Jocson argues that the students shifted their perceptions of themselves as "members of society with the ability to produce knowledge, to use particular forms of knowledge to challenge normalized ways of thinking and doing" (p. 47), pointing to the importance of identity formation with regards to cultural production.

Stepping outside the higher education classroom and into the courtyards and contested public spaces of the University of Puerto Rico, Melissa Rosario examines the symbolic strategies mobilized by students during a system-wide strike. In her article "Public Pedagogy in the Creative Strike: Destabilizing Boundaries and Re-imagining Resistance in the University of Puerto Rico," Rosario examines the spatial dimensions of these practices, showing how strikers disrupted the normative boundaries between protest space/public space, and actor/spectator through their direct engagement with the police force, whose purpose was to control the protests. Through several long days of public costumed performances and outdoor musical events from behind barricades, Rosario traces the ways in which protesters engaged police officers in ways that reconfigured the public space of the university. She connects this spatial reconfiguration to public pedagogy, suggesting that the activists were themselves transformed by the activism as much as their spectators/learners.

Shifting the focus to community arts centres in the United States, Paul Kuttner draws on political theory and cultural studies to examine the different kinds of cultural citizenship that emerge from different kinds of arts education programs. Rather than looking at cultural citizenship as a way to make demands on the state, Kuttner's article, titled "Educating for Cultural Citizenship: Reframing the Goals of Arts Education," focuses on the individual citizen and sheds light on the multiple possibilities for cultural citizenship. In this sense, cultural production is a key process in identity formation through which youth in this program seek out ways to be involved in their community, value different types of cultural production, and are taught that claims and obligations are put on them as artistic creators and consumers. In his examination of a community organization that trains youth as "cultural organizers," Kuttner traces the ways in which this educational project is invested in the development of a justice-oriented citizen (Westheimer & Kahne, 2004). This kind of cultural citizenship involves a critical examination of the cultural products being consumed in the mainstream media, using alternative modes of expression to tell counter narratives of particular communities. In this way, Project HIP-HOP uses cultural production to engage young people in a participatory politics that allows them to enact social change.

Staying with the focus on activism in the context of community-centred organizations, Nathalia Jaramillo draws on recent events in Venezuela to examine how youth use cultural production to enact their political agency and express their evolving subjectivity in relationship to the nation-state. In particular, in her article titled "The Art of Youth Rebellion," Jaramillo uses the cultural production of the *colectivos* to understand the role of expressive and symbolic work when the state is invested in, and encourages, the development of and participation in popular power movements. In this instance, the conditions of alterity are not the locus of resistance, but rather a mode through which young people in communities express their support for the state and become citizens. This is particularly important for youth from low-income communities who have felt marginalized and dispossessed by previous governmental policies and now find themselves playing a central role in support of the state. In engaging in these cultural practices, Jaramillos argues that the youth exercise collective freedom, witness a transfer of power to the community and "establish the foundation for continued social action" to improve their lives (p. 103).

By situating cultural practices enacted on the streets at the center of political participation, in the article titled "Shooting Back in the Occupied Territories: An Anti-Colonial Participatory Politics," Chandni Desai argues for an expansion of the conceptualization of participatory politics that takes into account contexts where the very idea of a citizen is under erasure. Drawing on Willis's (1990) notion of symbolic resistance, Desai analyses how Palestinian youth are "shooting back" through the production and distribution of films that capture their everyday experiences in the Occupied Palestinian Territories. This mode of cultural production goes beyond a politics of resistance to enact a politics of refusal that both articulates and mobilizes a Palestinian political identity. In utilizing technology to share these videos, Desai argues that Palestinian youth are crossing state and continental lines to bring their experiences to a broader public and mobilize international support, in effect to exert their voice on issues that concern them outside of the parameters imposed by a colonizing force.

Like Desai, Karyn Recollet situates her work within the streets of the settler colonial invention that is Canada. In her article titled "Glyphing Decolonial Love through Urban

Flash Mobbing and *Walking with our Sisters*," Recollet deploys a spatial analysis of the urban flash mob round dance of the Idle No More movement, as well as Christi Belcourt's *Walking with our Sisters* commemorative art installation. Recollet explores new geographies of Indigenous resistance in Canada. In particular, she focuses on the production of what she calls "spatial glyphs" through the embodied motions of Indigenous artists in the round dance flash mob, as well as the emergent pathways created by the strategically positioned vamps in *Walking with our Sisters.* In the tracing of these glyphs, Recollet demonstrates their implication for reconceptualizing processes of solidarity building, activism and pedagogical practices of resistance.

For us as editors, what emerges from a collective reading of these seven articles is the critical insight that cultural production is not simply a vehicle for communication in participatory politics, but central to the very process through which participants come to form their ideas and build political identities. Likewise, participatory politics is not just a context within which young people can share their creations, but the process of participation is itself a process of cultural creation.

Creation is Participation

While describing very different social and cultural contexts, each of the articles in this special issue offers examples of the ways in which cultural production always involves forms of participation that always have political implications. In the case of the *colectivos* in Venezuela, for example, Jaramillo shows how youth use cultural production as a way to connect to a political system that emphasizes communal participation. By contrast, as Rosario illustrates in the case of the students strikers at the University of Puerto Rico, cultural production is also a means of protesting against the state while challenging the repressive state apparatus. This is most evident in the video production of Palestinian youth, through which they do not only confront the military presence of an invading army, but also become active participants in the telling of a political narrative.

While Jaramillo, Rosario, and Desai illustrate how creation is a form of participation through engaging the state as a form of what Ito and her colleagues frame as "capital P" politics, the other four articles offer examples that require a broader conceptualization of politics. This is crucial because many of the youth involved in projects such as those described by Ito and her colleagues have grown disenchanted with mainstream politics "and want to distinguish themselves and their work from the figures who self-identify as politicians and from the kinds of events typically understood to be motivated by politics" (p. 14). This does not mean, of course, that their engagement in cultural production is any less participatory or any less political. Indeed, their work might be tied to community organizations invested in creating the kind of social justice oriented cultural citizen that Kuttner describes, which involves participation through the creation of cultural artifacts. Similarly, it might involve the kind of participation with local organizations that some of the students in Jocson's class engaged through their media production and without which the work would not have been possible. What ties all of of these contexts together is that young people are engaged in modes of cultural production that are inherently premised on participation and in engaging with the broader social context as a way to promote social change. It is this participative aspect of cultural production that underscores its importance for participatory politics.

When we examine cultural production as a mode for participation, we are able to see widespread political engagement in ways that focusing on more narrowly defined political engagement seems to miss entirely, as Ito and colleagues suggest. This focus on cultural production as participation allows us to consider how a wider range of cultural practices, such as murals (Jaramillo), people's journalism (Desai), hip hop culture (Kuttner), round dances/flashmobs (Recollet), and fan websites (Ito and colleagues) can all be understood as forms of participation. Moreover, it lets us move beyond the scope of practices narrowly framed as "the arts" toward the importance of symbolic creativity and recognize the everyday cultural practices of youth as potential terrain for political participation. This participation, taking place far away from polls and political campaigns, is rooted in community capacity building and, as Kuttner argues, gives youth a way to begin organizing and to "see themselves as part of larger struggles for justice, and be open to the kind of collaboration that undergirds successful social change efforts" (p. 86).

This is significant, as Ito and her colleagues remind us, because "young people's everyday experiences of agency in their social worlds, and of citizenship and community involvement turn out to be largely disconnected from what most educators might think of as sites of civic and political engagement" (p. 13). The authors in this issue demonstrate that in their participation, youth are not only exerting their voice in order to express ideas, but also trying to exert change into the world. It is through their cultural production that youth create and participate.

Participation is Creation

If the forms of creation described in the seven articles in this special issue are not just vehicles for participation, but rather constitute their own modes of participation, participation in politics is not just a venue for displaying what youth create, but rather it constitutes a mode of cultural production. In other words, the kinds of participatory politics described by the authors in this issue are also implicated in the process of creating not just artifacts, but also the very identifications and voices that are being expressed through participation. Indeed, as the authors make evident directly or indirectly, participatory politics is always about processes of identification and the production of particular views and positions. Using the lens of cultural production, we are able to see how participatory politics is a form of identification, conceptualized as a process. Participants create their voice as members in a society as they demand change.

For Kuttner, this process is key for becoming justice-oriented cultural citizens, as this requires a process of critically reflecting on the conditions that shape social life in the production and dissemination of cultural artifacts. Yet, participation is also about creating the very terms of engagement with the state, as expressed in the ways in which Rosario describes how Puerto Rican students challenged the police presence in the University campus. And as Desai explains, this challenge is even more fundamental when the state withdraws the rights of citizenship through the "state of exception", as in the case of Palestinians in Israel. Thus, whether as a way to resist the state, redefine the conditions for engaging the state, or engage the opportunities that the state makes available, participatory politics always requires the cultural creation of identifications, a process that becomes most evident when it involves cultural production.

These identifications are, of course, always in relationship to projects of nation building, as they pertain to how youth see themselves in relation to or in rejection of the state. In the context of the *colectivos* in Venezuela, for example, Jaramillo points to how the youth's cultural production is "a means to establish social relationships and uphold the ideas and beliefs of popular power that they associate with their struggle for collective humanization" (p. 101). It is through this process that the youth represent "the emerging class of political actors in a country undergoing a reconfiguration of the relationship between the underclasses of society and the state" (p. 97). Furthermore, cultural production is a means through which participants create these voices, as well as a way for them to imagine what is possible.

Conclusion

It would not be possible to understand what is at stake in the wide range of responses to the failure of the state to hold police officers accountable for their violence against Black men in the USA without attempting to make sense of how these responses constitute both a form of participatory politics as well as cultural production. For example, the kinds of political exchanges that have spread in response to the emergence of hashtags like #CrimingWhileWhite, #ICantBreathe, and #iftheygunnedmedown, require an understanding of "connected civics," to draw on Ito and her colleagues, that does not only view such hashtags as vehicles, but as both modes of participation *and* creation. Likewise, as Recollet clearly demonstrates, the practice of flash mob round dances in public spaces is not simply about creating a moment of protest, but also about the very possibility of reconstituting Indigenous/settler relations toward decolonization. And as Desai makes clear, "shooting back" through video production is not just about documenting violence in order to participate in politics, but it is about new forms of cultural resistance that declare a political subjectivity in the face of a brutal state that seeks to eradicate life.

The educational implications of the analysis and of the projects discussed in this special issue are varied and may be more or less evident for different readers of our journal. For scholars in the fields of civic and citizenship education, the insights presented in these articles provide entries for making sense of a wider set of practices through which young people engage in political participation. But such a broad conception of participation also has implications for how we think about engagement through cultural production, as well as how we come to view certain forms of creative expression as worthy modes for doing politics. We agree with Jocson, who draws on the important work of the late Jean Anyon (2009) to declare that, like the rest of the authors in this issue, her work is "moved by the potential of participatory politics not only as voluntary, but also as pedagogically operational in critical education" (p. 31). Together, the authors in this special issue of *CI* invite us to see beyond the surface appearance of dwindling participation and to recognize that cultural production is a key site for/of participatory politics.

This special issue also marks a new moment at *CI*, as we move to a new publisher with Taylor & Francis, under the leadership of a new Editor-in-Chief, with Rubén Gaztambide-Fernández, along with continuing Associate Editors, Sardar Anwaruddin and Alexandra Arráiz Matute, new Assistant Editors, Shawna Carroll and Neil Ramjewan, and the continued support of Gabrielle de Montmollin, as Editorial Assistant. We also have a newly reconstituted International Editorial Board with both veteran and emerging scholars in the field, to whom we express our gratitude for agreeing to support the work of the journal. With this editorial and this special issue, we wish to send a clear message that *CI* is not only interested in articles that deal with broad issues related to curriculum studies, but that we want to encourage articles that raise critical questions, engage controversial topics, and break new ground in critical areas of curriculum and pedagogy. As a form of participatory politics, academic scholarship should take up the pressing issues that we face today and present radical possibilities that invite readers to imagine things otherwise.

References

Anyon, J. (2009a). Critical pedagogy is not enough: Social justice education, political participation, and the politicization of students. In M. Apple, W. Au, & L. Gandin (Eds.), *The Routledge international handbook of critical education* (pp. 389–395). New York: Routledge.

Boutilier, A. (2014, August 21). Native teen's slaying a 'crime,' not a 'sociological phenomenon,' Stephen Harper says. *The Star*. Retrieved from http://www.thestar.com/news/canada/2014/08/21/native_teens_slaying_a_crime_not_a_sociological_phenomenon_stephen_harper_says.html

Chang, L. (2014, August 18). Do police shoot black men more often? Statistics say yes, absolutely. *Bustle*. Retrieved from http://www.bustle.com/articles/36096-do-police-shoot-black-men-more-often-statistics-say-yes-absolutely

Cohen, C. & Kahne, J. (2012). *Participatory politics: New media and youth political action*. Retrieved from http://ypp.dmlcentral.net/sites/all/files/publications/YPP_Survey_Report_FULL.pdf

Dimitriadis, G. (2009). *Performing identity/performing culture: Hip hop as text, pedagogy, and lived practice*. New York: Peter Lang.

Gabrielson, R., Grochowski Jones, R., & Sagara, E. (2014, October 10) Deadly force, in black and white. *ProPublica*. Retrieved from http://www.propublica.org/article/deadly-force-in-black-and-white

Gaztambide-Fernández, R. A. (2013). Why the arts don't *do* anything: Toward a new vision for cultural production in education. *Harvard Educational Review, 83*, 211–237.

Gilens, M. & Page, B.I. (2014). Testing theories of American politics: Elites, interest groups, and average citizens. *Perspectives on Politics,* 12, pp 564–581.

Gilroy, P. (1991). *There ain't no black in the Union Jack: The cultural politics of race and nation*. Chicago: University Press.

Hall, S., & Jefferson, T. (Eds.) (1976) *Resistance through rituals: Youth subcultures in post-war Britain*. London: Hutchinson.

Hebdige, D. (1979). *Subculture, the meaning of style*. London: Methuen.

Johnson, K., Hoyer, M., and Heath, B. (2014, August 15) Local police involved in 400 killings per year. *USA Today*. Retrieved from http://www.usatoday.com/story/news/nation/2014/08/14/police-killings-data/14060357/

Kahne, J., Middaugh, E., & Allen, D. (2014). *Youth new media, and the rise of participatory politics*. YPP Research Network Working Paper #1, March 2014. Retrieved from http://ypp.dmlcentral.net/sites/default/files/publications/YPP_WorkinPapers_Paper01.pdf

Kahne, J. & Westheimer, J. (2006). The limits of political efficacy: Educating citizens for a democratic society. *Political Science & Politics*. pp 289–296.

Macedo, S., Alex-Assensoh, Y., Berry, J.M., Brintnall, M., Campbell D.E., & Fraga, L.R. (2005). *Democracy at risk: How political choices undermine citizen participation, and what we can do about it*. Washington, DC: Brookings Institution.

Maira, S., & Soep, E. (2004). *Youthscapes: Popular culture, national ideologies, global markets*. Philadelphia: University of Pennsylvania Press.

Maira, S. (2000). Henna and hip hop: The politics of cultural production and the work of cultural studies. *Journal of Asian American Studies, 3*, 329–369.

Muñoz, J. E. (2000). Feeling brown: Ethnicity and affect in Ricardo Bracho's The Sweetest Hangover (and Other STDs). *Theatre Journal, 52*, 67–79.

McRobbie, A. (1993). Shut up and dance: Youth culture and changing modes of femininity. *Cultural Studies, 7*, pp. 406–426.

Simpson, L. (2014, March 5) Not murdered, not missing. *Indigenous nationhood movement*. Retrieved from http://nationsrising.org/not-murdered-and-not-missing/

Sium, A. (2013, November 22). "New World" settler colonialism: "Killing indians, making niggers". *Decolonization: Indigeneity, Education & Society*. Retrieved from: http://decolonization.wordpress.com/2013/11/22/new-world-settler-colonialism-killing-indians-making-niggers/

Smith, A. (2005) *Conquest: Sexual violence and american indian genocide*. Brooklyn: South End Press

Vizenor, G. (Ed.). (2008). *Survivance: Narratives of Native presence*. Lincoln: U of Nebraska Press.

Westheimer, J., & Kahne, J. (2004). What kind of citizen? The politics of educating for democracy. *American Educational Research Journal, 41*, 237–269.

Willis, P. (2003). Foot soldiers of modernity: The dialectics of cultural consumption and the 21st-century school. *Harvard Educational Review, 73*, 390–415.

Willis, P. (1990) *Common culture: Symbolic work at play in the everyday cultures of the young*. Boulder: Westview.

1 Learning connected civics
Narratives, practices, infrastructures

Mizuko Ito, Elisabeth Soep, Neta Kligler-Vilenchik, Sangita Shresthova, Liana Gamber-Thompson and Arely Zimmerman

Bringing together popular culture studies and sociocultural learning theory, in this paper we formulate the concept of "connected civics," grounded in the idea that young people today are engaging in new forms of politics that are profoundly participatory. Often working in collaboration with adult allies, they leverage digital media and emerging modes of connectivity to achieve voice and influence in public spheres. The rise of participatory politics provides new opportunities to support connected civics, which is socially engaged and embedded in young people's personal interests, affinities, and identities.

We posit three supports that build consequential connections between young people's cultural affinities, their agency in the social world, and their civic engagement: 1. By constructing hybrid narratives, young people mine the cultural contexts they are embedded in and identify with for civic and political themes relevant to issues of public concern. 2. Through shared civic practices, members of affinity networks lower barriers to entry and multiply opportunities for young people to engage in civic and political action. 3. By developing cross-cutting infrastructure, young people—often with adults—institutionalize their efforts in ways that make a loosely affiliated network into something that is socially organized and self-sustaining.

Drawing from a corpus of interviews and case studies of youth affinity networks at various sites across the US, this paper recasts the relationship between connected learning, cultural production, and participatory politics.

Slam poets who have grown up competing individually for high scores decide to join forces, launching sustained campaigns related to violence prevention and environmental justice. Harry Potter fans organize collective actions for fair trade chocolate and marriage equality. Young activists fighting for U.S. immigration reform appropriate iconography and storylines from popular comics to make their case. These are all examples of youth mobilizing their cultural contexts and productions to pursue civic and political action.

Today's networked ecosystem offers near-constant opportunities for young people to engage with peers in a range of ways. They can "hang out" together while physically apart, sharing photos, videos, captions and comments all throughout the day and night; and they can "geek out" together by swapping ideas, techniques and critiques related to projects that tap their deepest interests and aspirations (Ito et al., 2009). Whether by curating a public presence through Tumblr or Twitter, remixing videos and memes, or moderating an online discussion, young people cultivate skills and dispositions that do more than promote personal expression for its own sake. These same skills and dispositions are indispensible within "participatory politics" (Kahne, Middaugh, & Allen, 2014). Through participatory politics, young people use digital tools and other emerging forms of social

---

© 2015 The Author(s). Published by Taylor & Francis
This is an Open Access article distributed under the terms of the Creative Commons Attribution-NonCommercial-NoDerivatives License (http://creativecommons.org/licenses/by-nc-nd/4.0/), which permits non-commercial re-use, distribution, and reproduction in any medium, provided the original work is properly cited, and is not altered, transformed, or built upon in any way.

connectivity to express voice and influence on issues of public concern (Kahne, Middaugh & Allen, 2014).

Commentators bemoaning youth apathy worry that digitally-mediated, expression-based forms of civic activity will make young people less likely to take part in institutionalized politics (such as voting), but recent research has indicated the opposite. Involvement in participatory culture—meaning contexts that actively encourage members to make and share creative products and practices that matter to them, supported by informal mentorship (Jenkins, 2006)—can be a gateway to political engagement (Cohen, Kahne, Bowyer, Middaugh, & Rogowski, 2012). Moreover, participatory politics are much more equitably distributed across racial and ethnic groups than conventional measures of political engagement, like voter turnout (Cohen, Kahne et. al., 2012). A growing body of ethnographic case studies on participatory politics advances these quantitative findings by delving into the nuances and mechanics of how connections between participatory culture and politics are forged (Gamber-Thompson, 2012; Kligler-Vilenchik & Shresthova, 2012; Kligler-Vilenchik, 2013; Pfister, 2014; Shresthova, 2013; Zimmerman, 2012).

This groundswell of research on participatory politics shows young people linking the experiences of belonging, voice, leadership, and mobilization that they are developing through participatory culture to practices more conventionally thought of as civic and political in nature. Young people are also working in the opposite direction. Those who start off with civic and political commitments bolster those efforts by linking them to participatory culture. The research indicates that these connections between participatory culture and politics don't necessarily form automatically and can be actively brokered by peers and adults, and through organizational infrastructures.

In order to understand the unique conditions for learning that this emerging digital media landscape affords, this paper brings together the conceptual frameworks and case studies from two research networks established by the MacArthur Foundation that focus respectively on participatory politics and connected learning. What are the characteristics of the environments that support these connections between social and cultural activities, civic and political practices, and developmental outcomes for young people? And how can we better support these connections and outcomes?

We propose "connected civics" as a form of learning that mobilizes young people's deeply felt interests and identities in the service of achieving the kind of civic voice and influence that is characteristic of participatory politics. Of course there is nothing new about the idea that interest, affinity, and identity are drivers of political action, but too often when it comes to learning, we can default to civic educational experiences that fail to tap the kinds of cultural practices young people produce through their everyday symbolic expression. "Learning" connected civics does not entail individually-driven "transfer" between the personally meaningful cultural projects young people actively create and modes of concerted political engagement, but is centered instead on building shared contexts that allow for what we elaborate below as "consequential connections" between these spheres of activity.

We describe three kinds of supports for these consequential connections: 1. by constructing *hybrid narratives*, young people mine their cultural contexts and products for civic and political themes relevant to issues of public concern; 2. through *shared civic practices*, young people lower barriers to entry and multiply opportunities for young people to engage in civic and political action that can be temporary or more lasting in nature; 3. by developing *cross-cutting infrastructure*, young people—often working in collaboration with adults—institutionalize their efforts in ways that make a loosely affiliated network into something that is socially organized, self-sustaining, and recognized as such by those outside the original interest-driven community. Our focus throughout the article is on identifying the features of environments that build consequential connections rather than the "in the head" work (for example, knowing who controls the judiciary branch or which party holds the majority in the U.S. Senate) that very often draws attention within debates about the state of civic education or youth political participation.

Conceptual Foundation

Our central question is, how can we support young people's learning and development of deeply personal and culturally resonant forms of civic agency? In order to address this question, we draw from two bodies of theory and research—studies of youth popular culture and sociocultural approaches to learning.

Since well before the advent of digital networks, researchers have documented how young people's social and recreational pursuits offer avenues for participation in public and political life. Youth ethnographers have described the complex micropolitical dynamics of teen social status negotiations (Eckert, 1989; Milner, 2004; Pascoe, 2007). Cultural studies scholars have a long tradition of locating politics in popular culture, taking special interest in the subcultural engagements of youth and the civic and political activities of young people who've been marginalized on the basis of race, class, and gender (Ginwright, Noguera, & Cammarota, 2006; Hall & Jefferson, 2006; Hebdige, 1979; Willis, 1990). These studies have helped us to see how decorating the walls of a bedroom, or cultivating and sharing tastes in music, or styling hair in a particular way, can amount to potent forms of cultural production and contestation. Young people producing these practices are often expressing and in some cases organizing resistance to institutions and ideologies they deem problematic, obsolete, or oppressive.

More recent research has interrogated how these dynamics are playing out in contemporary digital environments (boyd, 2014; Ito et al., 2009; Kligler-Vilenchik & Shresthova, 2012). Through remix and other forms of media appropriation, popular culture fans and other consumers can exercise citizenship and create frameworks for activism (Jenkins, Ford, & Green, 2013). Deploying a "logic of connective action," young people circulate civic content across fluid social networks that don't necessarily require joining hierarchical political institutions (Bennett & Segerberg, 2012). In so doing, they enact forms of citizenship that privilege meaning, identity, and inter-subjectivity as everyday forces that shape political life and opportunity (Bakardijeva, 2009; Dahlgren, 2005). The notion of participatory politics identifies the conditions under which young people's everyday social and cultural engagements can foster forms of civic and political agency that are increasingly accessible due to emerging modes of social connectivity and the spread of digital and networked technology.

While we begin with this appreciation of the political *potential* of youth-driven online activity, we also feel it is critically important that we do not end there. Our approach to participatory politics recognizes that these activities can be tied to meaningful learning and development as products of participation in civic, political, and public life. Simply circulating civic content among peers does not necessarily do much of anything for the people who hit "share," nor does it necessarily advance the set of concerns they aim to address (though it can, and sharing information can sometimes be anything but simple and carry serious risk). The overwhelming dataflow that results can sometimes blur specific political messages and distract from the arduous work of organizing sustained, connected action; in other words, as Jodi Dean (2005) has argued, the waves of content can start to feel like part of a never-ending stream. Thus, we need to actively support learning and consequential connections between spaces of youth cultural production, their agency, and their civic and political worlds.

This brings us to a growing body of research in the learning sciences that has examined how learning is connected, reinforced, or disconnected across settings. Much of this research is concerned with the relationship between in-school and out-of-school learning, puzzling over: how classroom learning gets applied (or not) to everyday life (Hull & Shultz, 2002; Lave, 1988); how children's home and peer cultures inflect school achievement (Carter, 2005; Goldman, 2006; Varenne & McDermott, 1998); or how educators can intentionally design digitally-rich, production-oriented communities that bridge divides in access to robust learning environments (Barron, Gomez, Pinkard, & Martin, 2014). The process of connecting learning across settings is not a simple matter of acquiring generalized knowledge, skills, and frameworks that an individual can "transfer" across diverse settings of life. It turns out that the ability to connect learning across settings rests on a host of other contextual factors, social relationships, and mediating practices (Beach, 1999; Bransford & Schwartz, 2001; Engestrom, 1996). It also hinges on young people's own judgments about the extent to which they even want their civic and political activities to follow them across digital contexts (Weinstein, 2014). Indeed, as a 2012 National Academies report on "deeper learning" concluded: "Over a century of research on transfer has yielded little evidence that teaching can develop general cognitive competencies that are transferable to any new discipline, problem or context, in or out of school" (Pellegrino & Hilton, 2012, p. 8).

At first blush, issues of transfer and cross-site learning may seem less relevant to progressive approaches that already stress cultural relevance, real world learning, and civic and political engagement. We have observed however, that these questions of learning across settings are actually highly salient for understanding how young people's everyday settings and cultural practices relate to civic and political engagement. Just as, for example, school math and everyday math turn out to be quite different sorts of things (Goldman, 2006; Lave, 1988), young people's everyday experiences of agency in their social worlds, and of citizenship and community involvement turn out to be largely disconnected from what most educators might think of as sites of civic and political engagement. A young person who is active on Facebook and Instagram, or who organizes a gaming league or fan community, will likely not recognize these activities as relevant to political engagement, or to the activities for which they might earn community service credit at school. And civic educators are much more likely to stress involvement in civic and state institutions than they are to look towards popular culture and youth-centered identities and affinity for evidence of students' political imaginations and actions.

What counts as "civic" is a normative designation grounded in specific cultural values and institutionalized practices. We use the term to designate activities that include involvement in state apparatuses (what is traditionally deemed "politics"), as well as activities tied to community problem-solving and social justice that do not necessarily lead to or even involve direct governmental action, for example, through so-called "hashtag activism" campaigns inviting peers to share first-person experiences with racial profiling or violence against women. By social justice, we mean efforts geared towards equity, freedom, and sustainability. As articulated within the framework of participatory politics, these activities can involve: production and circulation of information about a matter of public import; carrying out dialogue and feedback related to that issue; investigating topics that are consequential to the community; using that information to hold accountable people in power; and mobilizing others on questions of justice, rights, and equality (Soep, 2014). This normative definition of the civic is unavoidably situated in our own U.S.-inflected progressive traditions, and we feel it is important to recognize and make explicit this cultural and historical specificity. It's also worth noting that the young people who have been a part of our research sometimes disavow "politics" as an apt description of what it is they are doing when they participate in just these kinds of activities, whether they are explicitly targeting the state or not. Many have grown disenchanted with the role of "capital P" politics in everyday life and want to distinguish themselves and their work from the figures who self-identify as politicians and from the kinds of events typically understood to be motivated by politics.

By stressing these boundaries between expressive and civic culture, our intention is to recognize these existing distinctions in order to find ways to cross and bridge the disconnection between them. We build on how King Beach (1999) has described learning as "consequential transitions." "Transitions are consequential when they are consciously reflected on, often struggled with, and the eventual outcome changes one's sense of self and social positioning" (p. 114). Also highly relevant to our framework is Kligler-Vilenchik's (2013) notion of "mechanisms of translation" that young people deploy to link participatory culture and participatory politics, forming a hybrid mode of engagement she and Shresthova (2012) describe as "participatory culture civics" (Kligler-Vilenchik and Shresthova, 2012).

Building on these frameworks, our view takes into account the fluid nature of young people's engagements, where new interests and affiliation are explored, abandoned, revisited, or brought together in ways that are not fully captured by a notion of "transition" from one role or activity to another—hence our use of consequential *connections* instead. Young people continue to value their interests—in slam poetry, for example, or gaming, or comics, or reading and writing back into wildly popular texts like *Hunger Games*—for their own sake and not just to the extent that these activities advance a civic or political agenda. Further, many sociocultural affiliations, such as immigration status, are not matters of individual choice, and young people's enlistment into civic and political commitments is not simply a matter of personal interest or engagement in peer or popular culture. The pivot between the cultural and the political can be enduring or ephemeral. In either case, it can be transformative for the young people involved, and for the issues of public concern they take on through their work and play (Jenkins, Gamber-Thompson, Kligler-Vilenchik, Shresthova, & Zimmerman, forthcoming).

This view of civic learning as "connected" brings together peer culture, personal interests and identities, and opportunities for young people to be recognized in sites of power in the wider world (Ito et al., 2013). Young people's entry points to connected learning and connected civics can be through their everyday social, creative, and community engagements, or through formal adult-guided programs and learning institutions. What is distinctive about a connected approach to civic learning is that it brings together these spheres in a meaningful and efficacious learning experience. In contrast to more fleeting or institutionally-driven forms of learning, connected learning experiences are tied to deeply felt interests, bonds, passions, and affinities and are as a consequence both highly engaging and personally transformative. Importantly, though, among the key learning tasks within connected civics is understanding *shared* experience and what it takes to "take turns accepting losses in the public sphere" while acknowledging and honoring "the losses that others have accepted" (Allen, 2012, p. 1). This means not mistaking interest for entitlement to be a part of something, but rather recognizing affinity as a point of access through which to pursue thoughtful collaboration.

Our use of the term "interest," then, is not meant to signal an individual or innate quality; we see interests as cultivated through social and cultural relationships and located within what we call an "affinity network" of commonly felt identity, practice, and purpose. We draw from Jim Gee's (2005) term "affinity spaces," which he uses to describe online places where people interact around a common passion and/or set of commitments, but broaden our focus to civic and political action and wider networks. We use the term affinity network to signal contexts that can span multiple sites and platforms but hold at their center joint interests, activities, and identities. Within these contexts, young people form social bonds, collective expressions, and shared practices. Like affinity spaces, affinity networks include groups with tight-knit relationships that might be characterized as a "community," or what Jenkins describes as "participatory culture." But as a result of open, online infrastructures, these networks are often visible and accessible to those outside the tight-knit community.

We want to be clear here that by highlighting affinity as a driving force among, for example, fans of Harry Potter advocating for fair labor practices and, for another example, undocumented youth fighting for their own rights and dignity, we do not mean to create an equivalency between the two (Jenkins, Gamber-Thompson, Kligler-Vilenchik, Shresthova, & Zimmerman, forthcoming). What is at stake, how close it is to the given struggle, and how embedded the affinity is in direct experiences of inequality and marginalization, are among some fundamental differentiators. By highlighting the role of identity, interest, and affinity across the range of cases we consider here, our aim is not to elide these differences but to offer a concept of learning that is sufficiently expansive to embrace the broad range of activities we are seeing among young people who are connecting the cultural and the political in transformative ways.

As pictured in Figure 1, "Connected civics" is a way to describe the learning that takes place at the intersection of three realms of activity: young people's agency within peer cultures and public spheres; their deeply felt identities, interests and affinities; and civic engagement and opportunity. Connected civics is a specific form of participatory politics where all three circles in Figure 1 intersect. Not all forms of participatory politics are tied to a deeply felt interest; signing an online petition or liking a cause of Facebook are expressions of civic agency and potentially impactful (Earl, 2013), though not necessarily tied to a personal interest, social bond, or affinity network. Likewise, other worthwhile learning opportunities take place at the intersection of two but not three circles within the figure. For example, young people can be engaged in interest-driven participatory cultures of fandom or gaming, and through that engagement they can achieve agency within public spheres—it just may not happen to be civic in nature. Or, young people can possess deeply felt and highly sophisticated civic or political interests, identities, and skills that are never connected to or activated in highly agentive ways. For example, they may be

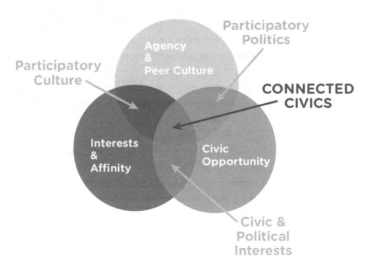

Figure 1: Connected Civics Diagram.

moved by a cause they are exposed to through the media or in their life experiences, but not take action or share their commitment to the cause to their peers or online. Neither connected learning nor connected civics is intended to encompass *all* of the learning that young people are or should be engaged in, but rather describes a *specific* form of social and consequential learning that is tied to deeply felt affinities and personal interests. For educators and designers, the framework points to ways in which we can help young people *learn connected civics* no matter where they start—be it peer culture, interest and affinity, or civic opportunity—by cultivating experiences that connect these spheres of activity.

Valuing the interests, identities and social relationships of youth is a means towards more equitable and diverse routes to civic and political participation as well as learning. As a dimension of participatory politics, connected civics sees the interests of youth in all walks of life as potential starting points for deep and consequential forms of civic and political involvement, though their pathways into this kind of engagement, the ways in which their politics form, and the kinds of supports they depend on to carry out critically-informed work, can be quite different. In this frame, a key role of education and positive youth development is to support the connective narratives, practices, and infrastructures that make learning and accomplishment in one sphere consequential in another.

Our Research

This paper represents a qualitative meta-analysis drawing from research conducted by two networks of scholars and educators supported by the MacArthur Foundation to explore the implications of digital and social media on youth learning and democracy: the Youth and Participatory Politics Research Network (YPP) and the Connected Learning Research Network (CLRN). These networks represent a range of disciplines and research in both in-school and out-of-school settings. Studies include two national surveys of young people, interviews with civically engaged youth, large-scale inventories of digital sites and platforms, meta-analyses of existing research, and international comparative ethnographic studies (Allen, 2012; Cohen et al., 2012; DeVoss, Eidman-Aadahl, & Hicks, 2010; Earl, 2013; Gardner & Davis, 2013; Jenkins et al., n.d.; Kahne et al., 2014; Soep, 2014; Zuckerman, n.d.) In order to understand the range of mechanisms that support consequential connections, we have considered cases that vary in the degree that they centered on youth culture or more formal and adult-driven organizational structure. Beyond our strategic selection of cases to represent that spectrum, our mode of analysis across these cases has focused by and large on evidence of youth-driven activities and their outcomes. We have explored qualitative data sets (interviews, observations) collected by researchers over time as well as publically available documents—digital assets, physical materials, testimonials—linked to civic and political campaigns. Out of these raw materials, themes emerged, which we elaborate below, related to the specific supports that enable young people to form the consequential connections that link their interests and affinities to agency and civic opportunity.

Cases from the CLRN Leveling Up project (Korobkova, 2014; Kow, Young, & Tekinbas, 2014; Martin, 2014; Pfister, 2014; Rafalow & Tekinbas, 2014), led by Ito and Katie Salen Tekinbas, and Ito's prior work on digital youth practices (Ito et al., 2009) provide a baseline understanding of youth affinity networks as sites for learning and include case studies of communities centered on creative arts, gaming, and fandom. Two case studies from the Media, Activism, and Participatory Politics (MAPP) project of the YPP Network, headed by Henry Jenkins at the University of Southern California, function as anchor cases, which have produced key conceptual insights that lay the groundwork for connected civics. The Harry Potter Alliance (HPA) is a non-profit organization, uniting fans and activists who take inspiration from the characters and events contained within that blockbuster series to mobilize for literacy, equality and human rights, all the while asking "What would Dumbledore do?" The study of HPA was led by Neta Kligler-Vilenchik (2013). Arely Zimmerman (2012) led the study of the second anchor case, based on her fieldwork in 2010-2011 with DREAM activists—young people who were undocumented and seeking immigration reform. Also known as the Developing Relief and Education for Alien Minors Act, the legislation young people in Zimmerman's study were working towards at the time of her research would grant conditional residency rights to qualifying immigrant students who'd grown up in the United States with undocumented parents. Also represented among the MAPP case studies we take up here are examples drawn from a study of Libertarian youth by Liana Gamber (2012) and a study of the Nerdfighters by Kligler-Vilenchik (2013). Nerdfighters are a community of millions that has grown up around video blogging brothers John and Hank Green and defines itself as working together to "decrease world suck." As noted above, frameworks emerging from these studies that deeply inform the notion of connected civics include the concept of "participatory culture civics" (Kligler-Vilenchik & Shresthova, 2012, 2014) and mechanisms of translation (Kligler-Vilenchik, 2013) that connect participatory culture and participatory politics, by tapping content worlds (Kligler-Vilenchik 2013), shared production and practice (Gamber-Thompson 2012; Zimmerman 2012; Kligler-Vilenchik 2013) and building institutional networks from existing communities (Kligler-Vilenchik et al. 2012; Kligler-Vilenchik and Shresthova 2012). Finally, Soep's (2012) research with youth media and its digital afterlife provides additional case materials from more structured programs that support connected civics.

Connecting Affinity-Based and Civic Practices

So far we have developed the concept of connected civics as a form of learning fostered via participatory politics that emerges when young people achieve civic agency linked to their deeply felt interests, identities, and affinities. Now we pivot to the question: What supports enable young people to move along a pathway towards learning connected civics? Three supports have emerged out of our research, which we take up in the following sections, centered on: 1. What young people produce when they engage connected civics (hybrid content worlds), 2. How they work together (shared practices), and 3. What conditions (cross-cutting infrastructures) render their activities increasingly sustainable and poised to achieve learning effects at scale.

Hybrid Content Worlds: Narrative Connections

One of the hallmarks of today's networked and participatory youth culture is the centrality of cultural production and sharing. With the advent of low-cost digital production tools and online platforms for sharing media, we have seen an explosion in the growth and visibility of youth creative production, including varied formats such as podcasts, YouTube videos, blogs, tweets, memes, fan fiction, and game mods. These settings can provide opportunities for young people to develop capacities for networking, media production, and public performance that are supported by peers and centered on interests (Gee & Hayes, 2010; Ito et al., 2009; Jenkins, Clinton, Puruchotma, Robinson, & Weigel, 2009; Rheingold, 2012). The connections between these affinity networks and the civic and political realm can be elusive, however. While recognizing how social media offer powerful new tools for activists, Ethan Zuckerman (n.d.) also suggests that it is challenging for political content to compete with cat memes. "The sharpest limit to the utility of social media as a tool for advocacy may be simple limits to attention. While access to social media tools provides the ability to publish content, it does not guarantee that anyone will pay attention to the content in question" (p. 18). Others have raised concerns about negative or harmful forms of cultural expression, such as images tied to self-harm, bullying, sexting, trolling or racist expression (boyd, 2014; Chun, forthcoming; Phillips, 2011). While young people are clearly exercising new forms of agency and voice through these creative activities, we certainly cannot assume that they will apply these capacities to purposes that are civic or even prosocial in nature.

Henry Jenkins (2012) and his collaborators have found that young people mine popular culture and everyday creative production to create "content worlds" that connect their deeply held identities and resonant narrative referents to issues of broader social, civic, and political concern. In her study of two fan groups, the Nerdfighters and Harry Potter Alliance, for example, Kligler-Vilenchik (2013) has described the "mechanisms of translation" that enable connections between the cultural and civic, which include tapping content worlds and communities, creative production, and informal discussion. Andrew Slack, the founder of the Harry Potter Alliance, has used the term "cultural acupuncture," to describe elevating themes from popular culture to a social justice agenda (Jenkins, 2012).

HPA campaigns bring together narrative elements from social justice and the Harry Potter content world. For example, their annual book drive to support libraries is called "Accio Books," referencing a charm in the Harry Potter story that summons objects from a distance. They are also running a campaign for fair trade chocolate to be used in Harry Potter branded sweets under the banner, "Not In Harry's Name." Through the Imagine Better Project, HPA members have more recently been conducting campaigns that are tied to other popular media content, such as the Hunger Games and Superman. One recent campaign is the "Superman was an Immigrant" campaign to support immigrant rights, tied to the release of Man of Steel. Lauren, one of the organizers, explains:

> We invited people to share their stories of their family histories, to change the conversation about immigration … So that campaign was very popular when we did it because both Superman and immigration were very popular at the time. And it continues to have value because the ideas are larger and broader.

In this way, the HPA encourages participants to produce their own media products like these immigrant stories, forming a hybrid content world that lies at the intersection of popular culture and social justice narratives.

To get to those "larger and broader" themes, participants in another youth-driven affinity network argue that content worlds need to be deeply personal and specific. Youth Speaks is a non-profit based in San Francisco that leads an international Brave New Voices network of spoken word poetry projects with wildly varying levels of formality and funding. "Being personal and vulnerable with your own experiences … creates a ripple effect," says Joshua, a longtime participant. "If your poem is very general, then it's easy to ignore or dismiss it. But if you're speaking about something you've actually experienced, that's work that is beautiful and can help change things."

In recent years, Youth Speaks has grown more deliberate in its use of digital and social media to organize concerted efforts to raise awareness and instigate action related to specific civic and political issues. Working with University of California researchers, they created an online video series about diabetes as a social justice issue. In collaboration with the Center for Investigative Reporting, they launched an Instagram campaign organized around the writing prompt, "What hurts you or your community more than fists?" Efforts like these aim to "make poems immortal," in Joshua's words. The organization's ultimate goal in these and other digitally-enabled narrative projects is to surface issues through fact-based poetry that can be used as organizing tools and spark legislative change.

Like the HPA and Youth Speaks, DREAM activists working towards U.S. immigration reform recontextualize cultural narratives in ways that draw out civic and political dimensions. For example, artwork developed by the Orange County DREAM Activists recontextualizes the iconic "illegal immigrant crossing" road sign to signify opportunity and educational attainment. The DREAM activists' image depicts the silhouettes of three youth in caps and gowns in a yellow sign, with the words CAUTION, echoing the iconic sign of a mother and father fleeing with their daughter. Jose explains: "For me, it portrays educated people who have legitimized themselves through an education because this system ... asked them to ... but still remain a little hidden, but they have that potential" (Zimmerman, 2012, p. 51).

Images such as these have made their way into websites, posters, campaigns and T-shirts. DREAM activists use T-shirts as a potent tool for displaying affiliation as well as new narrative framings. One T-shirt that was widely worn at DREAM activist events features white text on a dark blue shirt reading "I AM UN-DOC-U-MENT-ED" with the pronunciation, "(ŭn-dŏk'yə-mĕn'tĭd)" in small type below. Augustin, the designer, says his T-shirt is intended to reframe the stereotype that it is immigrants who are illiterate. "A lot of conservatives that I have seen online with images have signs that are anti-immigrants and sometime, they don't know how to spell the word undocumented ... these people are the ones standing for being American, yet they don't know how to spell their own language". (quoted in Zimmerman, 2012, p. 53)

These DREAM activist creations demonstrate how the work of cultural hybridization is multi-directional; popular culture and products can be used to infuse the dry domain of policy and govermentality with relevance, interest, and immediacy. This is similar to how the HPA mines popular culture in its work towards social justice, and how poetry lends itself to personal narratives tied to the civic and political. The case of libertarian youth, which Liana Gamber-Thompson (2012) has investigated in depth, provides examples that are explicitly about youth with political interests translating their identities into popular idioms. Gamber-Thompson documents the wide range of memes, art, and videos that libertarian youth have produced in order to depict their interests as fun and accessible. One of the more high profile examples is a series of fan tribute videos produced by 19-year old Dorian Electra. Instead of professing her love for a boy band or a TV character, she swoons over libertarian economic theorists such as Friedrich Hayek. She explains that her goal is to present academic ideas "in a more entertaining and accessible format" (Electra quoted in Gamber-Thompson, 2013, p. 151).

These hybrid cultural products, and the contexts out of which they emerge, are selected examples among a much larger array of narratives through which young people connect their interests and affinities with agency and civic opportunity. Taken together, they reveal the many ways in which young people take up characters, scenes, and tropes from within their culturally resonant story-worlds and mobilize these narrative materials to support public calls and campaigns for equity and justice.

Building Shared Practice

Hybrid narratives highlight the kinds of products and contexts that emerge out of connected civics. These products and contexts can only be understood against the backdrop of a set of shared practices that young people deploy in their work together. Part of what it takes to connect with an affinity network is to *learn* and in some cases help shape the norms, rituals, and codes of conduct that structure participation, including within activities aiming for civic and political outcomes. That learning balances mastery with humility—in other words, getting better and better at participating fully, while cultivating practices that keep key questions in play: how do my actions affect others, especially those with the most at stake? How can even my best intentions cause harm? When do I step up and when do I step back?

Young people are connected to their peers 24/7 through text messages, a diverse array of social network sites, and mobile apps that provide new platforms to pursue familiar practices of negotiating status, popularity, and romantic relationships. Through these modes of operation, affinity networks that are tied to a specific cultural or expressive pursuit can lay a foundation for a pivot—sometimes fleeting, sometimes enduring—to the civic and political (this process, of course, can move in the opposite direction as well, with groups that form around civic and political goals connecting their activities to participatory culture). For example, gaming groups generally have competitive play as a core practice, while also supporting sub-groups and more "elite" or high-investment practices such as designing and coding new levels, creating fan videos, or curating knowledge on a shared wiki. In the Star-Craft II community, for example, contexts for competition can range from casual games with others through the online platform, to international tournaments with millions of dollars of prize money awarded to professional players (Kow, Young & Tekinbas, 2014). Other gaming groups, like Little Big Planet, center on competitive play as well as creative production. An active creative community of level designers spans a wide range of online forums, where participants get together to create and submit work for shared challenges (Rafalow and Tekinbas, 2014). For young writers, fan fiction sites and writing forums for content worlds as varied as boy bands and professional wrestling provide contexts to reach an audience, get feedback, and collaborate (Kobrovka, 2014; Martin, 2014).

Even when centered on fun and games, the sense of agency that young people get from contributing to the culture and life of their community can be profound. For example, one young woman Ito interviewed as part of her study of fans of Japanese animation described the immediacy of the feedback she received when she released her translations of anime online:

> The compulsion was unbelievable ... because the feedback's immediate. ... You say something. People say something back a lot of the time. We weren't in the same time zone at the time so you'd have people jubilating because you're doing something at the time ... they're like, 'Oh my God. That's awesome. Thank you so much.' You don't get that kind of feedback. (quoted in Ito, 2013, p. 195).

This kind of immediacy and social connection, which is at the heart of fan and game activities, can also drive contributions to causes that are more explicitly civic in nature. For example, a pro-gaming group might host a livestream to raise dollars for a cause like Doctors Without Borders [Figure 2], and a high school physics teacher and League of Legends player in Des Moines sponsors LAN parties after school to keep failing students engaged in academics (see https://www.youtube.com/watch?v=eWysttc6aqw).

In the case of the Harry Potter Alliance, members have created a toolkit of strategies to mobilize campaigns addressing issues as varied as voting, body image, marriage equality, fair trade, literacy, child slavery, disaster relief, and hunger. Some campaigns involve shared media production, such as the Body Bind Horcrux campaign that encouraged participants to blog, create videos, and share stories about acceptance of their body and different ways of staying healthy. Campaigns also center on partnerships and contributing to causes outside of the HPA community. Helping Haiti Heal mobilized the fandom to provide disaster relief in the wake of the devastating 2010 earthquake. The HPA partnered with a Harry Potter themed "wizard rock" group as well as well-known vlogging duo

Figure 2: Photograph of Dario Wunsch (Starcraft II name TLO) by silversky of TeamLiquid Pro.

John and Hank Green to raise funds through an auction and awareness raising campaign. They raised over $123,000 for the relief group Partners In Health. In all of these campaigns, organizers work to define a concrete set of actions that structure participation, whether it is donating books, writing a blog entry, or helping register voters at a fan event.

Kligler-Vilenchik (2013) describes the close relationship between the HPA and the Nerdfighters, who share common values, cultural referents, and members. Unlike the HPA, however, the Nerdfighter community comes together through practices that are not explicitly civic in nature. The community grew around a daily video blog by writers, activists, and brothers John and Hank Green. Nerdfighters also engage in collaborative media production, particularly "collab channels" on YouTube, mirroring the ways in which John and Hank Green have vlogged collaboratively over the years.

> Members of collab channels often set a theme for the week (e.g. 'the Oscars' or 'your first kiss') that solves the problem of deciding what to talk about. Being assigned a regular day means you have a responsibility to the other group members and don't want to disappoint them. Some collab channels even impose playful "punishments" for not creating a video on your day, often consisting of dare-like tasks such as smearing peanut butter on the face while talking. (Kligler-Vilenchik, 2013, 34)

Kligler-Vilenchik describes how vloggers have been able to discuss electoral politics and social issues within the context of collabs centered on other topics. Vloggers often struggle with how to weave political topics into community or conversation that is not explicitly political in nature. But the fact that the community is connected through shared practices and affinity creates a context for meaningful political conversation and civic engagement at opportune moments.

Unlike activities that are framed in terms of "charity," or giving to groups distant and less privileged, connected civics are grounded in a strong sense of personal affinity and identity. Self-protection and self-interest are not anathema to meaningful civic and political engagement; young people leverage their own life circumstances and struggles as well as deep engagement with participatory culture to ground their activities in what they know, relationships that matter to them, and experiences they have shared. In this way connected civics opens new points of entry for youth who might not otherwise pursue official pathways into institutional politics. Even with Nerdfighter and HPA campaigns, where the concerns taken up by the issues can be socially and culturally distant for some members, we see altruism to others framed by a deep sense of identification, stitched together through cultural acupuncture.

Even when a mobilization is clearly centered on a policy issue, young people are often drawn through their participation in activities that tap personal interests and affinity spaces. In Korea in 2008, for example, 'Candlelight Protests' were organized against American beef imports, resulting in calls for President Lee Myung-bak's impeachment and the largest protests South Korea has seen in 20 years. Over 3.5 million people took to the streets, and over half were teens (Yun & Chang, 2011). Teenage girls in particular were central to this protest movement and were dubbed "candlelight girls." The Korean candlelight protests have been held up as an example of youth mobilization with social media as they organized in a highly distributed fashion through a variety of online sites and text messaging, bonding around everyday concerns over the educational system and food safety. It turns out that in addition to these real life concerns, they were mobilized around a different shared interest. HyeRyoung Ok (personal communication, 2009) followed this movement as part of her research on mobile media in Korea. Ok also happens to be a fan of a popular boy band, Dong Bang Sin Gi. In one of the massive online fan forums, she saw that the young women fans were mobilizing to attend the protests. They carried placards: "We don't want our boys to get sick because of mad cows." Their participation in the protests was grounded in a combination of the concrete conditions of their everyday lives, and in their solidarity with the shared practices that define a particular media fandom.

This stitching together of personal identity and civic action is even more evident in the case of DREAM activists, who are mobilizing to promote their own stories and needs to push for policy reform. The merging of personal interests and identities with a social justice agenda is, in this sense, seamless (though deeply challenging, strategic, and risky) for young people actively contending with threats to freedom, safety, and equal access to opportunity. The successful mobilization of DREAM activists is built on a layering of practices that sit between the social bonds and affinities developed among undocumented youth, and visibility and influence in the political sphere. The young DREAMers are their own best advocates, organizing events where undocumented youth are placed center stage. For example, in 2011 DREAMers staged a symbolic graduation in front of the Senate dressed in graduation caps and gowns.

The collaborative production of DREAMers centers on the stories of the undocumented youth themselves. One key activity of DREAMactivist.org is to provide media training for undocumented youth so they can produce content and messages and spread them through social media to build a following. They also support the sharing of "coming out" narratives where young people shoot videos of themselves declaring they are undocumented and telling their stories. Zimmerman (2012) quotes a young man who shared one of these narratives:

[When I watch it] I feel proud. I feel something that's a positive feeling, you know, it was a very — I didn't feel ashamed anymore. I feel like I came out and I felt safe to come out. We have to come out of the shadows. I think it's time where we should not be afraid of saying who we are. Why be afraid? ... I think we had enough, now let's stop being afraid and let's start taking action because if there is no action there is never going to be a change. (p. 46)

This young DREAM activist articulates his own movement along a trajectory from personal circumstances that he'd kept "in the shadows" for most of his life, into a community that is unafraid to come out and in so doing "take action," by mobilizing deeply felt identities, interests and affinity networks to achieve agency and seize civic opportunity.

Developing Cross-Cutting Infrastructure

In *Here Comes Everybody,* Clay Shirky (2008) argues that "we are living in the middle of a remarkable increase in our ability to share, to cooperate with one another, and to take collective action, all outside the framework of traditional institutions and organizations" (p. 20-21). The youth collectives described here leverage digital and networked tools to organize at a lower cost and larger scale than would have been possible in a pre-digital era (Earl & Kimport, 2011). Whether it involves a campaign orchestrated through a tight-knit affinity network or lightweight circulation of a political meme among peers on a social media site, participatory politics are enabled by the accessibility of media production, circulation, and communication. Participatory politics calls attention to what Bennett and Segerberg (2012) have described as "the logic of connective action" that mobilizes through "personal action frames" and distributed social networks and differs from collective action centered on organizationally brokered groups and actions. The narratives and practices of connected civics draw their power from personal investments and interests supported by social media and affinity networks. At the same time, building consequential connections to civic opportunities and agency also involves tying these networks and interests to durable infrastructures and existing institutions, constituting what Bennett and Segerberg have described as hybrid forms that sit between connective and collective action networks.

In high-tech countries like the U.S., youth access to networked and mobile communications infrastructure has increased steadily, and the vast majority of young people are connected to social media sites and apps where they communicate with peers from their local settings as well as more far-flung affinity networks (Madden, Lenhart, Duggan, Cortesi, & Gasser, 2013). Whether it is the "news" about a newly minted couple shared through a Facebook status update, or a call to participate in a political activation, more and more of young people's connection to public life is mediated through these online infrastructures. Youth affinity networks vary widely as to how formally they are organized and what kinds of digitally-connected, place-based, and hybrid infrastructures they rely on. They run the gamut from networks that rely entirely on free and widespread commercial infrastructure such as Twitter, Reddit, or Facebook, to home-grown sites like animemusicvideos.com or ravelry.com, which are designed, coded, and created by members of the affinity network themselves in order to serve the specialized needs of their core participants (video remixers and knitters in these cases) (Ito, 2013a; Pfister, 2014). From the growing array of social network sites, mobile apps, and affinity-centered platforms, young people are finding a rich set of tools and infrastructures they can use to connect with the civic and the political.

For example, DREAM activists have established multiple websites and networked organizations to build these connections. DREAMactivist.org was founded by students who only met in person several years after the site was established. It has grown over the years to become a coalition of 30 organizations that sponsor activities such as a new media intern program as well as campaigns such as the National DREAM Graduation, petitions, and fundraising (Zimmerman, 2012, pp. 22-23). A more formal organization like dreamactivist.org provides the focus for the more diffuse range of blogs, online videos, art, and twitter chats that comprise the broader movement. Without this formal organization, it is unlikely that the DREAMers movement would have had the kind of visibility or legislative successes that they have.

Like the DREAM Activists, Nerdfighters mobilize through a range of different online platforms. The Green brothers' videos are hosted on YouTube, and have over two million subscribers. Nerdfighters have uploaded hundreds of videos to their network of personal video blogs, donated hundreds of thousands of dollars to the Foundation to Decrease World Suck, and are the largest lending team for the small loans platform Kiva.org, at over $4 million in loans and over 45,000 members.

In contrast to the Nerdfighters, which is a loosely organized affinity network centered around a set of video blogs and varied online platforms, the HPA relies on a more formal, traditional organizational structure of chapters located at schools or other community organizations. Hundreds of HPA chapters have been established across the country and overseas and represent the core of the network that can be activated for campaigns. Becoming an HPA chapter requires having leadership in place, establishing some kind of online presence, and a commitment to participating in campaigns and other activities. In addition to this core network, the HPA also relies on the substantial infrastructure and organizational heft of the Harry Potter fandom as well as other fan groups such as the Nerdfighters. Collaborating with networked groups like the Nerdfighters and Harry Potter podcasters for campaigns and awareness-raising, the HPA will organize activities in tandem with fan conventions and Wizard Rock events in order to reach constituencies that are broader than its core membership. For example, in 2012 HPA members partnered with Wizard Rock artist Paul DeGeorge for their Wrock the Vote Campaign, and registered people to vote at concerts around the country (Kligler-Vilenchik, 2013, pp. 21-22).

Though different in important ways, the HPA and dreamactivist.org are examples of youth-led organizations that sit at the intersection of youth-centered peer networks and formal, adult-led institutions like schools and the state. Organizational structures that combine peer-to-peer engagement and youth-adult collaboration can also be initiated and led by educators and professional producers, as is the case with many youth-centered media programs and organizations.

At Youth Radio in Oakland, California, for example, young people are often drawn to apply for the organization's free, after-school multimedia classes initially based on a friend's recommendation or because they heard it was a place where they could get on the radio and learn to deejay and produce beats. Once young people come into the organization, they do get to make music. But they are also called upon to facilitate roundtable discussions, write opinion pieces and news spots, produce public service announcements, and learn to spread all this youth-generated content via social media. For the young people who opt to join the organization's newsroom after six months of classes taught by peer educators and adult faculty, there is the opportunity to reach audiences in the tens of millions. Youth Radio is National Public Radio's official Youth Desk and distributes stories through a range of other online and broadcast outlets including Marketplace, The Atlantic, Salon, Medium, The Huffington Post, National Geographic, Boing Boing, and local public and commercial radio stations around the U.S.

What started with a small group of teenagers collaborating with journalist Ellin O'Leary on a series of radio commentaries has developed a cross-cutting infrastructure that has been crucial in supporting young people's individual trajectories as well as the production of media that achieves civic impact. More than 80% of the teenagers and young adults (ages 14-24) at Youth Radio are low-income youth and young people of color. The organization provides academic, career, and health counseling as well as a network of peer and adult collaborators and escalating opportunities for young people to play leadership roles within the organization and in the wider community. The organization creates more than 250 paid jobs for youth per year in the center of Downtown Oakland.

One context that specifically supports young people's engagement in connected civics is Youth Radio's investigative unit. A recent project, the 2014 Double Charged series, was a year-long investigation into the hidden costs of juvenile incarceration (Soep is Youth Radio's Senior Producer and Research Director and was an editor on this series). The back-story behind the series highlights the importance of infrastructures for support. As part of their efforts to support young people at Youth Radio who are court-involved, staff members sometimes go to court with youth for hearings and other consequential events. They started to notice that many of the young people reporting for court dates were not there for sentencing but to pay fees. This observation triggered a large-scale, sustained investigation into the growing trend within juvenile courts across the country to offset costs by charging families, the majority low-income, for fees associated with their children's crimes.

Producing a series at this scale and with its daunting reporting demands requires considerable curricular infrastructure. Youth Radio has developed a methodology that combines peer education and adult collaboration or "collegial pedagogy" to prepare young people to conduct interviews and analyze data from fellow youth (in the case of this story, teens coming out of incarceration or probation) as well as senior government officials (e.g., District Attorneys, Public Defenders) and experts on criminal justice (Soep & Chávez, 2010). The capacity to produce this level of reporting depends on sustained, structured learning opportunities, which turned out to be crucial to the team's ability to create a series that culminated in two national radio pieces, articles in The Atlantic, Buzzfeed, and Medium, two data-driven info-graphics, a Tweet chat, an interactive news app, four lesson plans developed by young people to help teachers integrate the stories into their classrooms, and plans for briefing county officials on the implications of the investigation for law enforcement and youth communities.

Institutionalization and increased infrastructure can run the risk of undermining the youth-driven affinities that drew together a group in the first place, through the emergence of outward-facing concerns (for example, funding deliverables) or the development of internal factions. When affinity networks *are* able to successfully navigate these tensions, their infrastructures: tend to be organized around youth interest; facilitate alliances with adults on young people's terms; allow for youth participation to take a range of forms; connect with young people on- and off-line; and invite investigation and critique on the part of those involved. In turn, the participants are empowered to change course when circumstances call for iteration. When young people are able to connect *both* flexibly networked as well as more formalized and capitalized kinds of infrastructures and institutions, we see the largest impacts, both personal and societal.

Conclusion: Developing Civic and Political Affinity Networks

In this article we have proposed a framework for identifying and supporting points of connection and synergy between young people's agency in peer networks, their interests, and civic opportunity in an era of participatory politics. We have described this site of intersection as "connected civics," where young people can experience civic agency in a way that is embedded in meaningful social relationships, tied to deeply held interests and affinities, and powered by their various modes of creative expression and cultural production. We have dissected the properties of narratives, practices, and infrastructures that constitute "consequential connections" that tie together these more conventionally disconnected spheres. As a dimension of participatory politics, connected civics offers a powerful mode of learning and civic agency because it engages young people through deeply held identities and compelling cultural narratives, is driven by shared practices and purpose, and is grounded in a robust but accessible networked infrastructure. Further, by drawing together interests, agency, and civic opportunity, it infuses each sphere with the power of the other, making civics compelling—sometimes fun—and socially connected, and making social activity and cultural production reach for a higher calling. Groups that support connected civics include those that start with a youth affinity network (like the Harry Potter Alliance), as well as those that begin with a shared identity that is both embraced and politically imposed (like DREAMers), as well as programs structured around youth-adult collaboration with explicit educational and professional goals (like Youth Radio). In these consequential connections built by youth and adult leaders, we see a source of positive inspiration for other groups seeking to support youth civic engagement. We also see growing opportunities for supporting these connections and building multiple points of entry to connected civics with the growth of participatory politics that has accompanied the spread of digital and networked media.

By focusing on consequential connections, we have turned our attention to social and cultural contexts rather than individual skills, capacities, and ladders of engagement. Rather than limit our educational interventions to "engaging" or "developing" youth who are assumed to be in some way deficient, we might instead consider that the lack lies in the stories, identities, activities, and organizational roles that are open and available to them. Put differently, the "problem" may not be that young people are disengaged, but that there are critical disconnects between the social, cultural, and institutional worlds of youth and adults. Too often, young people are given the message that the issues they care about are trivial, lack broader relevance, and/or are beyond their grasp and therefore require officially recognized expertise to address. Very rarely are they invited to participate in activities of consequence that make a real difference in the adult-facing world, even though they may be engaged in meaningful and consequential forms of organizing and production in their digitally networked lives and peer communication.

Clearly young people are developing skills, literacies, and social connections in their peer social exchanges and affinity networks that can be mobilized for contexts outside of these settings. These include the ability to tell stories, mobilize publics, conduct research, code, and manage publicity (Soep, 2014). By stressing the importance of *consequential* connections, we call attention to the importance of building contexts where these capacities can be meaningfully applied and exercised. It is not enough to develop these capacities, whether that is in a peer setting, gaming community or in an educational program, if there are not narratives, practices, relationships, and infrastructures that enable the translation and shared purpose that knit these worlds together.

Indeed, if we do turn our attention to the individual journeys that young people take through their educational, social, recreational and civic worlds, we see a marked absence of clear "ladders" or sequential "pathways" of civic development. Instead we see moments of activation when an affinity space is under threat, or periods of engagement when a cause becomes relevant to a deeply held identity or value. Achieving a broader purpose does not require transcending or abandoning affinity and identity, and can involve finding specific causes and activities that make an individual's identity and social relationships consequential and urgently relevant.

Acknowledgments

This paper is indebted to the researchers in the YPP and CLRN networks who have offered not only rich data and case materials but key insights that have informed the analysis represented here. Special thanks go to Elyse Eidman-Aadahl, Cathy Cohen, Howard Gardner, Henry Jenkins, Joseph Kahne and the members of the Leveling Up team: Ksenia Korobkova, Yong Ming Kow, Crystle Martin, Rachel Cody Pfister, Matthew Rafalow, Katie Salen Tekinbas, Amanda Wortman, Timothy Young.

Funding

This work was supported by the John D. and Catherine T. MacArthur Foundation grants [13-103229-000-USP] and [10-97572-000-USP].

References

Allen, D. (2012). Towards participatory democracy. *Boston Review*. Retrieved from http://www.bostonreview.net/forum/port-huron-statement-50/toward-participatory-democracy

Bakardijeva, M. (2009). Subactivism: Liveworld and politics in the age of the internet. *The Information Society, 25*, 91–104.

Barron, B., Gomez, K., Pinkard, N., & Martin, C. (2014). *The digital youth network*. Cambridge, MA: MIT Press.

Beach, K. (1999). Consequential transitions: A sociocultural expedition beyond transfer in education. *Review of Research in Education, 24*, 101–139.

Bennett, L., & Segerberg, A. (2012). The logic of connective action. *Information, Communication & ..., 15*, 739–768.

Boyd, Danah. (2014). *It's complicated: The social lives of networked teens*. New Haven, CT: Yale University Press.

Bransford, J. D., & Schwartz, D. L. (2001). Rethinking transfer: A simple proposal with multiple implications. *Review of Research in Education, 24*, 61–100.

Carter, P. (2005). *Keepin' it real: School success beyond black and white*. London: Oxford University Press.

Chun, W. (in press). The dangers of transparent friends: Crossing the public and intimate spaces. In D. Allen & J. Light (Eds.), *From voice to influence*. Chicago: University of Chicago Press.

Cohen, C., Kahne, J., Bowyer, B., Middaugh, E., & Rogowski, J. (2012). *Participatory politics: New media and youth political action*. Retrieved from http://ypp.dmlcentral.net/sites/default/files/publications/Participatory_Politics_New_Media_and_Youth_Political_Action.2012.pdf

Dahlgren, P. (2005). The internet, public spheres, and political communication: Dispersion and deliberation. *Political Communication, 22*, 147–162.

Dean, J. (2005). Communicative capitalism: Circulation and the foreclosure of politics. *Cultural Politics, 1*, 51–74.

DeVoss, D. N., Eidman-Aadahl, E., & Hicks, T. (2010). *Because digital writing matters: Improving student writing in online and multimedia environments*. San Francisco: Jossey-Bass.

Earl, J. (2013). Spreading the word or shaping the conversation: "Prosumption" in protest website. In P. G. Coy (Ed.), *Research in social movements, conflicts and change* (pp. 3–38). Bradford, UK: Emerald Group Publishing.

Earl, J., & Kimport, K. (2011). *Digitally enabled social change: Activism in the internet age*. Cambridge, MA: MIT Press.

Eckert, P. (1989). *Jocks and burnouts*. New York: Teachers College Press.

Engestrom, Y. (1996). Development as breaking away and opening up: A challenge to Vygostky and Piaget. *Swiss Journal of Psychology, 55*, 126–132.

Gamber-Thompson, L. (2012). *The cost of engagement: Politics and participatory practices in the U.S. liberty movement*. Los Angeles. Retrieved from http://ypp.dmlcentral.net/sites/all/files/publications/The_Cost_of_Engagement-Working_Paper-MAPP_12.10.12.pdf

Gardner, H., & Davis, K. (2013). *The app generation*. New Haven, CT: Yale University Press.

Gee, J. P. (2005). Semiotic social spaces and affinity spaces: From the age of mythology to today's schools. In D. Barton & K. Tusting (Eds.), *Beyond communities of practice: Language, power and social context* (pp. 214–232). Cambridge, UK: Cambridge U. Press.

Gee, J. P., & Hayes, E. R. (2010). *Women and gaming: The sims and 21st century learning*. New York: Palgrave MacMillan.

Ginwright, S., Noguera, P. & Cammarota, J. (2006). *Beyond resistance! Youth activism and community change: New possibilities for practice and policy for America's youth*. London: Routledge.

Goldman, S. (2006). A new angle on families: Connecting the mathematics in daily life with school mathematics. In Z. Bekerman, N. Burbules, & D. Silberman-Keller (Eds.), *Learning in places: The informal education reader*. Bern: Peter Lang.

Hall, S. & Jefferson, T. (2006). *Resistance through rituals: Youth subcultures in post-war Britain*. London: Routledge.

Hebdige, D. (1979). *Subculture: The meaning of style*. London: Routledge.

Hull, G., & Shultz, K. (2002). *School's out! Bridging out-of-school literacies with classroom practice*. New York: Teacher's College Press.

Ito, M. (2013a). "As long as it's not linkin park z": Popularity, distinction, and status in the amv subculture. In M. Ito, D. Okabe, & I. Tsuji (Eds.), *Fandom unbound: Otaku culture in a connected world* (pp. 275–298). New Haven: Yale University Press.

Ito, M. (2013b). Contributors v. leechers: Fansubbing ethics and a hybrid public culture. In M. Ito, D. Okabe, & I. Tsuji (Eds.), *Fandom unbound: Otaku culture in a connected world* (pp. 179–204). New Haven, CT: Yale University Press.

Ito, M., Baumer, S., Bittanti, M., boyd, danah, Cody, R., Herr-Stephenson, B., . . . Tripp, L. (2009). *Hanging out, messing around, and geeking out: Kids living and learning with new media*. Cambridge, MA: MIT Press.

Ito, M., Guitiérrez, K., Livingstone, S., Penuel, B., Rhodes, J., Salen, K., . . . Watkins, C. S. (2013). *Connected learning: An agenda for research and design*. Irvine, CA. Retrieved from http://dmlhub.net/publications/connected-learning-agenda-research-and-design

Jenkins, H. (2006). *Convergence culture: Where old and new media collide*. New York: New York University Press.

Jenkins, H. (2012). "Cultural acupuncture": Fan activism and the Harry Potter alliance. *Transformative Works and Cultures, 10*.

Jenkins, H., Clinton, K., Puruchotma, R., Robinson, A. J., & Weigel, M. (2009). Confronting the challenges of participatory culture: Media education for the 21st century. *The John D. and Catherine T. MacArthur Foundation Reports on Digital Media and Learning*. Cambridge, MA: MIT Press.

Jenkins, H., Ford, S., & Green, J. (2013). *Spreadable media: Creating value and meaning in a networked culture*. New York: NYU Press.

Jenkins, H., Gamber-Thompson, L., Kligler-Vilenchik, N., Shresthova, S., & Zimmerman, A. M. (n.d.). *By any media necessary: Mapping youth and participatory politics*. New York: NYU Press.

Kahne, J., Middaugh, E., & Allen, D. (2014). *Youth, new media, and the rise of participatory politics*. YPP Research Network Working Paper #1. Retrieved from http://dmlcentral.net/sites/dmlcentral/files/resource_files/ypp_workinpapers_paper01_1.pdf

Kligler-Vilenchik, N. (2013). *"Decreasing world suck": Fan communities, mechanisms of translation, and participatory politics*. Los Angeles: MacArthur Foundation.

Kligler-Vilenchik, N., & Shresthova, S. (2012). *Learning through practice: Participatory culture practices*. Los Angeles, CA. Retrieved from http://dmlhub.net/publications/learning-through-practice-participatory-culture-practices/

Kligler-Vilenchik, N., & Shresthova, S. (2014). Participatory culture civics. *Conjunctions, 1*. Retrieved from http://dmlcentral.net/sites/dmlcentral/files/resource_files/learning_through_practice_kligler-shresthova_oct-2-2012.pdf

Korobkova, K. (2014). *Schooling the directioners: Connected learning and identity-making in the one direction fandom*. Irvine, CA. Retrieved from http://clrn.dmlhub.net/wp-content/uploads/2014/05/Schooling-the-Directioners_Korobkova.pdf

Kow, Y. M., Young, T., & Tekinbas, K. S. (2014). *Crafting the metagame: Connected learning in the starcraft ii community*. Irvine, CA. Retrieved from http://dmlhub.net/publications/crafting-metagame-connected-learning-starcraft-ii-community

Lave, J. (1988). *Cognition in practice*. New York: Cambridge University Press.

Madden, M., Lenhart, A., Duggan, M., Cortesi, S. C., & Gasser, U. (2013). *Teens and technology 2013*. Washington D.C. Retrieved from http://www.pewinternet.org/2013/03/13/teens-and-technology-2013/

Martin, C. (2014). *Learning the ropes: Connected learning in a wwe fan community*. Irvine, CA: Digital Media and Learning Research Hub.

Milner, M. (2004). *Freaks, geeks, and cool kids: American teenagers, schools, and the culture of consumption*. New York: Routledge.

Pascoe, C. (2007). *Dude, you're a fag: Masculinity and sexuality in high school*. Berkeley, CA: Univeristy of California Press.

Pellegrino, J. W., & Hilton, M. L. (2012). *Education for life and work: Developing transferable knowledge and skills in the 21st century*. Washington, D.C.: The National Academies Press. Retrieved from http://www.nap.edu/catalog.php?record_id=13398

Pfister, R. C. (2014). *Hats for house elves: Connected learning and civic engagement in Hogwarts at Ravelry*. Irvine, CA: Digital Media and Learning Research Hub.

Phillips, W. (2011). *LOLing at tragedy: Facebook trolls, memorial pages, and resistance to grief online*. First Monday 16, no. 12. Retrieved from http://firstmonday.org/ojs/index.php/fm/article/view/3168.

Rafalow, M. H., & Tekinbas, K. S. (2014). *Welcome to sackboy planet: Connected learning among littlebigplanet 2 players*. Irvine, CA. Retrieved from http://dmlhub.net/publications/welcome-sackboy-planet-connected-learning-among-littlebigplanet-2-players

Rheingold, H. (2012). *Net smart: How to thrive online*. Cambridge, MA: MIT Press.

Shirky, C. (2008). *Here comes everybody: The power of organizing without organizations*. New York: Penguin Press.

Shresthova, S. (2013). *Between storytelling and surveillance: American muslim youth negotiate culture, politics and participation*. Los Angeles, CA: Digital Media and Learning Research Hub.

Soep, E. (2014). *Participatory politics*. Cambridge, MA: MIT Press.

Soep, E. & Chávez, V. (2010). *Drop that knowledge: Youth radio stories*. Berkeley: University of California Press.

Varenne, H., & McDermott, R. (1998). The Farrells and the Kinneys at home: Literacies in action. In H. Varenne & R. McDermott (Eds.), *Successful failure: The school America builds* (pp. 45−62). Boulder, CO: Westview.

Weinstein, E. C. (2014). The personal is political on social media. *International Journal of Communications, 8*, 210−233.

Willis, P. (1990). *Common culture: Symbolic work at play in the everyday cultures of the young*. Boulder, CO: Westview.

Yun, S., & Chang, W.-Y. (2011). Political participation of teenagers in the information era. *Social Science Computer Review, 29*, 242−249.

Zimmerman, A. M. (2012). *Documenting dreams: New media, undocumented youth and the immigrant rights movement*. Los Angeles, CA. Retrieved from http://dmlhub.net/publications/documenting-dreams-new-media-undocumented-youth-and-immigrant-rights-movement

Zuckerman, E. (n.d.). Cute cats to the rescue? Participatory media and political expression. In D. Allen & J. Light (Eds.), *Youth, new media, and political participation*. Retrieved from http://ethanzuckerman.com/papers/cutecats2013.pdf

2 New media literacies as social action
The centrality of pedagogy in the politics of knowledge production

Korina M. Jocson

In this article, the author illustrates the blurring lines of youth cultural production and participatory politics from the perspective of new media literacies. Drawing on design-based action research, the author discusses pedagogical considerations in the conceptualization of new media literacies in a semester-long course that culminated in inquiry-based social action projects created by university students in the urban Midwest. Noteworthy in the course was an emerging ethos developed through *collaboration*, *participation*, and *distributed expertise* leading to the production of video documentaries and interactive websites. New media literacies served as core cultural competencies and social skills in a new media landscape, but more importantly emerged as key practices toward youth cultural production and participatory politics. The latter offers insights into the centrality of pedagogy in the politics of knowledge production.

Today's creative expressions blur the lines between youth cultural production and participatory politics. As the articles in this special issue illustrate, there are myriad ways of participating in civic life. It is no longer a surprise that many young people are making videos, taking photographs, creating websites, blogging, assembling mash ups, and sharing them online for others to view. From a new media literacies perspective, it is argued that an ethos of collaboration, participation, and distributed expertise shapes how individuals see themselves in the world and interact with each other as afforded by digital technologies (Lankshear & Knobel, 2006). At the center of this ontological and technocultural shift are youths who engage in alternative and activist practices (Lievrouw, 2011).

Such practices reflect what Cohen and Kahne (2012) call participatory politics, in which interactive, peer-based acts have the ability to reach large audiences, shape agendas through dialogue, and exert greater agency through the circulation of information and the production of original content − both online and offline. In this light, the notion of participatory politics is seen as wielding voice and influence on issues of public concern without being guided by deference to elites or formal institutions. Participatory politics are interest-driven and voluntary. In my continued work with secondary and tertiary students, I have been moved by the potential of participatory politics not only as voluntary, but also as pedagogically operational in critical education (Anyon, 2009a, 2009b; Apple, Au, & Gandin, 2009). What happens when participatory politics become a key component of the classroom experience? What pedagogical considerations are necessary to enable both students and educators to embrace varied uses of technology toward alternative and activist practices? In what ways can the curriculum be invigorated by interest-driven and peer-based acts within the confines of school, university, and other formal institutions? Philip and Garcia (2013) remind us of the centrality of pedagogy and the continued need for a dynamic relationship between students and teachers in supporting today's iGeneration. What I describe below is one instantiation of youth cultural production and participatory politics in the context of a new media literacies course. Given the pace of changing technologies and changing practices, it is important to examine specific ways through which youth leverage new media literacies in order to understand pedagogical possibilities.

In this article, I draw on design-based action research to offer insights on new media literacies as social action. On the one hand, the design-based approach was theory-oriented, iterative, interventionist, and pragmatic toward a greater understanding of learning (Cobb, Confrey, diSessa, Lehrer, & Schauble, 2003); on the other hand, action research as a form of teacher inquiry guided the work to be cyclical, contextual, ethical, and reflective to pursue learning and change (Cochran-Smith & Lytle, 1993, 1999; McIntyre, 2008). That is, students and I did not just arrive with set plans for the social action projects conducted at the end of the semester. Designing curriculum necessitated careful attention to cohort and context (Luke, Woods, & Weir, 2013). This meant situating ourselves during the course of our time together within the sociopolitical context of the university and the larger community.[1] This also meant co-constructing a learning space where varied resources and materials (official and unofficial) would come together in support of our purpose and needs. To that end, new media literacies as a course topic served as the context through which to explore participatory politics and issues of public concern that we as a cohort constructed together in a course titled "New Media Literacies and Popular Culture in Education."

In what follows, I begin with the conceptualization of "new media literacies" to demonstrate how the course topic was in itself mutually constitutive. I discuss curricular components with students' own new media literacies at work. Specific activities and assignments took place inside and outside of the classroom. Students enrolled in this course (ages 19–25) were asked to participate in a class blog (viewable by the public) as one way to share responses to readings, facilitate an in-class discussion with a partner using multimedia tools, create a digital story, and produce a short documentary along with an interactive website. For the latter, students were asked to examine a particular educational or social issue that would raise awareness about a historically segregated city in the urban Midwest.

As the instructor of record, I positioned myself as a learning partner open to ideas and suggestions; with that goal in mind, class sessions took a seminar format. In the end, a public screening and exhibit was held at a nearby museum to showcase student work. Planning the event was deliberate in order to promote dialogue across institutional spaces and to further legitimize youth voice and influence on local matters (Cohen & Kahne, 2012; Soep & Chávez, 2010). Noteworthy in the course was an ethos that developed through *collaboration*, *participation*, and *distributed expertise* leading to the production of video documentaries and interactive websites. Multilayered and occurring across off and online spaces, the inquiry and media-making process built on a set of new media literacies such as play, transmedia navigation, and visualization (Jenkins, 2006)[2]. These new media literacies served as core cultural competencies and social skills in a new media landscape, but more importantly emerged as key practices toward youth cultural production and participatory politics. In short, the uncertainty within the inquiry opened up opportunities for students and I to collaboratively recognize the value of new media literacies in everyday life and new media literacies as a form of social action toward a (re) interpretation of lived and constructed realities. The insights shared here point to the centrality of pedagogy in the politics of knowledge production. To understand the nature of the course, let me turn now to an overview of new media literacies as a concept that guided our work.

New Media Literacies

In the context of our semester-long course, the conceptualization of "new media literacies" was influenced by perspectives in media and cultural studies, education, and communication. Theoretically, we began the course with questions. What constitutes "new media literacies"? What counts as "new"? How are today's media similar to or different from the "old"? Why is the plurality of literacy necessary? Practically, what do "new media literacies" look like in everyday life and how do individuals, youth especially, utilize or leverage them for different purposes? These questions prompted early discussions in class and had been guiding my teaching and research in education. In this particular course, the questions served as a departure point for interrogating one's personal use of media technologies that typically evoke more questions about the quandaries of what it means to live in a digitally mediated world.

Open to upper-level undergraduate and graduate students, the course aimed to provide a dialogic space for exploring theories and practices of new media literacies. The course was iterative in design. Prior instances of the class varied slightly with modified sets of readings and assignments. An explicit difference this semester was the perspective on alternative and activist new media with a culminating social action project. As a basis for introducing the course, the terms "new," "media," and "literacies" provided a catalyst for theory building. For me, what became provocative over time were not the shifting meanings embedded in each term but the emergent thinking, and thus emerging concepts, when these terms were combined to produce three exciting areas of study: new media, new literacies, and media literacies. The breakdown of "new media literacies" into three different yet interrelated concepts during the first four weeks of the semester helped to organize the remainder of the course.

Briefly, according to Lister, Dovey, Giddings, Grant, and Kelly (2009), the new in "new media" points to change and continuity of practices that is shaped by but not reducible to technologies. The pace of change is unparalleled and, as they argue from a media and cultural studies perspective, has resulted in "new textual experiences, new ways of representing the world, new relationships between subjects and media technologies," new ways of embodying identity and community, and new patterns of organization, consumption, production, distribution, and use (Lister et al. 2009, p. 12). New media are characterized as digital, interactive, hypertextual, virtual, networked, and simulated.

Similarly, Lankshear and Knobel (2006) suggest that the new in "new literacies" is ontologically shifting everyday social practice and classroom learning. Their perspective renders two nodes of thinking relevant to education: new technical stuff (technology) and new ethos stuff (mindset). With the new technical stuff, the shift from analog to digital enables different ways of reading, writing, communicating, and sharing through various interfaces. With the new ethos stuff, the emergence of a distinctly contemporary mindset of collaboration, participation, and distributed expertise enables fluidity, openness, and hybridity. This type of mindset has implications for students and teachers who find themselves at the forefront of changing practices and changing technologies within and beyond the school walls. The "ethos" of *collaboration, participation*, and *distributed expertise* is part of what my students and I discovered along the way and grappled with until the end of the semester. Lastly, Kellner and Share (2007) note the value of "media literacies" in education as the ubiquity of media (and its many forms) has come to dominate screens present in youth's lives. Through what they call critical media literacies, the emphasis is on the explicit deconstruction of ideology found in media forms and the questioning of power relations within media representations. Kellner and Share see this approach as one way to equip students with the ability to consume and evaluate media, including social media, toward civic engagement.

From the outset, a working definition of new media literacies allowed for building and enacting theory into practice through course-related activities. New media literacies, then, were defined as the abilities to (1) utilize media technologies toward new experiences with texts and relationships, (2) build on a mindset of collaboration, participation, and distributed expertise in classrooms and beyond, and (3) consume and evaluate media forms as well as media representations more critically in order to challenge normalized discourses toward transformative cultural production. This working definition provided those of us in the course with a common ground, a framework, for conceptualizing new media literacies.

Further, recent scholarship on digital media and learning articulates the need for understanding new media literacies in a participatory culture. Jenkins and colleagues (2006) put forth that new media literacies are a set of core competencies and social skills in a new media landscape. A provisionary list of skills include play, performance, simulation, appropriation, multitasking, judgment, distributed cognition, collective intelligence, judgment, transmedia navigation, networking, negotiation, and visualization (see www.newmedialiteracies.org). As I will point out in my work with students, these core competencies and social skills (with the exception of simulation) emerged as key practices toward youth cultural production and participatory politics. The resultant social action projects – video documentaries and interactive websites – served as an example of engaging in the politics of knowledge production. Moreover, concerned with the changing demands of learning, Ito and colleagues (2013) offer a model of connected learning which fuses learning principles (youth's interests, peer culture, and academic achievement) with design principles (hands-on production, shared purpose, and open networks). Driving this model of connected learning are core values of equity, full participation, and social connection. Together, the learning principles, design principles, and core values of connected learning reflect possibilities in the classroom, which in the case of our classroom were centered on the conceptualization and application of new media literacies.

Doing the Work In/With New Media Literacies

To illustrate what led up to the social action projects, it is important to explicate some aspects of the learning process including course readings, discussions (in class and online), and assignments. A deliberate shift took place in week 4 from theory building to the practice of new media literacies. Blogging, group presentations, experiential learning to poster project, and digital story are described in the following subsections.

Blogging

A class blog served as our discussion canvas. Responses based on weekly readings were shared on the blog. For organizational purposes, I posted a visual (as opposed to written) prompt consisting of figurative images under the appropriate topic heading each week. The idea was to be suggestive and not be prescriptive about a reader-response approach to the assigned readings. Students used the blog as an opportunity to comment on what they found most striking about the readings; sometimes, students contested or critiqued statements previously posted by their peers. A minimum of five substantive entries was required for the semester. Open to the public, the class blog was meant to encourage students to write with a broader audience in mind, and to think of the online discussion as one way to contribute to the larger discourse on new media literacies.

Group Presentations

Aside from online discussions, activities and assignments throughout the course encouraged students to be dialogic, collaborative, and exploratory. Based on class enrollment, I pre-selected a number of readings for the purpose of group presentations. Thirteen students signed up to work in pairs for a total of six groups and one solo presenter (a graduate student); each group prepared summary points with the use of Powerpoint or Prezi slides. As it turned out, the class blog served as a resource with comments posted the night before a group presentation. Students facilitating the group presentation were responsible for monitoring blog comments for further take-up in class. As a common practice, I read all of the blog comments before each class session to see the level of engagement and to keep up with patterns in students' thinking. Each group presentation took on a seminar format where class members, including myself, sat around in a semicircle. We were fortunate to have an "active learning" classroom with swivel desk chairs inside the main campus library, which enabled spatial flexibility.[3]

Experiential Learning to Poster Project

As we moved toward weeks 5 to 8 of the semester, different articles and studies of new media literacies in youth's lives provided practical insights (Ito, 2010; Palfrey & Gasser, 2008; Scott & White, 2011). Genres of participation such as hanging out, messing around, and geeking out offered a framework for us to consider. By connecting theory to practice across contexts, students pointed out the permeability and nonlinearity in the genres; that is, they recognized that today's participatory culture is bi-directionally shaped by the availability of do-it-yourself digital media technologies and by the participants who tinker with them as creators and learners.

The notion of messing around or tinkering with digital media technologies, which to an extent draws on elements of play, transmedia navigation, and negotiation, was helpful to our growing understanding of new media literacies. This also became an important lens through which to examine what happens in different technology-rich environments such as museums, libraries, coffee shops, the Apple store, and even the metro or subway train. As part of an experiential learning exercise, students visited "technology-rich" environments and their observations led to a group analysis, including but not limited to: technology and public access, spatial design, portability, mobility, and connectivity. The class divided up into eight groups; each group produced a poster with general information and analysis, including representative artifacts and visual images of the technology-rich environment (see Figure 1). The theories and practices of new media literacies we had been discussing were unfolding before our eyes. For example, students reported that technology-rich environments were "rich" due in part to the material and human resources that allow for digitally-mediated interactions and networked activities (Ito, 2010; Ito et al., 2013; Lister et al., 2009). Students also noted the variability in spatial design conducive for specific purposes, including physical set ups for messing around as an element of learning. What seemed to be emerging at this stage in the course was attention to

Figure 1. Technology-Rich Environment Posters.

Digital Story

The notion of messing around (which we adopted as tinkering with digital media technologies) remained central in the course as students engaged in hands-on production. The digital story project that ensued was purposeful for tinkering with specific media editing tools. For 11 out of the 13 students, media production had been a first time experience. As I began to notice, tinkering with iMovie and Final Cut Pro was a turning point in the semester. Students had three weeks to tinker and complete a two to three minute digital story on a personal topic of their choice. One class session was devoted to visiting the university's Creative Lab for group and one-on-one tutorial. Several students on their own also accessed video tutorials on YouTube; two students went as far as visiting an Apple store for additional one-on-one tutorial on iMovie at no cost. Another class session was spent viewing a preliminary version of the digital stories in small groups for feedback. The next class session was the digital story videocast; this involved uploading the videos to our YouTube Channel, an in-house screening, and a collective feedback forum after the screening. The latter surprisingly ended with what seemed an on-the-spot jury selection of three digital stories based on quality. That is, the class requested to view three specific digital stories for a second time to discuss unique or standout technical aspects of the production. Given the personal nature of the digital stories, we as a class decided to keep the YouTube Channel private to accommodate concerns about privacy (a topic that we had discussed earlier in the semester). All but one of the digital stories revealed the student's likeness as well as friends and family members. For me, the exercise of tinkering with media production was an important part of the learning process. My hope in tasking students with a digital story was that it would expand their understanding of genres of participation while preparing them for the next and final project. Elsewhere (Jocson, in preparation), I discuss these digital stories as performative biographies with an emphasis on method. The digital stories served as stepping stones toward a more elaborate media-making endeavor intersecting with participatory politics because of the deliberate take up of alternative and activist new media.

Shifting to Alternative and Activist New Media

With the deployment of new media literacies as a concept and subsequent course-related activities, it became clear that the students and I were enacting various theories into practice. Blogging, group presentations, experiential learning to poster project, and the digital story all seemed essential but still incomplete pedagogically. The idea of wielding voice and influence on issues of public concern as participatory politics was catalytic. Around week 9, we proceeded to draw on what Lievrouw (2011) calls alternative and activist new media as a way to push our thinking toward the transformative potential of new media literacies. According to Lievrouw, alternative and activist new media "employ or modify the communication artifacts, practices, and social arrangements of new and information and communication technologies to challenge or alter dominant, expected, or accepted ways of doing society, culture, and politics" (p. 19). Genres of alternative and activist new media include culture jamming, participatory journalism, alternative computing, mediated mobilization, and commons knowledge. Attentive to changing practices,

Lievrouw argues that at the heart of such new social strategies are mediations, or the continuous and mutually reshaping of "relationship between people's uses of technology and their communicative action that produces social and technological change" (p. 231).

While reading Lievrouw's work, we also derived perspectives from Yang (2007) on youth walkouts and Cohen and Kahne (2012) on youth participatory politics. It was valuable to see examples of young people engaging in the pleasure and politics of everyday life, including school, and using technology to participate online through mediated expressions. This was significant for us in the process of expanding the notion of participatory politics as voluntary acts converging in institutional spaces. The link between theory and practice through the lens of alternative and activist new media led us to explicit connections about what we had done so far and the looming social action project. We recognized that our own class blog served as an example of participatory journalism and commons knowledge. As well, we claimed the digital stories and group presentations as participatory, mediated expressions that circulated information among us (regardless of group size). We were, in essence, producing knowledge with new media literacies at play. My point here (and in the analysis of the social action project below) is that pedagogy was integral to the thinking, theory building, and exchange. To illustrate this point further, I highlight aspects of my positioning as instructor and researcher-participant in relation to pedagogical strategies.

Instructor as Researcher-Participant

In this design-based action research, I utilized various methods to collect student work produced during the semester, including print and digital materials. The aforementioned activities yielded the following: 9 visual prompts on the class blog with a total of 64 comments; 7 group presentations with either Powerpoint or Prezi slides; 8 group analyses and posters on technology-rich environments; 13 personal digital stories; and, 6 social action video documentaries with accompanying interactive websites. To gain some sense of participants as individuals and as a group, I asked students on the first day of class to fill out an information sheet with general questions about their personal background, academic and social interests, media production experience, and reasons for taking the course. I collected and archived the information sheet, which for me had been a common practice in previous courses.

As mentioned, the new media literacies course was open to undergraduate and graduate students ages 19–25 with the exception of one, a 33-year-old middle school teacher whose 8-year teaching experience had been invaluable in our discussions about current practices of new media literacies in schools. Seven students had explicit interests in education or had been working in educational settings through after-school programs. Table 1 summarizes what students shared on the information sheet.[4] Later in the semester, I administered a self-evaluation (or what I refer to as "check in") in week 8 and another ("check out") in week 15 (separate from the university course evaluations). The "check in" centered on students' progress in the course and the "check out" served as an overall self-assessment with space to indicate any "take aways" about new media literacies. For both the digital story and social action project, an informal three-page reflection on the media-making process was submitted as part of the assignment. Additionally, I wrote field notes and memos about each class session.

As an instructor wearing a researcher and a participant hat, it was necessary for me to be transparent with the aims of the course and the particular ways in which I was deploying "new media literacies" through specific activities. On the first day of class, I described

38 CULTURAL PRODUCTION AND PARTICIPATORY POLITICS

Table 1. Student Information Sheet From First Day of Class.

Student Name*	Major / Area of Study	Race/Ethnicity (self-designated)	Gender	Level of Media Production Experience
Alvin	English	White	M	Intermediate
Amber	International Business; Educational Studies	Caucasian	F	None
Amy	American Culture Studies (graduate)	African-American	F	None
Anna	Urban Studies	African-American	F	Beginner
Devon	Urban Studies	African-American	F	None
Danny	Education (graduate)	Korean-American	M	Beginner
Eddie	International Business	White	M	None
Heather	Business: Organizational Behavior; Educational Studies	White	F	None
Jim	Business: Organizational Behavior, Healthcare Management	Caucasian	M	None
Janet	English Literature	White	F	Beginner
Kelly	Communication Design	Caucasian	F	Intermediate
Samantha	Educational Studies, Psychology, Children's Studies	White	F	None
Val	English Literature; Cultural Studies (graduate)	Thai-American / White	M	None

*All names are pseudonyms.

the nature of the course and informed students about conducting design-based action research with an emphasis on pedagogy. I underscored that their enrollment in the course implied that they were giving informal consent for participating in the action research.[5] About one third of the students did not show up beyond the first week of classes. During the weeks leading up to week 10, the set of readings and assignments was knowingly *and* unknowingly shaping the learning process toward alternative and activist new media. An ethos of collaboration, participation, and distributed expertise seemed to be emerging from theory building to grounded practice. Based on my observations, students were keen on the culminating event at a nearby museum as they became explicit about methods of attracting a broad audience. Initial conversations about location and venue, accessibility (free admission and transportation), date, time of day, event title, and types of publicity shaped the pre-planning. While we preferred an evening on the last of week of classes, the museum's schedule only allowed for a weekend event. We agreed to hold the public screening on a Saturday afternoon during a time when, as we were told, visitors across age groups flock the museum; the venue we selected inside was the grand hall where supposedly the most traffic occurs. We envisioned a large viewing screen and the voices within each video to fill up the space; we also envisioned easels in the periphery for sharing the technology-rich environment posters so that these would become part of the museum's exhibit at least for that time period. With such ideas and plans, I communicated with the museum's staff to coordinate the event (see Figure 2).

Figure 2. Public Screening at Museum.

By week 10, primed for a public screening of their work, students submitted final project proposals along with a project timeline. We spent the majority of that class session discussing different possibilities for moving forward and how to responsibly approach the social and educational issues they had identified (see Table 2). We eventually merged overlapping interests and topics to create five groups of two and one group of three students. To guide students in their inquiry, I specifically asked questions about ontology and epistemology in relation to knowledge production (i.e., what it means to examine social or cultural phenomena, how one can be positioned or privileged in particular environments, how one's view of the world informs ways of knowing or doing, etc.). It was important to connect what we were doing to what Kellner and Share (2007) describe as the work of critical media literacies. Drawing from class notes and a memo from that day, I shared the following with students: "Things do not just appear as they are; things are constructed and represented using language and other tools in particular ways for various purposes, including new media; those constructions and representations have implications for different people."

With this premise in mind, I proceeded to urge students to think about settings, participants, access, ethics, and representation with respect to each of their projects. For example, I posed questions such as "Who will help inform your topic of choice? How will you gain access to potential participants? What types of questions will you ask interviewees? In what ways will the social action project you have in mind provide an "alternative" view of the topic? How do you know it's "alternative"? The latter questions proved harder to answer because students depended largely on what the inquiry would yield. With some contemplation of the serious yet uncertain nature of inquiry, students were off to ask their own questions and seek the support of the larger community in the process of trying to

Table 2. Student Responses on Information Sheet and Check Out.

Student Name	Reason(s) for Taking the Course - Information Sheet [1/22/14] -	Take Aways - Check Out [4/23/14] -
Alvin	Interested in education, scope and influence of media as a persuasive tool (good and bad); I've never taken anything like this before.	I realize how pervasive new media is and the way certain people are privileged with different kinds of literacy. My role is worthy consumer but I hope to produce more.
Amber	I'm minoring in educational studies and this class seemed like something different and interesting. I expect to learn things that I have not been exposed to in other classes.	New media literacy shapes my views on culture, technology, and society. This class posed interesting questions that make me rethink my views.
Amy	I really am unfamiliar with the topic so I would love to learn more information. It seems like it could be really applicable to my career.	New media literacy is the way we view the world as digital beings at the intersection of the way we use technology. I love the open nature of the class. It provided a more inclusive dialogue.
Anna	Heard about the class and it sounds interesting and relevant to my major.	All of it makes me realize that our culture is dramatically shifting and how we need to change old ways of thinking.
Devon	I expect to learn how media can be used in the classroom to promote learning. I want to go into nonprofit management specifically dealing with education and learning effective and novel ways to teach students would probably help me later in my journey.	New media literacy has pushed me to see how I interact with new media as well as how it shapes what I see. It has shown that we are constantly expanding upon new media literacies and the interactions we have with them. The course was very interesting and a refreshing break from my usual school interactions. It allowed me to understand learning in a new way. The most interesting aspect was creating the social action video because it allowed me to apply new media literacies to something I am passionate about.
Danny	I am hoping that I will be able to use some of the materials and things from this class to help better my instruction and use of technology.	I learned that new media literacy is a living entity. It is constantly growing and changing as we evolve as a people. Utilizing these tools will always be a constant battle in my classroom to push my students to their full potential.
Eddie	This class is very different from my major, so I'm mostly just trying to learn some new information about a different study.	New media literacy makes me consider the footprint that everything I do leaves as well as the impact that media have on the world and what impacted them.
Heather	As an educational studies minor, I am really looking forward to learning about education in a new, more modern age. I think it will complement my other classes and help me learn more about the current methods.	New media literacy pushes me to constantly be thinking about how I can learn new things and be an active participant in this new, exciting age. I am looking forward to all the developments in the years to come.

(continued)

Table 2. (*Continued*).

Student Name	Reason(s) for Taking the Course - Information Sheet [1/22/14] -	Take Aways - Check Out [4/23/14] -
Jim	Enjoyed the last class and needed more [upper] level course elective. Expect the class to be fun and interesting. Hope the workload is second semester senior appropriate (though that doesn't mean I'm going to do a second-semester senior level job on the work).	The class really taught me that I can never stop learning. The world is constantly changing.
Janet	My high school has recently given every student an iPad. This has caused me to have several discussions with friends on this topic and has developed my interest in this subject.	New media literacy shapes my view of the world. How and where I obtain information daily shapes which the way the info is presented to me.
Kelly	I'm really interested in education and the education system we have in the U.S. I'm also interested in how technology may be positively and negatively impacting our future (and current) generations. I hope to gain more insight into these topics. My dad works at an online education company – combining the two has piqued my interest.	New media literacy made me consider how I fit in amongst our generation and the upcoming generations. I think this class made me more aware of different sides of NML which have been helpful in forming a more rounded opinion. I loved the incorporation of the (larger) community, something so important yet not focused on here at (the university) enough.
Samantha	I'm really interested in the way education is changing as technology rapidly advances. I think it seriously impacts the student experience, starting in preschool. I hope to learn more about that!	New media literacy is so relevant to much of how I think about culture and education. Understanding the concept of NML is integral to comprehending the way society functions and how we can contribute to it. I learned so much from each project. I genuinely enjoyed completing the assignments because they've challenged me to try new things and develop new skills and engage with new and different kinds of people.
Val	I'm interested in the complexity of the term "literacy." In a previous course on testing, politics, & science we discussed issues of accessibility, and how to accommodate testers with disabilities or for whom English isn't their primary language (and if the tests were administered in English). I have an interest in education and am considering putting together a program of study. I hope to learn how literacy and new media figure into today's classroom.	I now understand more concretely the importance of new media literacy, and the ubiquity of new media in everyday life. I appreciate the theoretical frameworks with which we explored the subject, and can identify more examples of new media literacy. Finally, I enjoyed the direction the course took with focusing on alternative and activist new media as a way of giving and/or finding voice. As we continue to strive to make education a means of improving the world around us, it is important to have perspectives that may sometimes be relegated to the margins incorporated in the conversation, and new media allows that.

find answers. The inquiry that unfolded was paired with readings on critical media pedagogy (Morrell, Dueñas, Garcia, & López, 2013), popular culture and teaching in urban schools (Mahiri, 2006; Philip & Garcia, 2013), remix and youth media (Jocson, 2013; Soep, 2011; Vasudevan, 2010), and copyright and fair use in education (Hobbs & Donnelly, 2011), to name a few.[6] Doing the work in/with new media literacies was in part about reflecting on our own sense of being a citizen and an advocate of social justice using arts-based work (see Kuttner, in this issue). Engaging in the politics of knowledge production seemed a fruitful exercise for seeing one's self as a member of a larger cultural milieu, and how that cultural milieu is ever-changing with mediation between the human, the material, the discursive, and the digital. The social action project was upon us.

Social Action Project

Students were not new to conducting inquiry. They had been part of a university that prides itself as a research institution. However, as revealed in the project proposals and reflection papers, this type of inquiry where students are positioned as questioning normalized discourses and using new media tools (versus a written report, thesis paper, or poster presentation) to inquire and disseminate findings had been rare. Doing critical inquiry involving input from the larger community to promote social awareness and civic dialogue was even more rare. Having some sense of the liminal space we inhabited at the university, I discussed in class the core values guiding our work, that we were drawing on a model of connected learning concerned with equity, full participation, and social connection (Ito et al., 2013; see also Ito et al., in this issue). By week 11, students had identified participants and churned out questions for use in their interviews. I reminded the class to obtain written permission to interview or record participants agreeing to have their likeness appear on video. For those conducting inquiry in schools, I emphasized ethics involved in working with minors. I distributed a template for obtaining parental consent for minors, as several students had planned on interviewing high school-aged youth to inform their project. There were no risks or benefits to participants, and the social action project was intended for educational purposes.

Through dialogue and collective feedback during week 11's class session, it became apparent to me that the social and/or educational issues selected by the students were building on concurrent courses, working theses, or preliminary research in their academic trajectory. The selection of a social or educational issue, then, was not random or arbitrary, which sometimes happens when the learning objective turns into appeasing the instructor or fulfilling a course requirement; rather, the selection was purposefully connected and contingent upon other discourses in which students had participated. Additionally, the selection of group partners was also purposeful to complement students' interests.

By week 12, I had become more attentive to the emerging ethos that was developing through *collaboration* with peers and community members, *participation* in interest-driven inquiry centered on social or educational issues, and *distributed expertise* in the learning process that ultimately led to video documentaries and interactive websites. At this stage, most of the students' planned interviews had been completed and researching the topic online or reviewing literature began. Students in their respective groups had tasked themselves with different responsibilities, and by week 13, several groups had begun culling together video footage and other visual materials to create an edited timeline using iMovie or Final Cut Pro. We discussed in class the difficulty of cutting down footage to fit into a 5 to 8 minute narrative. We consulted each other for collective feedback. By week 14, students had produced a rough cut of the video documentary and a preliminary interactive website. Once again, we consulted each other for collective feedback; this was a key moment, as students had less than a week to make revisions and complete the video documentary for the public screening. The anxious countdown to the public screening was evident as students worked around the clock until the evening before the event. As students submitted their video documentaries, I created a DVD containing all six projects to use for playback at the public screening the next day.

Analyzing What and How Students Produced

A content analysis of the social action video documentaries shows the interweaving of voice-narration, written text, visual text, and sound/instrumental track. Table 3 provides details of the analysis. Elsewhere, I have discussed a data analysis matrix that pays attention to the script, image, and sound of multimedia texts, and the various aesthetic, conceptual, and technical elements involved in media production (Jocson, 2012; 2013). Here, the interweaving of voice-narration, written text, visual text, and sound/instrumental track reflects the multiple layers constituting each video documentary. The inquiry part of the project yielded video interviews and original footage of the local setting as well as appropriated video and still images that were (re)assembled using an editing tool to frame the select topic.

The ethos of collaboration, participation, and distributed expertise that had been a part of our learning process surfaced in support of the social action projects. As revealed in student reflection papers, *collaboration* with peers and community members, *participation* in interest-driven inquiry, and *distributed expertise* through the production of a video documentaries and interactive websites plus a public screening helped to realize the transformative potential of new media literacies as social action. From inquiry to media-making, the learning process centered on shared purpose, hands-on production, and open networks.[7] According to students, it was important to build on each other's strengths, to be diligent about exploring the select topic, and to apply their knowledge from tinkering with digital media technologies to create and disseminate "alternative" texts. For example, as Val of group #6 pointed out in his reflection paper:

> We were able to handle technical aspects of the project simultaneously, employing new media literacy in sharing a Google document on which we proposed ideas and drafted a script. We maintained a healthy amount of trust between the division of responsibilities, and were able to meet regularly to flesh out the final product. Because (Danny) had access to teachers and students at (school), he was able to interview/survey individuals, and we incorporated that content into our project. I found myself handling the script writing, which required balancing a well-framed argument with an engaging narrative arc. We both accessed footage through YouTube to serve as additional supports for our message of the importance of arts education in public schools [4/23/14].

Danny shared a similar appreciation for their work on the project and pointed to the extent of engaging participatory politics through video production and website creation to circulate among a larger audience. In his reflection paper, he wrote:

> (Val) and I met on several occasions, breaking the project up into smaller chunks so that we could work on multiple aspects simultaneously . . . knowing several art teachers, and having direct contact with students each day, I chose to help complete this section. I used a digital camcorder to interview (a teacher) and chose to create a brief questionnaire for the students . . . the last component was the website. On the "About" tab we wrote a quick summary

Table 3. Social Action Projects - Video Documentaries.

Group#	Title*	Topic	Length	Content	Number of Video Interviews and Original Footage	Number of Appropriated Video Footage and Still Image	Website Homepage
1	"The District: A Unique Perspective" *(by Anna and Della)*	Loss of accreditation, examining the issue with voices of students	6:09	Voiceover-narration (single) Written text Visual text Sound/instrumental	3 video interviews (3 community members-high school youth)	4 videos 13 still images	
2	"The Divide" *(by Amy and Janet)*	Segregation by race and class, questioning the dividing line	6:02	Voiceover-narration (double) Written text Visual text Sound/instrumental	1 original footage 5 video interviews (4 community members; 1 university student)	2 videos 1 still image	
3	"Social Change" *(by Alvin and Eddie)*	Community needs, exploring and representing community ideas	5:24	Voiceover-narration (double) Written text Visual text Sound/instrumental	12 video interviews (9 community members; 1 university student; 2 university students-creators	8 still images	

(*continued*)

Table 3. (*Continued*).

Group#	Title*	Topic	Length	Content	Number of Video Interviews and Original Footage	Number of Appropriated Video Footage and Still Image	Website Homepage
4	"Innovative" *(by Amber, Heather, and Jim)*	School to prison pipeline, interrupting through education	5:33	Voiceover-narration (single) Written text Visual text Sound/ instrumental	1 video interview (1 university faculty)	3 videos 11 still images	
5	"The Politics of Change" *(by Kelly and Samantha)*	Homelessness, acknowledging lack of awareness and disconnect between university and community	8:15	Voiceover-narration (single) Written text Visual text	10 video interviews (7 university students; 1 university faculty; 2 community members)		
6	"We're All Born Artists" *(by Danny and Val)*	Arts education, challenging cutbacks to support development of creative capacities of children	7:45	Voiceover-narration (double) Written text Visual text Sound/ instrumental track	2 video interviews (1 teacher; 1 student)	5 videos 20 still images	

* Titles slightly modified for purposes of anonymity

outlining the problem of the arts declining within public schools. I gave each of my students a four-question survey asking them why the arts in school are important. We selected several answers to include on the "Student Voice" section (of the website). We also created a "Resource" tab where we linked up many of the resources we found for our project and a couple of arts programs (in the local area). Last we embedded our iMovie within the website [4/15/14].

In another example, Kelly of group 5 noted the necessity of working collaboratively yet marked challenges along the way:

We tried to do it all together. Of course, there were scheduling issues or technology issues . . . [for example] extenuating circumstances like how all of our footage was on one computer making it hard to work simultaneously and productively . . . we interviewed several students, one faculty and two homeless participants. We had all this footage but it was hard to figure out what to include. [4/22/14].

Likewise, Samantha echoed similar sentiments about collaboration and distributed expertise. Noteworthy in her reflection paper is a critical recognition of media-making and community building as participatory politics:

We took advantage of one another's strengths. (Kelly), for example, is in Communication Design, and is artistically inclined. All of the drawings and doodles that you find in our movie are her creations. I am a seasoned public speaker, so it's my voice you hear in the narration. Overall, the documentary came out of a strong sense of urgency regarding the issue of connecting our (university) peers to our greater (local) surroundings. We wanted to shine light on the fact that our school exists in a much bigger community with different kinds of people, many of whom come from privileged backgrounds. So did we. [4/21/14].

Upon a closer look at the student reflections along with the video documentaries, I noticed that two groups (#1, #3) exercised division of labor in order to complete the project in a timely manner, while four groups (#2, #4, #5, #6) jointly conducted different aspects of the project, including: interviewing participants; writing a script; editing the video; and later creating an interactive website. Additionally, I noticed the deployment of new media literacies to be pragmatic in order to complete different tasks. The following new media literacies became evident: tinkering or experimenting with digital media technologies (*play*); adopting roles or performing identities to conduct interviews with different people inside and outside the university context (*performance*); sampling and remixing media content (*appropriation*); shifting focus while tending to multiple commitments as students (*multitasking*); expanding one's mental capacities through new tools and new experiences (*distributed cognition*); pooling knowledge and sharing notes toward a particular purpose (*collective intelligence*); evaluating the reliability and credibility of information sources (*judgment*); following the flow of stories and information across multiple media (*transmedia navigation*); collecting and circulating information to others (*networking*); traveling across different communities and respecting multiple perspectives (*negotiation*); and translating information into visual models as a form of communication (*visualization*).

These new media literacies were central in the completion of the social action projects; they were key practices in the planning, design, implementation, and dissemination. The social action projects created opportunities for "doing" participatory politics – from brainstorming topics to researching online, interviewing local participants in context, editing original and found footage to produce a video, building an interactive website, and sharing the combined material with a public audience. The "doing" is akin to what Ratto and Boler (2014) have termed "DIY (Do-It-Yourself) citizenship"; that is, students assumed active roles as tinkerers and media-makers in critical making, a kind of cultural production. Within the learning and production process were also opportunities for self-reflection. Thus, the pursuit of "alternative" media-making was, in turn, a pursuit of shifting views about ourselves as participants in the research as well as members of society with the ability to produce knowledge, to use particular forms of knowledge to challenge normalized ways of thinking and doing, and to be open to and informed by multiple ways of knowing in recognition of possible entangled lives and experiences (Deleuze & Guattari, 1987). New media literacies as social action pedagogically oriented us to engage in the politics of knowledge production.

Evident in the reflection papers and my observations of class sessions were insights gained from doing critical inquiry. The inductive approach was helpful for students to recognize the limitations as well as tensions that emerged through collaboration with peers and community members. In a group share-out during class, one group (#2) pointed out the difficulty of having differing views on information-gathering, who they should interview and where, who should conduct the interview based on social perceptions about race and gender, and to what extent their identity markers and rapport within the local community can shape how interview participants respond to them and their questions. Two groups (#1, #4) revealed the limited or narrow perspective represented in their videos due to the low number of participants and interviews in the inquiry process. In contrast, three groups (#3, #5, #6) noted having more than enough interviews and footage from which to select for inclusion in the video; that is, they had far more available footage to whittle down during editing. Three groups (#1, #4, #5) whose topics involved either minors or vulnerable populations also expressed ethical considerations that limited their access to participants or their ability to record using a video camera.

In hindsight, these revelations about the nature of inquiry affirmed a conception of knowledge as constructed and that the subjective representations of any experience through the exchange of meanings always remain incomplete (Denzin, 2014; Hall, 1997). Processes of cultural production always omit someone or something. Despite efforts toward alternative and activist new media, the mediation between the human, the material, the discursive, and the digital in the social action projects illustrates the value of learning with/from each other and across multiple perspectives in an ever-changing cultural milieu. The social action projects did not end when the video documentaries were screened at the museum. Soon after, the interactive websites were cast to promote continued dialogue. At the writing of this narrative, each respective website had accumulated traffic and comments from visitors. Both the community sharing and the distribution of videos rendered a kind of participatory politics that was enabled by a course theorizing on new media literacies.

Finally, as expressed on the last day of class, all students in the course recounted theory building and grounded practice as helpful to seeing themselves differently in a digitally mediated world. In particular, the tinkering with digital media technologies through purposeful assignments expanded their media production experience and furthered their thinking about what it meant to consume, produce, and share media content in the realm of DIY citizenship. The following excerpts from the end-of the-semester check out highlight students' take aways:

> I now understand more concretely the importance of new media literacy . . . to strive to make education a means of improving the world around us.

48   CULTURAL PRODUCTION AND PARTICIPATORY POLITICS

I learned that new media literacy is a living entity. It is constantly growing and changing as we evolve as a people. Utilizing these tools will always be a constant battle in my classroom.

I genuinely enjoyed completing the assignments because they've challenged me to try new things and develop new skills and engage with new and different kinds of people.

I think this class made me more aware…I loved the incorporation of the (larger) community, something so important yet not focused on here at (the university) enough.

Noteworthy in the responses are the conceptualization and application of new media literacies that had guided the course (see Table 2 for all student responses paired with reasons for taking the course gathered from the information sheet on the first day of class). Comparing various sets of responses allowed me as an instructor and a researcher-participant to reflect on what had taken place throughout the semester in relation to learning and change. The course had ended yet I was left wondering about pedagogical possibilities.

Limitations and Lessons Learned

In this design-based action research project, I was privileged to work with students who were willing to go with me pedagogically. I was also privileged to have had university resources to help accommodate our needs, including a classroom inside the main campus library that enabled collaborative learning and a Creative Lab with digital media technologies that provided students with equipment and tutorials. I remain grateful for the opportunity to have facilitated (and participated in) a kind of learning with the support of the larger community. The lessons are many. This narrative is an attempt to share some insights into new media literacies, youth cultural production, and participatory politics. Reflexively, it is important to note the limitations in the research. These include the small number of students enrolled in the course as represented here, the university context in which the course was offered, the specific readings and assignments that guided the course, and the particularities of our experience subject to a specific space and time in the urban Midwest. To protect the identities of students and community members, the links to the video documentaries and interactive websites are not included in this writing. Sharing specific aspects of the learning process has been my task in order to point out pedagogical possibilities.

For me, the implications of new media literacies extend beyond research. As a teacher, I continue to grapple with lessons learned about theory building and classroom practice. What does it mean to draw on new media literacies as a way to understand the politics of knowledge production with DIY tools readily more available now than ever? In what ways does an ethos of collaboration, participation, and distributed expertise bust the very bubble that we as learners, creators, and tinkerers operate within, and in what ways do they allow us to become more thoughtful in the process of becoming the learners, creators, and tinkerers we have yet to be? How should curriculum be shaped with digital media, democracy, and justice at the center of pedagogy?

From this particular new media literacies course, it became apparent that continued work is necessary to understand the blurring lines of youth cultural production and participatory politics. For example, I wonder, what would have happened if students and I had an opportunity to revisit the interactive websites, to ask each other questions about meaning and representation, or to repurpose the written and visual texts gathered during the inquiry toward the further remaking of the material, the discursive, and the digital? What knowledges and positionings would future opportunities of critical making yield? What new DIY tools would allow for a kind of youth cultural production and participatory politics in the classroom? Whose voices and whose matters would be included, and from whose perspectives? It seems that these questions point back to the theorizing of new media literacies that had taken place and the practices that had emerged along the way to further explore the politics of knowledge production. There are various pedagogical possibilities; whatever the case, I look forward to the next iteration of the course in similar or different contexts.

New media literacies as a topic and an area of study are still evolving. In this article, it has been important to identify the ways in which university students leveraged new media literacies to engage in theory building and grounded practice. I drew on design-based action research to discuss specific aspects of the learning process, an opportunity to see that what we were doing in the course had social consequences. The work produced through course assignments and activities demonstrate that youth cultural production and participatory politics were shaped by our very own social and cultural experiences. In part, alternative and activist media practices allowed for an exploration of voice and influence on issues of public concern (Cohen & Kahne, 2012). New media literacies as social action emerged as a key insight. What became evident in the learning process were lessons about how mediation between the human, the material, the discursive, and the digital can offer new experiences and new possibilities.

There is room to grow and to (re)imagine critical making differently. An ethos of collaboration, participation, and distributed expertise may have been fleeting in the context of a semester-long course. My hope is that, while school, work or life unfolds in each of their respective contexts, students continue to leverage new media literacies in ways that question or challenge normative discourses. This hope represents a shift toward seeking alternative possibilities, perhaps a (re)interpretation, a (re)representation, or a (re)construction of lived and constructed realities. The uncertainty of becoming active citizens with the use of digital media technologies and shifting everyday practice was (and is still) part of the journey.

Acknowledgments

I would like to acknowledge the editorial team of *Curriculum Inquiry* and three anonymous reviewers for the constructive feedback on the manuscript. As well, special thanks to Jonathan Rosa for additional insights. Any and all errors are mine.

Notes

1. The university is a private research institution. Some students have referred to the university as a bubble and removed from the larger community. Like many universities, there are opportunities for service learning and community engagement or other public service initiatives.
2. For more information, see www.newmedialiteracies.org
3. The classroom also had an interactive Smart Board and computer-media panel to accommodate our needs. Each group presentation included a contemporary multimedia example (typically a video from YouTube) to incite thinking about the topic at hand; there were instances when small group activities (i.e., quick online search, think-pair-share, interactive performance) were embedded in the group presentation. The classroom was equipped with Wi-Fi connectivity and 4 iMac computer stations; several students typically had their own laptops or Smart phones available for use for related activities.
4. All names are pseudonyms.

50 CULTURAL PRODUCTION AND PARTICIPATORY POLITICS

5. I informed students of my research interests in youth literacies and my ethical responsibilities as a qualitative researcher. A few weeks into the semester, permission was granted to me via written consent forms by a number of students whose digital stories were analyzed in more detail.
6. In order to accommodate project timelines, it became necessary to streamline assigned readings and modify the schedule of two group presentations. I felt compelled to have students spend more time with the inquiry given the short window toward the completion of the video documentaries and interactive websites.
7. The interactive websites had at least three tabs: the Homepage as a blog, an About page, and a "Resources" page. The Homepage contained the embedded video from YouTube. Visitors could post comments and access related information via links. Wordpress, Tumblr, or Google Sites hosted the interactive websites.

References

Anyon, J. (2009a). Critical pedagogy is not enough: Social justice education, political participation, and the politicization of students. In M. Apple, W. Au, & L. Gandin (Eds.), *The Routledge international handbook of critical education* (pp. 389–395). New York: Routledge.

Anyon, J. (Ed.). (2009). *Theory and educational research: Toward critical social explanation.* New York: Routledge.

Apple, M., Au, W., & Gandin, L., (Eds.). *The Routledge international handbook of critical education.* New York: Routledge.

Cobb, P., Confrey, J., diSessa, A., Lehrer, R., & Schauble, L. (2003). Design experiments in educational research. *Educational Researcher, 32,* 9–13.

Cochran-Smith, M., & Lytle, S. (1993). *Inside/outside: Teacher research and knowledge.* New York: Teachers College Press.

Cochran-Smith, M., & Lytle, S. (1999). The teacher research movement: A decade later. *Educational Researcher, 28,* 15–25.

Cohen, K., & Kahne, J. (2012). *Participatory politics: New media and youth political action.* Oakland, CA: YPP Network/MacArthur Foundation.

Deleuze, G., & Guattari, F. (1987). *A thousand plateaus: Capitalism and schizophrenia* (B. Massumi, Trans.). Minneapolis: University of Minnesota Press.

Denzin, N. (2014). *Interpretive autobiography.* Thousands Oaks, CA: Sage.

Hall, S. (Ed.). (1997). *Representation: Cultural representation and signifying practices.* London, U.K.: Sage.

Hobbs, R., & Donnelly, K. (2011). Toward a pedagogy of fair use for multimedia composition (pp. 275–294). In M. Rife, S. Slattery, and D. DeVoss (Eds.) *Copy(write): Intellectual property in the writing classroom* (pp. 275–294). West Lafayette, IN: Parlor Press.

Ito, M. (2010). *Hanging out, messing around, and geeking out.* Cambridge, MA: The MIT Press.

Ito, M., Gutierrez, K., Livingstone, S., Penuel, B., Rhodes, J., Salen, K., Schor, J., Sefton-Green, J., & Watkins. S.C. (2013). *Connected learning: An agenda for research and design.* Irvine, CA: Digital Media and Learning Research Hub.

Jenkins, H. (2006). *Confronting the challenges of participatory culture: Media education for the 21st century.* Chicago, IL: MacArthur Foundation.

Jocson, K.M. (2012). *Youth media as narrative assemblage: Examining new literacies at an urban high school. Pedagogies: An International Journal, 7,* 298–316.

Jocson, K.M. (2013). Remix revisited: Critical solidarity in youth media arts. *E-Learning and Digital Media, 10,* 68–82.

Jocson, K.M. (in preparation). *Youth media matters.* Minneapolis, MN: University of Minnesota Press.

Kellner, D., & Share, J. (2007). Critical media literacy is not an option. *Learning Inquiry, 1*, 59–69.
Kuttner, P. (2015). Education for cultural citizenship: Reframing the goals of arts education. *Curriculum Inquiry, 45*, 69–91.
Lankshear, C., & Knobel, M. (2006). *New literacies: Everyday practices and classroom learning.* Maidenshead: Open University Press.
Lievrouw, L. (2011). *Alternative and activist new media.* Malden, MA: Polity.
Lister, M., Dovey, J., Giddings, S., Grant, I., & Kelly, K. (2009). *New media: A critical introduction (2nd Ed.).* New York: Routledge.
Luke, A., Woods, A., & Weir, K. (Eds.). (2013). *Curriculum, syllabus design, and equity: A primer and model.* New York: Routledge.
Mahiri, J. (2006). Digital DJing: Rhythms of learning in an urban school. *Language Arts, 84*, 55–61.
Morrell, E., Dueñas, R., Garcia, V., & López, J. (2103). *Critical media pedagogy: Teaching for achievement in city schools.* New York: Teachers College Press.
McIntyre. (2008). *Participatory action research.* Thousand Oaks, CA: Sage.
Palfrey, J., & Gasser, U. (2008). *Born digital: Understanding the first generation of digital natives.* New York, NY: Penguin/Basic Books.
Philip, T., & Garcia. A. (2013). The importance of still teaching the iGeneration: New technologies and the centrality of pedagogy. *Harvard Educational Review, 83*, 300–319.
Ratto, M., & Boler, M. (Eds). (2014). *DIY citizenship: Critical media making and social media.* Cambridge, MA: MIT Press.
Scott, K., & White, M. (2011). COMPUGIRLS' standpoint: Culturally responsive computing and its effect on girls of color. *Urban Education, 48*, 657–681.
Soep, E. (2011). Youth media goes mobile. *National Civic Review (Fall)*, 8–11.
Soep, E., & Chávez, V. (2010). *Drop that knowledge: Youth radio stories.* New York: Teachers College Press.
Soep, E., & Ito, M. (2015). Learning Connected Civics: Narratives, Practices, Infrastructures. *Curriculum Inquiry, 45*, 10–29.
Vasudevan, L. (2010). Education remix: New media, literacies, and the emerging digital geographies. *Digital Culture & Education, 2*:1, 62–82.
Yang, W. (2007). Organizing MySpace: Youth walkouts, pleasure, politics, and new media. *Educational Foundations, 21*, 9–28.

3 Public pedagogy in the creative strike

Destabilizing boundaries and re-imagining resistance in the University of Puerto Rico

Melissa Rosario

In this article, I examine key symbols and strategies mobilized by students during the first system-wide strike in the University of Puerto Rico's history. I argue that these acts of creative cultural production not only supported the growth of participatory politics within the mobilization but that they also were tools for enacting public pedagogy. In particular, I examine the spatial dimensions of these practices, showing how strikers disrupted the normative boundaries between protest space/public space, and actor/spectator by engaging police officers in innovative ways. I suggest that by performing this spatial reconfiguration, pedagogues were implicated in the process of transformation as much as their targeted learners/spectators. In the conclusion, I reflect on the ethical implications of public pedagogy, arguing that artistic expressions facilitate a flexible and dynamic mode for becoming otherwise in ways that cannot be anticipated.

When students occupied the University of Puerto Rico's (UPR) flagship campus in Río Piedras on April 21, 2010, no one realized their 48-hour stoppage would become a 62-day long occupation and the first system-wide strike in the institution's history.[1] Indeed, immediately after students' occupation of the campus,[2] the interim rector Ana Guadeloupe closed the campus for an indefinite administrative recess, and soon after a number of police were deployed to the campus gates. While this move may have temporarily frustrated students—as it ignored their calls for dialogue—it ironically propelled them into the spotlight, offering them a chance to dialogue with a much broader public.

In many ways, students had already begun to engage with the public months earlier. In the fall of 2009, students participated in a series of multi-sector actions protesting Governor Luis Fortuño's austerity plan. The public fervently opposed it because the plan authorized the layoffs of nearly 30,000 workers in a span of less than six months. The students' most impressive action in opposition to the law was their six-hour occupation of the major highway *Expreso las Américas* during the October 15th march, *El Paro Nacional* (General Strike).[3] Although a nation-wide general strike never came to fruition, students honed that pervasive energy of desperation and refusal to organize in their own context. Still, they continued to make connections between the island-wide conditions and changes they were facing at the university.

Historically, the UPR has served as a vibrant space of political action and compared to other arenas in the public sphere, maintains a relative degree of autonomy (Fiet, 2013).[4] But as the commonwealth's initial economic boom began to decline in the mid-1970s, crisis became an everyday reality. As a result, protests within the school focused increasingly on a lack of course offerings and a rise in tuition fees. The 2010 strike must be understood as part of a history of struggle to maintain that sphere of autonomy. While these historical continuities are important to note, the 2010 UPR strike represented a remarkable shift in political organizing because it subverted Puerto Rico's fragmented political terrain rarely open to new participants or to lasting forms of coalition building.[5]

Key to the strikers' success was that instead of organizing through established channels, students developed new organizing committees around areas of study increasing the range of political perspectives and levels of experience among participants. Second, they mobilized a range of creative strategies that led to the strike's moniker of *la huelga creativa* (the creative strike). Before the 2010 strike, there were only two major organized struggles—*la huelga del pueblo* (the strike against the privatization of the telephone company) in 1998 and the struggle for Peace in Vieques (demanding the exit of the U.S. Navy from the municipal island), immediately following it—that were able to break with the polarized political terrain and organize a broad-spectrum of actors. As Mareia Quintero Rivera (2014) argues about both of these cases, artistic interventions facilitated "symbolic disobedience," which she defines as public actions that articulate alternative imaginaries through intense metaphoric signs and participatory politics (p. 715). In this way, symbolic forms of disobedience were a necessary complement to the occupation, subverting dominant feelings of acquiescence and ambivalence, strict boundaries between political groups, and the relative isolation of social issues.

In this article, I examine how students' creative strategies fomented alternative imaginaries of resistance, creating a public forum where students and non-students alike could refuse the status quo of the political terrain. When I say status quo, my intention is to signal both political fragmentation in the local context, as well as the generalized power of hegemonic norms and unquestioned assumptions that govern social life. Following Deborah Gould, I believe that social movement spaces are sites that "nurture counterhegemonic affects" (2009, p. 41) and that the feelings generated through this occupation were shaped in large part by the creative strategies undertaken by students.

Accolades aside, I acknowledge strikers' unresolved debate about the need to connect more explicitly with those who rarely participate in protest politics. Although a sizeable contingent of strikers with community organizing backgrounds urged their peers to go beyond the three familiar arenas of protest—the campus, the streets surrounding the gates, and the President's office at neighboring *Jardín Botanico* (Botanical Gardens)—and enter neighboring barrios and housing projects to discuss their struggle, their plans never fully materialized.[6] While I agree that the alternatives created by the students were often physically separated from the public by the gates of the campus and strikers' barricades, I am interested in how creative interventions symbolically destabilized the distinction between these two spheres of life.

Although I participated in nearly all dimensions of strike life, sleeping in *Bellas Artes* (the Faculty of Fine Arts) and occasionally in *Humanidades* (the Humanities Faculty), working the occasional shift at the security gate, sitting in on plenary sessions and marching in morning picket sessions, I was in no way a leader or a decision maker, but merely a learner and a witness. Indeed, I had not expected any of the widespread protests I witnessed upon my arrival to the island in 2009 and did not plan to write about the university. But the moment was too important to miss. As a result, I spent many days during the strike moving back and forth between the occupied campus and my original site of research: an eight year old occupation on five acres of public coastal lands that were being privatized through a secret deal between the Government of Puerto Rico and the Marriott Corporation. After the strike ended, I supplemented these observations with interviews with strikers who had assumed leadership roles in various arenas of the strike.

In what follows, I show how UPR strikers disrupted everyday divisions between protest and public space, intentionally entangling multiple publics through artistic forms of cultural production. In contrast to other modes of socialization, cultural production is an active process of interrupting normative divisions in the social world. Drawing on Jacques Rancière's concept dissensus (2010) as well as what Elizabeth Ellsworth's (2005) terms anomalous spaces, I argue that strikers' mobilization of creative forms of expression served as a tool for enacting public pedagogy. Drawing on discursive materials published by strikers, collective forms of engagement with police officers, and mundane acts of expression, I analyze how strikers questioned the values and norms that promoted neoliberalism as a solution to the University crisis. As such, I show that public pedagogy facilitates a process of learning for social movement actors, not just those they try to reach through their manifestations. By way of conclusion, I reflect on the ethical implications of this view of public pedagogy and suggest that any form of teaching and learning that occurs outside formal education spaces agitating for progressive change must allow for the transformative capacity of the encounter to emerge organically.

Interrupting the Public: Dissensus as Public Pedagogy

A poignant example of how students produced discourses that reimagined the relationship between different publics is the famous "letter to the country," which was drafted collaboratively by members of *el Comité de Acción de Humanidades* (the Humanities Action Committee) before the strike began.[7] The opening lines of this letter are extremely intimate—"by the time you open your eyes"—words that might be penned for a lover and left on a pillow to be read upon awakening. It conveys a sense of care for other members of the public that immediately contrasted with popular notions of student-protestors as lazy, self-entitled kids who didn't want to graduate.

Describing the rationale for the strike and the motivations of strikers, the letter condemned the school administration and Board of Trustees who were responsible for authorizing cuts to institutional services. According to the letter, it is they who "threaten both regular academic offerings as well as those offered in the summer, tuition waivers, the cost of tuition, and services that are vital to the functioning of the university." These claims repositioned strikers as the ones taking responsibility on behalf of the university, reminding others of their proposals for solving the issues the public institution confronted as compared to the administration's willful neglect of students' call for dialogue and negotiation.

As in the refrain *la UPR es un país* (the UPR is a country), students were keen to note that these challenges were not limited to the university, but merely reflected what everyone on the island was facing. They identified a causal relationship between the two, "We denounce the deterioration of your living conditions and the conditions under which we study, which are the result of mismanagement, waste and corruption." In constructing the university crisis as a mirror, what may appear to be disparate problems are actually symptomatic of one another. In other words, they claimed that the university was a microcosm of the nation.

As the letter to the country demonstrates, the discourse of the student strike was consciously directed outwards—beyond the student body and even beyond education—towards a broad scale public. Students often invited non-students to participate actively in strike events and to become a sounding board for student demands. This quality was not mere rhetoric but became an organizing principle. By using the metaphor of the "sounding board," students' called for allies to undertake actions that would echo their own work. What can be seen in this call is that the public (ostensibly strangers and non-students) was situated as co-conspirators and pedagogues in their own right. This move supports Gaztambide and Matute's (2014) assertion that public pedagogy is primarily an intersubjective and relational project.

The discourse that students developed through the idea of the UPR as a country seemed to resonate with other people's experiences, as many were facing the layoffs directly authorized by Governor Fortuño's neoliberal plan. Indeed, in the first month, the strike was not only supported by progressive organizations, as well as faculty and staff at the university, it was front-page news. For example, an early headline published by one of the most conservative papers on the island, *El Nuevo Día*, described strikers in other-worldly terms: "Inside the campus, students operate on a different air." They followed students doing the most mundane tasks. Pictures and videos of students recycling, and sweeping the sidewalks became news in ways that other mobilizations might only dream.

Through the discursive and visual images produced through the occupation, students succeeded in disrupting of normative representations of protestors as selfish and entitled, aligning them with others who were effected by Fortuño's austerity measures. This strategy not only produced interconnected publics, it signaled the important role of interrupting the status quo in students' work as public pedagogues. Indeed, interruption is one of the more salient dimension of public pedagogy, as discussed in the impressive review of public pedagogy scholarship by Sandlin, O'Malley, and Burdick (2011; see for example Brady, 2006; Ellsworth, 2005; Gablik,1995; Lacy,1995). This suggests that when public pedagogy is not used to signal the teachings imparted through hegemonic discourses, it implies that before critical learning can take place, pedagogues must first dislodge unquestioned political divisions.

Rancière's (2010) notion of real political action rests on the idea of interruption and, as such, provides the groundwork for my understanding of enacting public pedagogy as a practice of calling the status quo into question by interrupting its logic. Although it is beyond the scope of this paper, I advocate for adopting a more narrow understanding of public pedagogy that coheres to this definition so it becomes a term for indexing and analyzing public learning for progressive social transformation. Rather than adhere to the idea of democracy as a process of consensus building, Rancière defines it as a practice of foregrounding difference and questioning what silences and exclusions are made possible by the seductive power of consensus. If the politics of the state (*la police*) is concerned with maintaining things as they are, real politics, or "dissensus," is about disrupting the line between what is perceived and not perceived as worthy political action. For Rancière, dissensus works by highlighting *le partage du sensible* which Panagia translates as the "distribution of the sensible" (2010). As Panagia explains, disrupting this invisible line is a vital dimension of being able to transform the status quo (p. 96).

Dissensus is fundamentally an aesthetic action because it necessitates a reconfiguration of the conditions through which the political terrain is sensed. As Rancière (2010) explains, "genuine political or artistic activities always involve forms of innovation that tear bodies from their assigned places and free speech and expression from all reduction and functionality" (p. 1). The choice of language—a tearing—evokes the feeling of discomfort that comes with inserting a break in the logic of the status quo. We might say that public pedagogy is a style of education that aims to alter the realm of the possible, which requires a commitment to unlearning and experimentation.

In this sense, my definition of public pedagogy is most aligned with Ellsworth (2005), who argues that non-traditional pedagogical spaces—what she calls anomalous spaces—are transformational because they are always changing. These transitions are not just a way of conceptualizing the durability of such spaces, but also in foregrounding their disruptive capacity. In the case of the UPR strike, public pedagogy refers not just to the space produced by students' occupation of the campus, but also how student pedagogues were themselves transformed. This process of personal change was facilitated by undertaking the role of "communitarian public intellectual." Coined by O'Malley and Nelson to refer to the educator role assumed by the students in the *pingüinos* (penguins) movement in Chile (2013), this role describes a decentered form of public pedagogy wherein community groups agitate for social justice while eschewing the hierarchical positioning usually associated with the traditional role of a teacher.

In the case of the UPR strike, students assumed the role of communitarian public intellectual, but they also went beyond it. Inhabiting the line between those that are counted and those that are not, they became the vessel for producing dissensus. Questioning normative political divisions in this way inevitably shapes one's own subjectivity regardless of whether the action is a success or not. Public pedagogy in the UPR strike signals the process of continual un/making at the heart of resistance work, what I suggest in my work is predicated on producing a ripple effect through the form of resistance in society (Rosario, 2013). By engaging a diverse array of subjects through their protest, strikers' could amplify the similarity between the conditions each was facing, while also producing a space that would preserve the differences between them.

Key to this project was an ethical orientation to action, which in Ellsworth's (2005) terms, operates as "an undirected dynamic of interrelation" (p. 57). Public pedagogy provides a space wherein participants are in a process of becoming another self as a result of their interaction with others. As Rasza (2012) has argued of emergent mobilizations that rest on direct democratic practices, the key political praxis is one of becoming. Becoming is a dynamic mode where the self is always in a process of emerging through the activism itself. In the case of the UPR student strikes, and as I hope to illustrate in this article, this dynamism relied on the plethora of performances that dominated protest actions. Unlike the established knowledge of canonical thinking, students' pedagogy was intent on transforming the status quo, by deemphasizing the self (student body) and foregrounding their struggle as a mirror for what the country was facing.

In sum, the outwardly directed discourse of the 2010 strike suggests that students were not only thinking of "saving" their institution. By fighting to secure accessibility to the broader public and to future generations, by disrupting the normalization of the political sphere and in particular, and by enacting interventions that exceeded popular understandings of protest itself, the strike gained a broader significance. As illustrated earlier through the letter to the country, this learning was initially performed by discursively entangling multiple publics—political, popular and concrete[8]—growing in power as they invited others to participate in interrupting the division of power through creative acts of solidarity. It also highlighted the hypocrisies of the normative political sphere's emphasis on neoliberalism as a solution to the economic crisis plaguing the island. In other words, they fostered a participatory mode of engagement with macroscopic issues associated with the current conditions as well as producing a space that subverted historical problems of tenuous collaborations and fragmented political sphere.

Yet, despite the promise that creative interventions offer in disrupting dominant logics, Rubén Gaztambide-Fernández (2013) cautions against uncritically taking on the neoliberal sense that everything can be quantified when analyzing forms of consciousness raising that have to do with the arts. Such practices offer a promise, but they in and of themselves, don't *do* anything (2013). While I do not claim a facile relationship between the mobilization of artistic modes and the success of the movement, I will show in the next section how these claims were enacted and suggest that the creative inflection of students' protest strategies worked to dislodge members of the public from their habitual positions and made students' demands legible to others who might automatically disengage when they encountered student protestors in the past.

Reconfiguring Protest Space: Spectacular and Mundane Acts

In this section, I examine two recurring performances—the clown police and open mics—and show how they enabled a reconfiguration of the boundaries between protest space and public space by subverting the perpetual police presence encircling the campus gates.[9] I argue that these actions disrupted the clear distinction between participant and spectator alleviating the constant tension for students and allies alike while questioning forms of repression that were being used against protestors. Part of the reason this open questioning of police presence was possible was the school's *Política de no Confrontacíon* (No-Confrontation Policy) or PNC, designed to break with the legacy of officers' violent responses to student protests during the 1970s and 1980s. The PNC policy established dialogue as the mode for resolving conflict in the university and expressly forbid the police to enter into physical conflict with students. Since the institution of PNC in 1992, the 2010 strike was the first time many officers were deployed to the campus gates and many worried that it signaled a changing face of governance. The fact that student-strikers took this opportunity to question the shifting line of the sensible, as it were, and openly ridiculed the repressive politics of the state was bold to say the least.

When *los payasos policías* (the clown police) arrived to the strike for the first time during the concert *Que Vivan los Estudiantes* (Long Live the Students)[10]— held just one week after the occupation began—I, like others standing on the street in front of the gates, watched fascinated. They lined up directly in front of the officers who were blocking the major entrances to the institution, wearing all black, a round red nose, and face paint. They adorned their uniforms with a patch on their arms, mimicking the riot police in front of whom they stood. Instead of guns, they wielded brooms. Evoking the standard role of the police—guardians of public space who ensure that these arenas remain nothing but "space(s) for circulating" (Ranciére, 2010, p. 37), they "cleaned" the perimeter by sweeping the streets in order to keep it open for the flow of traffic. Following a series of orders from their chief, they moved in formation to his calls: *izquierda, derecha, alante, atrás* (*left, right, front, back*).

Like many other creative interventions mobilized in the strike, *los payasos policías* originated months earlier. As Israel Lugo—actor and graduate of the main UPR campus in Río Piedras—one of the founders of *los payasos policías* explained on *Piedra, Papel y Tijera* (Rock Paper Scissors) a radio show broadcast on Radio Universidad, the performance troupe was conceptualized in protest to a new ordinance requiring establishments in the Old San Juan area to close by 2am during *Las Fiestas de San Sebastian*—an extremely popular festival held in the old city to commemorate the end of the Christmas season. The performance troupe's official name *La Unidad de Operaciones Tácticas de los Payasos Policías* is an adaptation of the riot police's official name in Puerto Rico (*Unidad de Operaciones Tácticas*) and critiqued this increased regulation of public space.

At the UPR, *los payasos* also critiqued the deployment of officers and the increased regulation of public space. The performance literally included police officers in the protest itself, disaggregating the officers from those invisible bodies who deployed them, in an effort to temporarily shift the division between protester and repressor by locating real state power as outside their purview. As Israel Lugo explained, the clown police sought

58 CULTURAL PRODUCTION AND PARTICIPATORY POLITICS

to humanize police officers while underscoring the absurdity of the order to repress a non-violent protest. The clown police also disrupted the dominant affect of protest as a confrontational space allowing all present to experience a break from the tension produced by the police presence. Although riot police did not break form, I noticed their interest in these clowns as their eyes shifted slightly toward the performers. Some officers slightly smirked while others appeared to be holding back laughter. These temporary disruptions were vital for producing a distinct kind of protest space, diminishing the threat of imminent violence while also dismissing officers' ability to shock participants into submission.

As Haugerud (2012) argues, political satire is a useful strategy to mobilize when normative forms of dissent do not seem adequate to address sensitive issues. Aggressions directed at officers would have likely exacerbated fear amongst participants and ensured their repression, but satire provided a way of commenting on the degradation of public life without succumbing to the tactics of the state. Although less subtle than some forms of culture jamming—like so-called subvertisements or billboard liberation—this satirical performance shared one of its major goals: interruption. As Sandlin and Milam (2008) suggest, "culture jammers interrupt how public spaces are typically used and understood" (p.331). In making a spectacle of habitual uses of public space, culture jammers seek to rupture normative modes of thinking, feeling, and inhabiting public spaces in order to inspire a different, more just use. Culture jammers, like satirically-inflected performers, produce an ironic commentary on the status quo by reproducing the lines usually drawn in normative political framings to highlight their problematic nature. The clown police did this quite literally, by standing directly in front of the officers producing a spectacular opposition to their presence.

In contrast to the performance of the clown police, which was a dramatic, if laughable confrontation of the *partage du sensible*, the nightly open mic sessions held at the porous boundary of the main security gate at *la Barbosa* offered a mundane strategy for reconfiguring protest boundaries. As the only gate left open where administrators, police and university researchers could enter the campus, it was the site of many confrontations. With the exception of a few spectacular moments of repression, the violence students encountered at this gate was mostly limited to verbal aggressions, shoving, hitting, and the occasional arrest. Although I took a few shifts at the security gate during the day, I never heard about the open mics until after the strike was over. When Guillermo mentioned them during an interview I conducted with him about his experiences as a poet in the strike, I was visibly upset. He comforted me by reminding me that there was so much happening then, that it was impossible to know all that was taking place. My description of the space is based on this interview and is situated within my larger interpretation of the destabilizing nature of the 2010 strike as a creative protest, aimed at reimagining protest spaces through public pedagogy.

The open mic sessions started sometime in the first weeks of the occupation and lasted until the string of Riot Police that encircled the campus were asked to retire from their posts in late July. It is useful to note that temporal lag and its coincidence with police presence, as it supports my claim that these open mics served as a daily practice of reconfiguring protest space at the porous boundary of *la Barbosa*. In contrast to large-scale protest, the media never reported on the open mics. Perhaps as a result of its invisibility from popular publics and representational spheres, daily open mics offered an impressive route for reversing the power imbalance between police and students.

Using the equipment borrowed from the Electrical Industry and Irrigation Workers Union (UTIER), who established a permanent post outside this gate, students' connected mics to the *tumba coco*[11] (speaker system), singing songs and reading verses from both published and personal works. Police stood in formation on one side of the open gate, while protestors stood in front of them behind a barricade only a few feet away. As Guillermo Rebollo Gil, one of the principal organizers of the event explained, the open mics served as one way to safely comment on the line between the strike and the outside while talking back to the officers indirectly. "It gave us the opportunity to contest the legitimacy of them being there without necessarily getting immersed in a violent encounter." This quickly became necessary as the proximity to the officers produced a tension that anticipated officers' response to students. Guillermo explained the dynamic:

> You almost got to know one another. Sometimes we'd engage in small talk and things would feel as casual and mundane as one would have with a stranger on the street. We'd talk about the weather or about a sports game and you'd start to wonder if they were really so bad. But quickly and without clear cause, these same officers would return back into the aggressive posture. They would suddenly threaten violence. That they couldn't wait to receive the order so they could beat us up with their batons.

On the one hand, this porous boundary amplified the similarities between protester and officer—they both were standing guard, they both were tired, and they had shared interests in seeing the conflict end. On the other hand, most officers used their dual position as spectator and authority to remind strikers that they desired to hurt them. Given that students were living on campus and officers were always present, they were able to watch students as if they were in their house. There was no sense of privacy, an intimacy that officers often took advantage of in visceral ways, hitting on female strikers or reminding students of their violent inclinations, as in the above example provided by Rebollo Gil.

Open mics enabled students to reclaim protest space by reversing the spectator/actor binary they were locked into in their day-to-day interactions with officers. Resignifying the space became consonant with students' ability to take control over how and what the officers were watching. During the open mics, police officers were no longer agents of the scene they were patrolling, but became witness to participants' declarations, ideas that officers could normally ignore by virtue of their position as agents of the state. Strikers took the very intimacy that created tension in other moments and used it to displace their own tension onto the officers.

At the same time, open mics enabled participants to connect themselves and the present moment to prior historic moments that had been cemented into popular forms of cultural production. Guillermo Rebollo Gil cited a peculiar aspect of the transmission of other meanings through reading and listening to protest pieces:

> I grew up listening to nationalist songs—these songs didn't mean much to me while drinking and playing dominos, and then all of a sudden you hear these songs differently, they come to mean something else. The songs all of a sudden meant something else, they became real in a way. To this day particular poems also mean something more to me because of that experience. And don't think that is a unique experience. At least from the conversations I had after that.

By vocalizing with prior moments of resistance in the strike encampment, the messages became intertwined with the feelings of the present moment. The words no longer signaled a tradition of listening to something out of habit, but instead were imbued with a radical possibility. By noting the resonance between disparate times and places, this spatial shift also encouraged strikers like Guillermo to experience a non-linear, palimpsestic temporality. As Jacqui Alexander (2005) has argued, palimpsestic time—the entanglement of past and present that is symbolized by a parchment that is written on again and again—can be liberatory when intentionally cultivated because it refuses normative divisions between present and past, invoking the continual interplay between different moments of resistance. This, too, is part of the work of dissensus, by making links which have been erased, thereby disrupting the normative order of the political terrain.

Satirical and introspective strategies alike worked to destabilize the boundaries of protest space and the roles that protestor and officer occupied vis-à-vis one another. Indeed, these projects actually created a sense of the mobility of the strike, and of its applicability to questions beyond the strike. In the case of the open mic, the resignifying of one's fears by connecting to popular protest music and forms of cultural production subverted a sense of powerlessness, drawing strength from the past. In the case of the clown police, mirroring the officers' role served as a means to playfully question their presence as well as the state attitudes toward protest itself, disrupting the normalcy associated with state intervention.

Imagined Alternatives: Allegories of the Death and Life of Resistance

As we have seen, one mode in which strikers enacted public pedagogy was to efface the boundaries that existed between protest and public spaces. By playing on the police presence that separated these two spheres, students' cultivated an anomalous space in which to construct other spatial configurations of resistance. In this section, I turn my focus to two of the most utilized tropes in the strike: the death of the university and the fragile life of protest (signaled by the mobilization of flowers). The focus of these creative forms of cultural production were the effects of neoliberalism. By abandoning previous understandings of the university as a space that values critical-thinking and challenging basic assumptions, in favor of teaching vaguely defined "skills" like teamwork and productivity, strikers hailed the death of the university while hailing the fragility and beauty of social protest. Each of these tropes was essential in reimagining resistance by providing an allegory of the future promised by neoliberalism—one where the university ceased to exist as a "critical public sphere" turning the pursuit of truth into the pursuit of profits (Giroux, 2008). In what follows, I examine how these strategies sought to shift arguments about the strike and the economic crisis toward deeper questions regarding the aforementioned stakes of the neoliberalization of the university while refusing to be silenced or to take on the hardened logics of the state.

I became cognizant of the power of the death of the university trope during my witnessing of a silent performance at the concert *Que Vivan Los Estudiantes*. As I stood in the streets waiting for another local music act to take the stage, I observed a group of young women painted as skeletons walking slowly down the avenue dressed in all black, each appearing more alone than the other despite their proximity to each other. They did not make any effort to connect with the crowd and seemed lost in their grief. As I closely examined the giant papier-mâché skull they pushed along, I noticed that it was composed of classic books. I noted fragments of poems, nationalist literature, and fiction. Sharing none of the playful logics at work in the clown police performance, this action simply noted the death of the university; even the books which once were the topic of classroom debates and final papers were on their way to the grave. Here the death of knowledge served as an outcome of the crisis foretold.

The trope of death served as an allegory of the impeding damage that budgetary cuts and the implementation of austerity measures would signal not only for the conditions of study at the university, but also for people's livelihoods across the island. This was a peaceful way of inserting a distinct imaginary into the political discourse, one that extrapolated the effects of economic restrictions and closures onto the student body, the imagination and by extension, the university itself. As Ranciére (2010) reminds us, "a dissensus is not a conflict of interests, opinions or values; it is a division inserted in 'common sense': a dispute over what is given and about the frame within which we see something as given" (p. 69). In commonsensical logic, neoliberalism is understood as necessary for sustaining life. Despite frustrations, many accept the erosion of public services to be an inevitable consequence of the crisis we live in. The figure of death highlighted the intense effects such an orientation towards cutbacks would have on daily life, thereby disrupting its core logic. Death here was used to channel frustration without necessarily proposing an idealistic alternative.

The death of the university continued to serve as a powerful commentary on the attacks being waged against students, especially when such aggressions became literal.[12] For example, on May 4, a violent confrontation between students and the riot police occurred during the daily early morning picket held at the security gate. According to eyewitness reports, officers began pushing and hitting some students as they attempted to join the picket line. No one was arrested. None of the authorities that were interviewed knew what caused the outburst and all denied that there was an order given to storm the gate. Tensions were high because the night before students on the negotiating committee had given then President of the UPR system, José de la Torre, their counter offer to his first negotiating offer. In response to this attack, which many thought signaled a narrowing terrain for free expression and a growing lack of respect for the No-Confrontation policy (PNC), students enacted another performance that took death as its central image. The street theater action, *de luto por el fallecimiento de la educación pública* (mourning the death of public education) was held just outside of the president's office at *Jardín Botanico* (botanical gardens).

The performance was quite simple. A group of female skeletons accompanied by three students in mourning arrived at the picket line. The students were dressed in black and sobbed as the skeletons stood somber holding bunches of yellow daisies. The skeletons broke form only to comfort the mourning students and to turn near the end of their performance to face the officers and offer them the flowers they held. After the performance was complete, the skeleton performers laid on the ground forming a line on the floor in front of the officers, barefoot (see Figure 1).

This performance highlighted how death can be mobilized for pedagogical ends. On one level, this teaching was tied to a questioning of commensencial notions of protest as fundamentally destructive. The performance also dramatically suggested the effects that silencing dissent could have. As one of the performers explained after the action was over, "we wanted to dramatize the death of dignity and respect" that the officers' aggression on students signaled. The visual effect of giving form to the pain that such changes would have not only affirmed that what was happening in the university was a death, it also made visible the normalization of the death of things, a process that goes on unquestioned. Using the trope of the death of the university again and again in hyperbolic ways aimed to reverse that normalization and to mourn for the future. This move sought to make it more difficult for onlookers to distance themselves from the protest.

In the student journalist collective, *Rojo Gallito,* Aura Colón Solá described the flowers as "the last vestige of life which they offered to the police who mostly ignored their pleas." Her beautiful interpretation of the flowers as an offering proposes that the officers, while complicit in a larger structure of power, were themselves much more

Figure 1. El dolor que la muerte se llevó.
(Yarelys Rivera Rodríguez; photo courtesy of the artist).

closely aligned to students than normative political divisions might suggest. Were they to accept the offering, they might be forced to recognize the ways in which their lives were bound up with one another. Although none of the officers took the offering, I was surprised to note that one officer appeared to be fighting back tears.

Although it was rare to see flowers intertwined with protests that hailed the death of the university, students often responded to the presence of officers by offering them flowers. Recalling the oft-cited phrase, *podrán cortar todas las flores, pero no podrán detener la primavera*, (they can cut all the flowers, but they cannot keep spring from coming), this tactic suggested that nonviolent protest was more potent than the violent tools used to repress it. At the same time, it reflected the fragility of life and of protests themselves while drawing police into the protest, implicating them as unwilling recipients of the gift of their resistance.

The deployment of flowers is a familiar trope for protesting unjust acts of violence, first popularized by anti-war activists in the 1960s, and were likewise mobilized in Puerto Rico. For example, the photo essay of the UPR strike in 1981 published as a part of *Huelga y Sociedad: Análisis de los Sucesos en la U.P.R. 1981-1982* includes an image of a female protestor holding a bunch of flowers approaching an officer inside the university.[13] She is turned back toward the camera, looking away from the officer. Appearing timid, her attitude is very different from the images of students facing officers at the picket line.

Although some have argued that students' use of flowers was a tactic that affirmed their pleas for dialogue even in the face of repression (see for example, Quintero Rivera 2014), it may be more accurate to call these demands instead of pleas. As the photograph reveals, flowers did not always symbolize peace offerings. Remembering the combative

Figure 2. Flowers vs. boots.
(Photo courtesy of Gamelyn Oduardo Sierra).

attitude students took at the picket line, I searched for images that reflected their posture. One photograph in particular, shows student strikers aggressively chanting as they hold flowers in front of the line of officers.[14] Students' offerings expressed a dissonance between the fragility of the flower, its aesthetic function in other contexts, and its use here as a weapon of resistance.

It may seem unclear at first glance how this may be an act of reimagining resistance, since the mobilization of flowers served to visually magnify the different positions of the two sides. Yet the positions of the uniformed police and flower-wielding students offer a potent allegory of resistance based on the position each occupies in relationship to life and death. As the next image suggests these futures are opposed: increased militancy, hardness, and violence, or vulnerable fragility. Even though these images are clichéd and, perhaps, even satirical, the meaning of flowers at the picket line still exceeds interpretative capacity as certainly as they are to fail to prevent violence and repression.

These dichotomies become even more palpable after the protest line was broken and students released their flowers to the ground (see Figure 2).

The officers' black boots appear tall next to the protestors' discarded flowers; lying on the ground they symbolize an offering rejected. The fragility of the protestors' demands was clarified through this opposition. Like the heart of the conflict, these flowers lie exposed to the repression of the state. They are powerful reminders of the heart of the conflict—a call for dialogue—is as fragile as life itself.

The images of the discarded flower and of the flower offering create two different temporal sensations. In the hand, they create a pause—a maybe. On the ground, they signal a failure that is ironically still an enactment of an alternative, imbued as they are with a vibrant beauty. As cut flowers on the ground, we know that they will soon be trampled. Still, their radical difference from the police suggests that even if their death is a certainty, it cannot dampen the importance of the students' demands for dialogue and for another way of enacting social transformation.

The use of tactics that foreground the dimensions of life/death in students' protests not only sought to shift popular understandings of what was at stake in the student strike, they also suggested that to choose the politics of the state, or *la politique,* would mean accepting violence to quell dissent. A simple gesture of beauty in the face of repressive conditions, flowers signaled strikers' refusal to become apathetic even when they were being ignored by the administration. Likewise, performing death, hyperbolic as it might seem, produced a cumulative effect, one that eroded the boundaries between this protest and the conditions of life on the island. As such, through artistic interventions the strikers created an oppositional narrative that implicated spectators from the public at large in their struggle, aligning the beautiful with the nonviolent.

Conclusion: The Ethics of Public Pedagogy in Social Change Work

This exploration into the symbolic meaning and pedagogical lessons of the creative strike suggest that acts of dissensus produced through artistic interventions and participatory modes of organizing are fundamentally ethical projects designed to disrupt the lines that divide the individual from the social. The first and most obvious target of these interventions was the neoliberal restructuring of the university, which seeks to produce equivalencies between research projects and classroom experiences, and whittle away any possibility of self-governance in the sphere of learning. As critical educators and activists know all too well, the claim that educational experiences can be reproduced irrespective of the context in which they are embedded is completely false. One group's dynamics can make the same course content into a very different classroom experience. Thus, the deeper crisis that neoliberalism fosters is to ignore difference and to teach us that they really don't matter. What artistic interventions provided in the case of the UPR strike was a public venue in which to critique these logics while building an alternative to it. Not only did performances disrupt boundaries normally associated with political publics, they made direct democracy more legible to a divided political sphere. As public pedagogy, creative forms of cultural production can restore a sense of fantasy and possibility simply by highlighting the dangerous implications of modalities of being that animate narratives of neoliberalism: scarcity and crisis. In this context, the refusal to stop imagining is extremely important.

Indeed, the representational regimes that order our lives are ethical. As we have seen, artistic interventions re-present the problems being faced by actors across multiple spaces in Puerto Rico in order to intentionally disrupt the limitations of political horizons that keep us from recognizing an intersectional political project. As Gert Biesta (2014) has argued, "Becoming public ... is about the achievement of forms of human togetherness ... in which action is possible and freedom can appear" (p. 23). In reconfiguring protest space, our communities and tools for liberation, we must not forget that relationships make these achievements possible.

As Gaztambide and Arraiz Matute (2014) argue, producing an ethical encounter is at the heart of a public pedagogy useful for direct democratic practices and social movements alike. They call for scholars to acknowledge both the importance of the motivations of the pedagogue as well as the relationships that are produced through the learning/teaching encounter to identify its ethical possibilities. Facing an/Other, coming into contact with difference signaled by the intersubjective encounter is uncomfortable. Yet, it is in what they describe as a "pushing against" one's individuality that a transformation becomes possible. They write that public pedagogy is "a relation that was ethically laden with the responsibility of a response to the other in the rupturing of the self" (2014, p. 61). Discomfort is a productive sign of the success of public pedagogy. In breaking down the self for another, both are transformed.

In *Problematizing Public Pedagogy*, Burdick, Sandlin, and O'Malley (2014) pose a question about the enactment of public pedagogy that is worth considering here to extend the ethical conundrum implied herein: "How does pedagogical public art convey political meanings to a broad audience without resolving itself in progandistic techniques/discourse?" (p. 8) While I acknowledge that the intent to transform is shared in both cases, artistic interventions are not dogmatic; they remain open to interpretation. These efforts to reach a broad audience through creative means critique the normative sphere of action but do not give explicit solutions for the thing that is being critiqued. In public pedagogy, we must acknowledge that the intent to transform needs to be ethically grounded or else we wind up reproducing colonialist logics and oppressive conditions that are inhospitable to social change. If pedagogy is also on some level a philosophical orientation to one's teaching, then to place ethics first is to relinquish control over outcomes in a way that allows for the transformative capacity of the encounter to emerge organically.

The UPR strikes did not succeed at every moment in producing this ethical encounter, but the structure of their resistance made such moments possible, creating conditions for self-reflection and transformation in activists themselves, who engaged in practices that embodied the division of the sensible, pushing against their own sense of self and ethical action. They also used the form of the occupation to produce a pedagogical space that broadened the sphere of participation in strike actions by non-students while also engaging in role reversals that questioned the legitimacy of the state and the administration's ability to adequately govern. When compared to educational pursuits in the classroom, public pedagogies that are linked to oppositional projects can only succeed to the degree that they initiate this ripple effect between disparately located actors and distinct social issues.

As Levinas (1996) argues in *Totality and Infinity*, this reconfiguration of the ethical encounter implies a reversal of the terms that structure our thinking about politics. He argues that we must place "existents before being . . . and justice before freedom" (p. 47). In other words, it is existence that sheds light on and changes our understanding of metaphysical concerns of being. In the same way, prioritizing justice makes it possible for us to understand and experience freedom. When I think of public pedagogy's utility in social movement spaces, I take Levinas' reformulation of the ethical encounter to mean that the production of a just encounter is key to experiencing freedom.

Organizing within the rubric of participatory politics is challenging and can be tiresome, and working with others can feel like freedom's opposite. As such, the process holds important keys for understanding the meaning of the movement, as well as its directionality. To achieve something without marginalizing difference is an achievement. As analysts we must identify how "forms were deliberately figured to facilitate the reception of pedagogical intent" (O'Malley & Nelson, 2013, p. 48). I have used a series of important symbols mobilized by student-strikers to show that there is a fundamentally ethical pedagogical message driving them: creating a new country, and an alternative to the politics of inequality propagated through neoliberalism can only be achieved by finding new ways to engage with one another.

In conclusion, our ways of being cannot be disentangled from ways of being-with but they must be separated from expecting to know totally what that new world will be before we engage in building it. As I have argued in other contexts (Rosario, 2013), this shift is evidence of an orientation to politics "in the meantime," a temporality that precludes the development of new master narratives while preserving the sense that one needs to fight anyway. It is this openness to imagining alternatives even if the outcome is uncertain that is needed to sustain any revolutionary praxis that breaks away from old patterns of being with others and doing politics in the future. What the UPR protests clearly demonstrate is that an unwillingness to be silenced and to forgo other possibilities despite the radical uncertainty "which animates our time" (Rebollo Gil, 2012, p.25)[15] is for me the most important lesson to be gleaned from this return to direct democratic practices.

The deliberate breaking of particular boundaries and subject positions that are set up to keep us from knowing one another is key to producing a public where justice can be realized. I hope that this glimpse into the world of the creative strike has helped to demonstrate that this is more than a possibility. It is an imperative.

Notes

1. Despite the fact that the medical sciences campus only held a 24-hour stoppage, they often participated in actions organized by the neighboring Río Piedras campus and openly expressed support for the strike.
2. The strike resulted from three major concerns: cuts in the operating budget of the University authorized by Law 7, feared privatization of the institution and a Board of Trustees' policy, Certification 98 which eliminated double eligibility for tuition waivers and financial aid. These concerns reflected a more longstanding concern about the rising cost of study that was center stage in the 2005 strike *la huelga del CUCA* (the committee against the tuition hike).
3. A long occupation of a major highway would be disruptive anywhere, but in Puerto Rico, an island with a notoriously severe traffic problem due in major part to rapid development of the island in a fifty-year period, it was even more of a threat to the functioning of daily life.
4. This is despite its original designation as a school that would promote English language and train technicians to work on the sugar plantations when it was founded shortly after the U.S. military invasion of the island and the passage of the Foraker Act, which established a civilian government in the island.
5. Although a close analysis of how this fragmentation was produced is beyond the scope of this paper, it relates to the political designation of the island as a "free associated state," which operates in practice in ways much more aligned to the island's original status of unincorporated territory. More than fifty years since its founding and after three plebiscites held to decide its fate, the most powerful parties are those that support continued integration into the US. The opposition is extremely weak and appears to be plagued by old school languages and tactics that emphasize short-term coalitions but lack lasting forms for creating a viable alternative.
6. The few times students did abandon the campus, they faced extremely violent repression by the state, making the proposition of leaving campus regularly more fraught. The practical issue of who would protect the campus from police and infiltrates further complicated matters. In the strike against the fiscal stabilization fee that followed this one, efforts were made to make these connections, but many thought that the opportunity had already been missed.
7. To read the letter in its entirety, see http://occupyca.wordpress.com/2010/04/23/more-upr-campuses-strike/
8. Whereas political publics refer to macro-level configurations like the nation-state, popular publics refer to the distribution of everyday texts, and concrete publics refers to spatially grounded spaces of experimentation where actors build an alternative community together (Savage, 2014, p. 81–88).
9. I am focusing on interventions that commented on the police presence since students' efforts to make them part of the struggle is one concrete way to demonstrate their intention to shift boundaries between public and protest space. I am fully cognizant of the fact that this was a representational strategy that in no way should suggest that students' felt a false sense of collectivism with police officers. However, students' manner of engaging with the police was

CULTURAL PRODUCTION AND PARTICIPATORY POLITICS 67

significant especially when compared to their representations of the administration of the UPR system, who were consistently ridiculed in performances and online forums. One popular form of student critiques of administrators was to produce culture jammer-esque movie posters based on the conflict, such as: "How to Lose the University in Ten Days," or "How the Grinch stole the UPR."

10. The concert's name is a reference to a popular protest song written by Violetta Parra, a Chilean multi-genre artist who was known for her love and respect for peasants as well as workers. She became a major figure in Latin American song writing and was one of the key founders of the folk inspired, socially political music genre known as *la nueva canción* (the new song). The title of the concert was not only homage to prior student movements, but also signaled a shared love for "the people." Estimates of the number of attendees in popular presses ranged between 6,000-8,000 and suggested that a broad range of constituents identified with the students' claims.

11. *Tumba coco*, or coconut knocker, is a colloquial name for a large speaker system, usually outfitted to a van or truck. The sound is so loud it could knock down coconuts from the tree. It also has the added implication of being against the statehood party, which has adopted the palm tree as one of its key symbols.

12. Of course, it bears mentioning that it wasn't until the second strike, which ran from December 2010 to February 2011, that the trope of the dying university became more than a trope. Approximately 10,000 students were forced to drop out after the implementation of the $800 quota, and officers occupied the campus after the second stoppage was lifted on December 9, 2010, making it nearly impossible to engage in creative forms of protest.

13. The photo montage is not paginated. The image I describe is in the section titled October 1981, seventeen pages in.

14. To access the photo, go to http://www.primerahora.com/noticias/gobierno-politica/nota/huel gaenlauprdia22minutoaminutoygririveraanunciacierrehastael31dejulio-387498/

15. The title of this poem is borrowed from a line in Amiri Baraka's work *Black Music* published by Akashic Books in 1959. It appears on p.181 as part of a description of the present moment. "Contemporary means that; with the feeling that animates our time".

References

Alexander, J. (2005). *Pedagogies of crossing: Meditations on feminism, sexuality and the sacred.* Durham: Duke University Press.

Biesta, G. (2014). Making pedagogy public: For the public, of the public or in the interest of publicness. In J. Burdick, A. Sandlin; & M.P. O'Malley (Eds.). *Problematizing public pedagogy* (pp. 15–26). New York: Routledge.

Brady, J.F. (2006). Public pedagogy and educational leadership: Politically engaged scholarly communities and possibilities for critical engagement. *Journal of Curriculum & Pedagogy, 3,* 57–60.

Burdick, J. Sandlin, A., & O'Malley M.P. (Eds.). (2014). *Problematizing public pedagogy.* New York: Routledge.

Chambers, S. (2011). Jacques Rancière and the problem of pure politics. *European Journal of Political Theory, 10,* 303–326.

Cólon Pérez, D. (2012). Puerto Rico: Arte, diáspora y esfera pública. Ph.D. dissertation Universidad Autónoma de Barcelona (Philosophy Department)

Ellsworth, E. (2005). *Places of learning: Media, architecture, pedagogy.* New York: Routledge.

Gablik, S. (1995). Connective aesthetics: Art after individualism. In S. Lacy (Ed.), *Mapping the terrain: New genre public art* (pp. 77–87). Seattle, WA: Bay Press.

Gaztambide-Fernández, R. (2013). Why the arts don't do anything: Toward a new vision of cultural production in education. *Harvard Educational Review, 83,* 211–236.

Gaztambide-Fernández, R. & Arráiz Matute, A. (2014). 'Pushing against:' Relationality, intentionality, and the ethical imperative of public pedagogy. In J. Burdick, J. Sandlin, & M. O'Malley (Eds.). *Problematizing public pedagogy* (pp. 52–65). New York: Routledge.

Giroux, H. (2008). Academic unfreedom in America: Rethinking the university as a democratic public sphere. *Works and Days, 51/52*, 1–27.

Giroux, H. (2004). Public pedagogy and the politics of neoliberalism: Making politics more pedagogical. *Policy Futures in Education, 2*, 494–503.

Gould, D. (2009). *Moving politics: Emotions and ACT UP's fight against AIDS*. Chicago, IL: Chicago University Press.

Haugerud, A. (2013). *No billionaire left behind: Satirical activism in America*. Stanford, CA: Stanford University Press.

Lacy, S. ed. (1995). *Mapping the terrain: New genre public art*. Seattle, WA: Bay Press.

Levinas, E. (1996). *Totality and infinity: An essay on exteriority*(A. Lingus, Trans.). Pittsburgh, PA: Duquesne University.

Morrell, E. (2002). Towards a critical pedagogy of popular culture: Literacy development among urban youth. *Journal of Adolescent and Adult Literacy, 41*, 72–77.

Nieves Falcón, L. et. al. (1982). *Huelga y sociedad: Análisis de los sucesos en la U.P.R. 1981–1982*. España: Editorial Edil.

O'Malley, P & Nelson, S. (2013). The public pedagogy of student activists in Chile: What have we learned from the Penguins' Revolution. *Journal of Curriculum Theorizing, 29*, 41–56.

Panagia, D. (2010). 7. "Partage du sensible": The distribution of the sensible. In J.-P. Deranty (Ed.), *Jacques Rancière: Key concepts* (pp. 95–97). Durham, UK: Acumen.

Polletta, F. (2002). *Freedom is an endless meeting: Democracy in American social movements*. Chicago: University of Chicago Press.

Quintero Rivera, M. (2013). "Cartografías culturales del entresiglo: arte y política en las décadas de 1990 y 2000" In Gonzalez Vale, L. y Maria Dolores Luque (Eds.). *Historia de Puerto Rico*. Madrid: Editorial Doce Calles.

Rancière, J. (2010). *Dissensus: On politics and aesthetics*. (S. Corcoran, Trans.). New York: Continuum International.

Rebollo-Gil, G. (2012). *Sospechar de la euforia*. San Juan: La Secta de los Perros.

Rosario, M. (2013). Ephemeral spaces, undying dreams: Social justice struggles in contemporary Puerto Rico. Ph.D. Cornell University.

Sandlin, J. A., O'Malley, M. P., & Burdick, J. (2011). Mapping the complexity of public pedagogy scholarship 1894–2010. *Review of Educational Research, 81*, 338–375.

Sandlin, J. A., Schultz, B. D., & Burdick, J. (Eds.). (2010). *Handbook of public pedagogy: Education and learning beyond schooling*. New York: Routledge.

Stanchich, M. (2011). University Besieged: Dimensions, Contexts and Stakes. *Sargasso*, 12(1), ix–xxxiii.

4 Educating for cultural citizenship
Reframing the goals of arts education

Paul J. Kuttner

Arts education does more than transfer the skills and knowledge needed to create artistic works. It also helps to shape young people's orientations towards participation in the cultural life of their communities. In this article, Paul Kuttner argues for reframing arts education as a process of developing cultural citizenship. Cultural citizenship, a concept from political theory and cultural studies, is concerned with the development of diverse cultural practices and identities alongside full participation in cultural and political life. Using this lens, we can look at different forms of arts education and ask, "What types of cultural citizens are these programs developing?" Building on the work of civic education scholars Westheimer and Kahne (2004), Kuttner suggests a few initial types before delving into a fuller description of what he calls the "justice-oriented cultural citizen." This concept is illustrated with data from an ethnographic case study of one arts organization that is developing such citizens: Project HIP-HOP, a Boston-based youth organization that trains young artists as cultural organizers who can use their art to catalyze change in their communities. This reframing of arts education as a form of civic education helps to situate artistic practices in their larger socio-political contexts, while contributing to an ongoing dialogue about the role of arts education in supporting participatory democracy and social change.

What does it mean to be part of a society? What are the responsibilities, roles, and rights of community members? How does one become a "good" citizen? These questions are central to the field of civic education, which prepares individuals to "acquire and learn to use the skills, knowledge, and attitudes that will prepare them to be competent and responsible citizens throughout their lives" (Gibson & Levine, 2003, p. 4). There is wide agreement that civic education is of vital importance to the viability of democracy. As Levinson (2012) writes, "The legitimacy, stability, and quality of democratic regimes are all directly dependent on the robust participation of a representative and large cross-section of citizens" (p. 48). Preparing young people for such participation is a long-recognized goal of schooling, and drives an array of private, public, and non-profit institutions.

At the same time, there is significant diversity among civic education programs, reflecting fundamental differences in how educators envision the "good" or "ideal" citizen (Westheimer and Kahne, 2004). Galston (2004) captures some of this diversity when he writes,

Americans do not wholly agree about the kind of citizenship they want our schools to foster. Some stress loyalty to current institutions and practices, while others emphasize critical reflection on them. Some focus on principles of national unity, while others want civic education to underscore the importance of demographic and ideological diversity. Some would teach our civic history as the story of fitful but palpable progress towards equality and inclusion, while others would insist on equal time for the effects of past and present oppression. Moral decency, voluntary service, voting, social movements...each of these can be taken as the paradigm of civic practice and placed at the core of civic pedagogy. (p. 265)

Those of us working in the field of arts education – whether in schools or museums, community centers or informal spaces – should be asking questions similar to those posed at the start of this article. Citizenship is not only a matter of formal rights and responsibilities; it is also a matter of culture. One may be formally recognized as a citizen of a country while still having one's cultural perspectives and practices marginalized, leading to second-class citizenship (Rosaldo, 1994). One may have access to the ballot box but not the right, enshrined in the Universal Declaration of Human Rights, to "freely participate in the cultural life of the community" (UN General Assembly, 1948). Moreover, engagement in cultural production and consumption includes a vital political dimension. The visual art we create, the music we listen to, and the online media we share can all serve to reinforce and challenge existing social systems. In fact, groups that have been denied access to traditional political participation have often turned to the arts and other cultural practices as forms of civic engagement (Dolby, 2003; Scott, 1990). For these reasons and others, many scholars have begun writing about the importance of *cultural citizenship*: the right and capacity of people to develop and pass on diverse cultural traditions and identities while participating effectively in a shared cultural and political arena (Miller, 2001, 2002; Rosaldo, 1994, 1997; Stevenson, 1997, 2001, 2003; Turner, 2001; Wang, 2013).

Arts education is about more than transmitting the skills and knowledge needed to create artistic works. It is also a process of developing young people's orientations towards the arts as a form of cultural production. Whether implicitly or explicitly, arts education teaches people their roles and responsibilities as artists and/or audience members (Efland, 1990). It helps define what counts as art, what it means to be an artist, and what exactly art is *for*. Thus, arts education offers an entryway for young people into an important aspect of cultural life. One useful way to think about arts education, then, is as a process of developing *cultural citizenship*. Arts educators are helping youth to acquire skills, knowledge, and attitudes that will prepare them to be competent and responsible members of their cultural communities.

If we think of arts education as a process of developing cultural citizenship, then we can begin asking questions similar to those with which I began this article: What kind of cultural citizens do we need? What does it mean to be a "good" cultural citizen? What skills, capacities, and orientations do young people need in order to engage effectively as full cultural citizens? As with civic education programs (Galston, 2004; Westheimer & Kahne, 2004), I argue that different models of arts education promote different types of cultural citizenship. Understanding these differences can contribute to a broader dialogue about the role of arts education in supporting participatory democracy and social change – a particularly important topic in this era of global media conglomerates, participatory online culture, and vibrant social movements related to questions of individual and national identity.

In this article, I lay out my argument in three steps. First, I discuss the literature on cultural citizenship and argue that arts education can be usefully interpreted through this lens. Second, I suggest that different models of arts education promote different types of cultural citizenship, and lay out three potential types as a springboard for discussion. Developing a full typology is beyond the scope of this article. Third, I focus in-depth on one proposed type of cultural citizen – the justice-oriented cultural citizen – breaking it down into what I see as its key components. I illustrate this concept by presenting one example of an arts-based program that supports young people as justice-oriented cultural citizens. In my concluding sections, I reflect on the implications and limitations of this argument, and describe potential next steps in researching and practicing arts education through a cultural citizenship lens.

Before I begin, I will take a moment to explain how I am using the terms *culture, art, and citizenship*. Following the "semiotic turn" in cultural anthropology and cultural studies, this article is based on an understanding of culture as an ongoing process of collective meaning making (Boele van Hensbroek, 2010; Geertz, 1973). At the most visible level, this meaning-making process is carried out through *cultural production*: the creation and consumption of various forms of symbolic creativity including mass media, language, slang, fashion, and the arts (Willis, 1990). Cultural production is inextricably intertwined with less visible, yet more fundamental questions related to shared values and assumptions about the world (Schein, 1990). When a (more or less) defined group of people with a shared history reaches a significant level of agreement about values, assumptions, and common modes of expression, we speak of them as sharing a culture. However, culture is always in a state of internal flux and contestation.

The arts are understood here as a sub-set of cultural production. They include a variety of forms of symbolic creativity, including what are sometimes called the "fine" or "high" arts (ballet, opera, theater), the "folk" arts (spirituals, folk dances), and the "popular" arts (pop music, television, the creative use of social media).[1] Distinctions between these forms are largely a matter of social stratification, rather than useful divisions for my purposes (Bourdieu, 1993). Therefore, what I term "arts education" is inclusive of a range of activities from theater training to documentary film courses to collaborative mural design to community-based folk arts festivals.

In defining the arts this way, I am working from what Gaztambide-Fernández (2013) calls a "cultural production" approach to the arts and arts education. Rather than seeing the arts as separate from everyday life, a cultural production approach frames artistic practice as part of a larger, ongoing process of creating and redefining our shared cultural space through symbolic creativity and interaction. Art is understood as a culturally-situated activity involving "actual people, under real social circumstances, in particular cultural contexts, and within specific material and symbolic relations" (Gaztambide-Fernández, 2013, p. 226). Therefore, while the term "culture" implies something much broader than "arts," the term "arts" should always be interpreted as being embedded in larger processes of cultural (re)production.

Finally, when I write of citizenship I am not restricting the term to membership in a nation-state. While recognizing that the idea of citizenship developed in tandem with the rise of the nation-state, and that the nation is still an important unit of belonging and political struggle (Stevenson, 1997, 2003), I am using the term more broadly. Citizenship, as used here, refers to "our connection to particular social and cultural locations, [and] the possibility of a participatory involvement in shaping our society and our understanding of our rights and responsibilities" (Stevenson, 2011, p. 5). Processes of globalization, localization, and (im)migration have radically complicated our ideas of citizenship. As Miller (2001) writes:

- Citizenship is no longer easily based on soil or blood. Rather, it is founded on some variant of those qualities in connection with culture and the capitalist labor market. And the state is no longer the sole frame of citizenship in the face of new nationalisms and cross-border affinities that no single governmental apparatus can contain. (pp. 4—5)

In order to understand these diverse new forms of belonging and allegiance, we must be able to appreciate the profoundly cultural nature of citizenship.

Culture and Citizenship

Citizenship is commonly understood as a legal structure that formally recognizes certain people as members of a nation-state, and in doing so bestows certain rights and demands certain obligations from those individuals. T. H. Marshall (1950) famously divided citizenship in England into three elements: civil, political, and social. Beginning in the late 1980s, scholars such as Renato Rosaldo, Tony Bennett, and Will Kymlicka began to extend this analysis by exploring the "cultural dimension" of citizenship (Miller, 2002; Stevenson, 2001). Many were inspired by the so-called "new" social movements of the prior few decades, which demanded not just formal civic, political, and social rights, but also an end to cultural marginalization and oppression (Stevenson, 2001). A new field of study emerged at the intersection of political theory and cultural studies, addressing questions like: What does belonging look like in a multicultural nation? Where do race, class, sexuality, gender, and (dis)ability fit into discussions of citizenship? What is the role of cultural policy in supporting democracy? How do marginalized groups engage in cultural practices as a form of resistance and political action?

From this field, scholars have articulated different versions of what they term "cultural citizenship." While variously defined, cultural citizenship is broadly concerned with the development and recognition of cultural diversity on the one hand, and full cultural and political participation on the other. As Rosaldo (1997) explains, the concept of citizenship has long been based on assumptions of cultural homogeneity. The rhetoric of universal citizenship and open political participation have obscured the very real ways that people are marginalized and denied access to democratic processes through cultural exclusion. Cultural citizenship, for Rosaldo (1994), is an active response to this situation, in which marginalized groups claim "the right to be different and to belong in a participatory democratic sense" (p. 402). For Rosaldo (1997), cultural expression – including the arts, broadly defined to include fine, popular, and folk art forms – is an important way that marginalized groups claim cultural citizenship.

In a similar vein, Pakulski (1997) describes cultural citizenship as entailing a set of "cultural rights," which he describes as "a new set of citizenship claims that involve the right to unhindered and legitimate representation, and propagation of identities and lifestyles through the information systems and in public fora" (p. 80). He divides these rights into three streams: the right to "symbolic presence and visibility (vs marginalisation); the right to dignifying representation (vs stigmatisation); and the right to propagation of identity and maintenance of lifestyles (vs assimilation)" (p. 80). Cultural rights can imply a set of obligations as well, such as the obligation to make public space for diverse forms of cultural expression (Turner, 2001). In this sense, cultural citizenship is a deepening of traditional citizenship, addressing previously ignored aspects of belonging. Cultural citizenship is a process of contention and struggle, with groups making claims for rights that may or may not be recognized by a society or state (Pakulski, 1997). Cultural citizenship is a process of redefining what it means to belong.

A complementary vein of scholarship on cultural citizenship focuses less on belonging, and more on opportunities to actively participate in a shared cultural sphere. Turner (2001), for example, writes that cultural citizenship can be described as "the capacity to participate effectively, creatively and successfully within a national culture" (p. 12). Boele van Hensbroek (2010) similarly writes that cultural citizens are "co-producers, or co-authors, of the cultural context or contexts in which they participate" (p. 321). This concept has been captured most famously in Article 27 of the 1948 Universal Declaration of Human Rights, which includes the statement, "Everyone has the right freely to participate in the cultural life of the community, to enjoy the arts and to share in scientific advancement and its benefits" (UN General Assembly, 1948).

The importance of this type of participation is based on an understanding that power and politics function not only through visible political processes but also in the "cultural domain" – the realm of discourse, story, and ideology (Collins, 2009). Stevenson (2003) argues that this domain is particularly important today given our increasingly information-rich societies.

> The power to name, construct meaning and exert control over the flow of information within contemporary societies is one of today's central structural divisions. Power is not solely based upon material dimensions, but also involves the capacity to throw into question established codes and to rework frameworks of common understanding. (p. 4)

Full citizenship, then, must entail opportunities to participate not only in the formal political realm, but also in the cultural realm—to be a part of the cultural dialogue. This raises questions about who does and does not have access to media and communications systems, as well as other outlets of cultural production such as schools and museums. Turner (2001) writes, "We can conceptualize cultural citizenship in terms of the ownership and control of the means of cultural production: how is citizenship participation expressed with respect to the ownership, production, distribution and consumption of cultural goods?" (p. 20).

We can think of participation in the cultural sphere as a form of civic activity related to but distinct from political participation in the state (Boele van Hensbroek, 2010). In fact, groups that have been kept out of traditional political and civil processes have often turned to the cultural sphere as a space within which they can claim rights to participate and belong. For example, popular culture has been shown to be a "vital political space" in which youth—who may be too young to vote—engage in civic life (Dolby, 2003, p. 269; Gramsci, 1972). In a similar vein, media scholars such as Jenkins (2009) have begun exploring how involvement in participatory online communities can constitute an important form of civic engagement, even when not explicitly "political" in the traditional sense. Dolby (2003) argues that the concept of cultural citizenship can be useful in clarifying important connections between engagement with these types of "everyday cultural practices" and larger political processes.

> The concept of "cultural citizenship" . . . underscores the fact that everyday cultural practices are not disconnected from pressing economic and political issues about the future of democracy in an increasingly privatized, globalized world. Instead, those cultural practices are a force in shaping and reshaping that world. (p. 272)

While much attention has been given to what cultural citizenship is and how states can facilitate it through, for example, cultural policy (Mercer, 2002), far less has been given to how we might prepare young people to *become* cultural citizens (Stevenson, 2011). It is clear that education is key to cultural citizenship, given the central role of schools in developing national identities and educating youth in language and communication skills. This raises important questions for educators, such as: How should education be designed to promote the kind of cultural citizens we want young people to become? What skills, knowledge, and attitudes do individuals need in order to claim their cultural rights? How can we best prepare young people to engage fully in the cultural life of their communities? While these questions are relevant to all educators, I want to address here how they specifically relate to arts education. Amid ongoing debates about the value and role of arts education, I argue that we can usefully think of the job of arts educators as developing cultural citizenship.

Arts Education and Cultural Citizenship

Education in the arts—the training of individuals for their roles as producers and consumers of the arts—has long incorporated an array of social, economic, and moral goals (Efland, 1990). Today's arts education landscape, however, is arguably much more complex than in the past. Arts educators today work in a wide variety of locations including public schools, community organizations, private residences, museums, universities, and on the Internet. Even more varied are the goals towards which they work, from socio-emotional development to economic growth to the improvement of math and reading skills. In many cases, arts education efforts include explicit civic goals such as increasing social capital and amplifying collective voice in marginalized communities (McCarthy, Ondaatje, Zakaras, & Brooks, 2004; Quinn, Ploof, & Hochtritt, 2012).

Researching with young people along the US-Mexico border, Fránquiz and Brochin-Ceballos (2006) show how arts programming can be used to foster cultural citizenship, defined as "students' evolving sense of belonging to differing social groups and to claiming cultural space for personal and collective expression" (p. 6). They describe how educators facilitated this process through a videopoetry project in a small rural community by, "(a) providing access to culturally relevant oral, visual, and written texts; (b) proposing multiple opportunities for children to use cultural assets in producing their texts; (c) fostering cultural preservation; and (d) engaging students in activities with transformative potential" (p. 6). Students in the study were able to draw on local cultural resources, build strong cultural identities, and preserve valued aspects of community life, thus "claiming" cultural citizenship through the arts.

Building on this insight, I would like to take the argument a step further. Not only can arts education serve as a space for developing and claiming cultural citizenship; we can think of arts education *in general* as a process of developing cultural citizens. No matter what other outcomes arts educators seek, we are teaching students about their roles and responsibilities in relation to artistic creation and consumption. We are helping to shape students' capacities and orientations towards participating in an important aspect of cultural life. The arts are far from the only way that young people participate in the cultural sphere. Still, creation and consumption of artistic products, broadly defined, remain key ways that people engage in communication, individual identity formation, and the construction of shared cultures (Foster & Blau, 1989).

This argument requires us to make a conceptual departure from most of the cultural citizenship literature. In general, theorists have sought to define cultural citizenship as a fixed good, whether a set of rights and opportunities, or a set of practices. Cultural citizenship is then treated as a binary (individuals do or do not have access to cultural citizenship) or as a spectrum. In this formulation, cultural citizenship is something to "increase" or "achieve" (Boele van Hensbroek, 2010). If we are thinking in terms of cultural policy or citizen demands on the state, such an approach makes sense. However, from the perspective of the individual "cultural citizen" it may be more helpful to think of cultural citizenship as multiple. There are many ways to engage actively in the cultural life of one's community and many ways to claim space for individual and group expression, each of which can be seen as a different type of cultural citizenship. One type may look like Rosaldo's (1997) vision of the polyglot citizen, while another may look more like

Stevenson's (2003) vision of a new cosmopolitanism. There may be types of cultural citizenship not yet captured in the literature.

In making this conceptual departure, I draw my inspiration from the field of civic education, and particularly the work of Westheimer and Kahne (2004). In their article, *What Kind of Citizen: The Politics of Educating for Democracy,* the authors argue that among civic educators there is significant disagreement about what it means to be a "good" citizen in a democracy. They divide civic education programs into three types, based on their answer to the question, "What kind of citizen do we need to support an effective democratic society?" (p. 239). Some programs, they argue, advocate for *personally responsible citizens,* who are helpful, honest, and self-disciplined. Others advocate for *participatory citizens,* who join voluntary civic organizations. Still others advocate for *justice-oriented citizens,* who are able to critically analyze and address systems of injustice.

Following Westheimer and Kahne, I suggest that different arts education programs promote different visions of cultural citizenship, whether such visions are explicit or not. What roles are youth taught to play in the creation and consumption of artistic products? What art forms are they taught to value? Towards what ends do they engage with artistic practice? What rights are they taught to claim and what obligations are put on them as artistic creators and consumers? Based on the answers to these and related questions, we can begin to sort out the different visions of cultural citizenship inherent in arts education practices. While developing a full typology is beyond the scope of this article, I will suggest a few tentative types in order to illustrate my point, before exploring one type in-depth. These types are not, for the most part, mutually exclusive. I have somewhat overstated the distinctions between them for the sake of conceptual clarity. In practice, arts programs may combine aspects of different approaches, and students can benefit from taking part in programs across the spectrum. Some of the highest quality arts education programs are those that pursue multiple goals simultaneously and allow for diverse experiences (Seidel, Tishman, Winner, Hetland, & Palmer, 2009).

Some arts programs are designed to develop what we might call *informed cultural citizens.* The informed cultural citizen has the capacity to understand, appreciate, and critique works of art within a larger social, political, artistic, or cultural context. She has full access to what artists and scholars call the "aesthetic experience," along with its attendant benefits. She is confident in her right to attend museums, plays, concerts, and other artistic fora without feeling alienated or excluded. She is not a passive consumer of whatever media comes her way; she is engaged in choosing, critiquing, and discussing art, thus involving her in the evolution of artistic tastes. She has also tried her hand at a few art forms so, although it is likely she does not identify as an "artist," she has a deep appreciation for the artistic process.

This approach to arts education has a long history in the fields of *art appreciation* and *aesthetic education,* among others, and remains prominent (Gaughan, 1990; Smith, 2004). It is clearly articulated, for example, in the Wallace Foundation's 2008 report, *Cultivating Demand for the Arts: Arts Learning, Arts Engagement, and State Arts Policy* (Zakaras & Lowell, 2008). Responding to concerns about decreasing audience numbers, this report calls for investment in arts education as a way to "expand demand by cultivating the capacity of individuals to have aesthetic experiences with works of arts" (p. xvi). As the authors explain, this is not only about supporting arts institutions, but also about addressing inequity in the distribution of the benefits of arts experiences. The authors state that, "by deemphasizing the education of children in the arts and humanities, American public schools are no longer adequately preparing their students to participate in the rich cultural life that is one of civilization's greatest achievements" (p. 4).

The need to develop what I am calling informed cultural citizens was one of the key arguments behind the Discipline Based Arts Education (DBAE) movement, launched by the Getty Trust in the 1980s. DBAE combines artistic practice, art history, art criticism, and the study of aesthetics. Early advocates argued that this type of arts education should be taught to all K-12 students as a way to expand artistic literacy, increase cultural capital, and broaden access to the "pleasures" of the arts, among other goals (Eisner, 1987). DBAE has influenced more recent state and national efforts in the United States to develop arts education standards (Zakaras & Lowell, 2008). This idea of broadening access to artistic experiences and spaces that have long marginalized certain groups is what Evrard (1997) calls the "democratization of culture."

In other programs, we see the development of what we might call *participatory cultural citizens*. The participatory cultural citizen sees herself as an active participant in the arts, whether or not she considers it to be a profession. She is involved in producing, remixing, and sharing original artistic works. She has a strong connection to her own cultural heritage, along with the freedom to explore new forms of expression and to share in cross-cultural exchange. While she may use the arts as a means of individual expression, she also sees the arts as a way to connect with and understand the broader communities of which she is a part. The participatory cultural citizen does not see a firm divide between "artist" and "audience," and is resistant to hierarchies among art forms. In fact, she is likely to engage in "popular" or "folk" art forms that encourage wide participation.

We see this vision of participatory cultural citizenship powerfully illustrated in the arts programs run by the settlement houses of the late 19th and early 20th centuries in the United States. Dedicated to offering social services and working for social reform among growing immigrant communities, institutions like Hull House in Chicago offered an array of arts education opportunities that directly challenged the hierarchy and elitism of the professional arts world (Ganz & Strobel, 2004; Koerin, 2003).[2] As Rabkin (2013) writes,

> Hull House encouraged and taught the poor to make art themselves in music, drama, dance, and visual art programs staffed by artists. It quickly replaced reproductions of Old Masters in its art gallery with exhibitions of art by neighborhood residents. The arts at Hull House helped immigrants remain connected to their cultural roots and identities; they helped them understand their new environment and its inequities; they helped them develop the sense of agency and imaginative capacity needed to believe in their own potential and hopes for the future; and they helped build the social bonds and empathy that are the foundation of community and democratic life. Four hundred settlements across the country made the arts central to their work by 1914. (para. 3)

Similar approaches to arts education emerged repeatedly over the course of the next century, and are practiced today by numerous community arts organizations and teaching artists. These efforts, often focused on particular geographic neighborhoods, seek to enrich the lives of individuals and to strengthen the social and cultural fabric of communities.

The rest of this article considers a third type of cultural citizen, which, in deference to Westheimer and Kahne, I will call the *justice-oriented cultural citizen*. The justice-oriented cultural citizen can critically analyze the ways that the arts are implicated in processes of oppression and resistance. She actively values and promotes cultural perspectives and narratives that are kept out of mainstream discourse, while maintaining a strong sense of cultural pride and identity. The justice-oriented cultural citizen feels a responsibility to use her art to improve her community and directly confront injustice, while understanding that social change must be a collective effort utilizing multiple forms of cultural and social action. Programs promoting justice-oriented cultural citizenship, as defined here, can be found in the fields of social justice arts education, community-based arts, youth participatory action research, youth media, youth organizing, critical media literacy, hip-hop education, community cultural development, and cultural organizing, among others.[3] In the following sections, I delineate four key characteristics of the justice-oriented cultural citizen and illustrate the concept through a case study of one youth arts organization.

Developing Justice-Oriented Cultural Citizens: Project HIP-HOP

Project HIP-HOP (Highways Into the Past, History, Organizing, and Power) is a community-based organization in the Roxbury region of Boston, MA. Originally launched in 1993 as an effort to engage young people in the history of the civil rights movement (Murray & Garrido, 1995), Project HIP-HOP (PHH) trains youth as "cultural organizers" who can use the arts to address injustice in their communities. PHH works mainly with Black and Latina/o youth from Boston's low-income Communities of Color, who bring a range of artistic interests and skills; they are rappers, dancers, musicians, deejays, poets, singers, actors, and visual artists. PHH supports them in honing their artistic skills, analyzing oppression in their lives and communities, and taking collective action. Over the years they have taken part in traditional community organizing campaigns, convened open mics, performed street theater, planned flash mobs, and run a radio show, among other activities.

PHH is one of a growing number of organizations around the world utilizing hip-hop culture as a forum through which to engage in youth and community organizing (Clay, 2012; Dixon-Román & Gomez, 2013; Ginwright, 2006; Maira, 2013). The group has also recently taken on the concept of *cultural organizing* as a frame for their work. The term cultural organizing refers to social change efforts that place art and culture at the center of an organizing strategy, and that are rooted in the cultural practices, identities, and worldviews of those doing the organizing (Benavente & Richardson, 2011). The term has been used to describe the artistic practices of the African American civil rights movement, and partnerships between artists and activists during the Popular Front organizing of the 1920s (Denning, 1990; Street, 2007). Today, a multi-disciplinary, multi-issue field of practice is forming under the name, led by intermediary groups such as the Highlander Research and Education Center, Arts & Democracy, and the Culture Group.

The data below come from an ethnographic case study (Stake, 1995) that I conducted, looking at PHH's model of cultural organizing (Kuttner, 2014). My goal was to assist in building a descriptive and theoretical foundation for the practice of cultural organizing with young people, a topic that has received little attention in the emerging literature on modern cultural organizing (Arts & Democracy Project, 2011; Benavente & Richardson, 2011; Cohen-Cruz, 2010; Kohl-Arenas, Nateras, & Taylor, 2014; The Culture Group, 2014). At the same time, I hoped to speak more broadly to diverse forms of arts-based youth activism. For this reason, I chose a site that explicitly utilized the concept of cultural organizing, while also engaging with hip-hop culture, a common practice among many youth activist groups (Delgado & Staples, 2008; Flores-Gonzáles, Rodríguez, & Rodríguez-Muñiz, 2006; Ginwright, 2006). The study was centered on the following questions:

(1) How is youth cultural organizing conceptualized and designed at one organization?

(2) What does youth cultural organizing look like in practice at this site?
(3) How do young people involved in the organization experience and make sense of youth cultural organizing?

The majority of fieldwork was conducted between July 2011 and May 2012. During this time, PHH worked directly with 7 – 20 young people at a time, depending on the season, many of whom were given stipends for their participation. These youth identified as having African American, Latina/o, Caribbean American, and Native American roots. The study was designed in partnership with PHH staff and youth, and adapted over time to address the evolving needs of both the organization and the research. I conducted 31 formal interviews and two focus groups with youth members, board members, current and former staff members, and individuals outside the organization. These interviews focused on the concepts and intentions behind PHH practices, as well as the experiences of those directly involved. I took part in ongoing participant observation of meetings, rehearsals, political education sessions, public events, and performances, as well as many informal conversations in the field. I also analyzed documentation produced by or relating to the organization across its lifespan. Data was thematically coded with a blend of deductive codes based in existing literature and inductive codes emerging from the data. Analysis consisted of an iterative process of coding, writing, and discussing findings with peers and participants. All quotes used below are from interviews that I conducted with participants, unless otherwise noted.

Through this study, I constructed a theoretical framework for how youth cultural organizing at PHH works towards transformative change at the individual, group, and community levels. A full picture of PHH's multi-layered cultural organizing work is beyond the scope of this article. Here, PHH serves as an example of a program that seeks to develop what I'm calling justice-oriented cultural citizenship. PHH itself does not use the language of citizenship, speaking instead of leadership and organizing. However, the concept of justice-oriented cultural citizenship emerged from the process of delineating implications of PHH's work for civic education more broadly. In particular, PHH's dedication to building "cultural leadership" among young people as a way to support the growth of progressive social movements led me to consider how their work (and that of other organizations like them) might form a link between the concept of cultural citizenship and the practice of civic education.

In the following sections I lay out four key aspects of justice-oriented cultural citizenship. I argue that the justice-oriented cultural citizen:

(1) Has a critical, systemic analysis of power in the cultural domain;
(2) Advocates for marginalized cultures and stories, based in a strong sense of cultural pride and efficacy;
(3) Feels responsible for, and capable of, using art towards justice in her multiple, overlapping communities; and
(4) Is dedicated to change through collective action utilizing multiple social change approaches.

Each aspect of justice-oriented cultural citizenship is illustrated with data from PHH. While the specifics of PHH's methods are particular to its organizing model and context, I argue that the broader concepts introduced in each section will resonate across a wide range of arts-based initiatives. I support this argument by linking each aspect of justice-oriented cultural citizenship to existing literature.

Critical Analysis of Power in the Cultural Domain

It is widely agreed that effective democratic systems require informed citizens who have the knowledge necessary for political involvement. However, exactly what people need to be informed about is up for debate (Caprini, 1996). Critical educators argue that individuals cannot effectively participate and effect change in a society without the ability to critically analyze the multiple, interlocking systems of power within which their lives are situated (Freire, 1970; Giroux, 1988). Westheimer and Kahne (2004) capture this idea in their concept of the justice-oriented cultural citizen, who has a critical social and structural analysis of the workings of power, and is able to "analyze and understand the interplay of social, economic, and political forces" (p. 242).

The same is true of the justice-oriented cultural citizen, with the caveat that this critique must extend beyond the visible political and social arena and into the cultural domain of power (Collins, 2009). Having a critical analysis of power in the cultural domain means understanding the ways that symbols, narratives, and ideologies, disseminated through cultural institutions such as schools, mass media, and the art world, undergird systems of domination and privilege—what Gramsci (1971) calls *hegemony*. It means being able to examine the art and media that one consumes for messages about race, gender, class, sexuality, (dis)ability, and other axes of discrimination and oppression. Moreover, it means knowing how these messages and ideologies affect one's own life and self-concept. This kind of critical capacity may be a necessary foundation for claiming cultural rights and for taking justice-oriented action through the arts.

Numerous authors have shown how education through the arts can be a forum in which to develop a critical analysis of power (e.g. Dewhurst, 2010; Flores-Gonzáles, Rodríguez, & Rodríguez-Muñiz, 2006; Jocson, 2006). Of particular interest here are educators in the field of *critical media literacy* (Alvermann, Moon, & Hagood, 1999; Duncan-Andrade, 2006; Kellner & Share, 2005), who address cultural power by,

> cultivating skills in analyzing media codes and conventions, abilities to criticize stereotypes, dominant values, and ideologies, and competencies to interpret the multiple meanings and messages generated by media texts. Media literacy helps people to use media intelligently, to discriminate and evaluate media content, to critically dissect media forms, to investigate media effects and uses, and to construct alternative media. (Kellner & Share, 2005, p. 372)

Other forms of arts programming focus more on the ways that cultural hegemony leads to internalization of stereotypes and dominant narratives—for example, Augusto Boal's Theatre of the Oppressed (1979) and Rainbow of Desire (1995) techniques make space for personal and psychological explorations of oppression in everyday life.

At PHH, critical analysis of cultural power takes place in the context of what they and other organizing groups call *political education* (Weiss, 2003). The curriculum is designed around the central concept of oppression, with a particular focus on how oppression functions in the cultural realm. Youth explore *ideological oppression* in the form of dominant narratives in mass media, art, and schooling that frame young People of Color and their communities through a deficit lens. At the same time, they explore *internalized oppression*: the ways that individuals internalize these dominant narratives as self-doubt, self-hate, and stereotypes of their own communities. This work often begins with a critical analysis of hip-hop music and culture, a common practice among hip-hop educators (Akom, 2009; Brown, 2009; Low, 2011). Youth analyze lyrics from their favorite songs, read poems and raps critiquing hip-hop culture, and express their own concerns through discussion and writing prompts.

80   CULTURAL PRODUCTION AND PARTICIPATORY POLITICS

For example, in one exercise youth listen to Bridget Gray's (2007) poem, *My Letter to Hip-Hop*, in which the poet "ends her relationship" with hip-hop due to its strains of sexism and hyper-consumerism. In response, youth write their own letters to hip-hop. Lena Rojas,[4] a young Puerto Rican dancer and activist taking part in the PHH summer program following her senior year in high school, writes the following:

> Dear Hip Hop
> I never had an issue listening to you
> Songs about struggle, love and happiness, I was cool with it
> But then it happened
> Words contradicting themselves in the same sentences
> From supporting your baby girl to making women call you daddy
> Who would have known you had such audacity
> Moans and groans, bitches and nigga and yet you say your mother raised you NO fool?
> Here's another one I see you use:
> From being so deeply in love with him
> You go and cheat on him
> And months later flip the channel and you got beat by him
> But now you love whips, chains, and the smell of sex
> And my question to you is . . . you're role modeling to who?

For PHH, there is a particular urgency to addressing hegemony in hip-hop given that many of the youth identify as hip-hop artists, and all are using hip-hop-related art forms in their cultural organizing. If they are to challenge, rather than perpetuate, oppressive narratives found in much popular hip-hop music, they need a critical understanding of their own art form. However, this critical analysis does not remain in the realm of hip-hop. As Mariama White-Hammond, the Executive Director, explains, "We are really clear that hip-hop did not make oppression." Instead, hip-hop is seen as a microcosm for society, a smaller context within which larger dialogues around race, gender, class, and sexuality are played out. As youth learn about these larger social and cultural systems, they begin to contextualize their individual experiences and develop a shared language for talking about community issues. As Jalen Williams, an African American rapper and high school senior in the program, explains:

> For me PHH has been very real. It's been enhancing? Educational, there you go. That's the word. Because the things that we're learning about—oppression and community issues—it's real and it goes on in our face and sometimes we might not be able to identify it for what it is . . . like, "That just happened yesterday, and I didn't even know how to describe it, what to say about it."

Youth are encouraged to embody the forms of oppression that they experience in their everyday lives as a basis for discussion, self-reflection, and action. This is done through artistic practices such as Theatre of the Oppressed and the creation of collaborative hip-hop performances. This work is emotionally intense, and can lead to personal transformation as youth members rewrite their own sense of self in the context of larger systems of power. Through this process Ashleigh Brown, a young singer and high school senior with African American and Native roots, discovered deep-seated negative feelings about her skin color.

> I'm one of the darkest people in my family and a lot of people in my family are light skinned or brown skinned. We all have really nice skin but everybody is lighter than me. I grew up not really saying much about it, but I always used to wear jeans in the summertime because I

didn't want my legs to get darker. I would always wear my hair a certain way because I wanted to look like the other girls... when we got into the Theatre of the Oppressed with Project HIP-HOP that's when it really hit me. I really started thinking I have a problem... I really started thinking about what it was that was bothering me and how I could fix it. It was little exercises they would do that nobody really knew how much it was helping me but me... little exercises that got me over it... I know that it's okay to be dark skinned. That's the biggest thing, to really love yourself, love your culture love where you came from and don't be afraid to be dark skinned.

For staff members at PHH, this kind of work is understood not only as education, but also as a form of healing—of loving yourself and becoming, as one staff member put it, "comfortable in your own skin." As Ginwright (2010) explains, oppression can be conceptualized as "a form of social and collective trauma." His response, based in years of youth cultural work, is what he calls *radical healing*, a process that helps young people "reconcile painful experiences resulting from oppression through testimony and naming what may seem to be personal misfortune as systemic oppression" and "builds the capacity of young people to act upon their environment in ways that contribute to well-being for the common good" (p. 85). According to PHH Artistic Director D. Ferai Williams, this kind of healing is a necessary step in preparing young people as political actors.

I want to focus on folks from my community feeling better about themselves and healing, and being in a place to even be able to enter a conversation about, "now what the hell do we do about the fact that the buses don't stop here often?" Someone has gone to war and they come back and they've got a gaping hole in their side and their arm has been severed in a place and one of their ankles has been bit by a wolf. My thinking is that first you have to deal with the wounds. You have to at least stop the bleeding. If I don't stop the bleeding I don't see how I can expect this person to go back to the front lines. It just doesn't work.

Through critical literacy and radical healing youth are able to build a foundation of understanding and confidence, leaving them better prepared to challenging the stories they've been told and to insert their own stories into the public sphere.

Advocating for Marginalized Cultures and Stories, Based in a Sense of Cultural Efficacy

Cultural citizenship scholars argue that a truly participatory democracy must encompass respect and support for diverse cultural practices, identities, and heritages. These scholars stand in opposition to assimilation on the one hand, and marginalization on the other, using discourses such as multiculturalism and cosmopolitanism (Pakulski, 1997; Stevenson, 2003; Wang, 2013). The justice-oriented cultural citizen works towards this vision by taking an activist approach to learning about and advocating for marginalized cultural practices, identities, and perspectives. She is a "counterstoryteller," uncovering, articulating, and sharing stories that challenge dominant discourses (Bell, 2010; Delgado, 1989).

For the justice-oriented cultural citizen, this commitment to marginalized cultural perspectives is rooted in a deep connection to her own cultural heritage. As Stevenson (2011) writes, in his vision of a new cosmopolitanism, appreciating global cultural diversity does not mean losing local cultural attachments. "We must grasp a sense of our own overlapping histories and traditions as well as a sense of how our own lives are linked to citizens of the past and future... we will not be able to realise ourselves without the wider community making available to us a sense of our own 'living traditions'" (p. 14).

82   CULTURAL PRODUCTION AND PARTICIPATORY POLITICS

By maintaining strong cultural connections, the justice-oriented cultural citizen develops what Jenkins (2013) calls "cultural efficacy," which includes "positive feelings about one's culture; strong understanding of the components, values, and structures of one's culture; confidence in one's culture to contribute to the world (sic)" (p. 10). Cultural efficacy allows the justice-oriented cultural citizen to move beyond her own cultural community and engage across cultures from a place of strength; to draw on the "cultural wealth" of her communities, including artistic and storytelling traditions (Yosso, 2005); and to proudly advocate for the cultural rights of her own communities (Rosaldo, 1994).

The arts have long been used as spaces for counterstorytelling and building a sense of cultural efficacy, particularly for communities whose voices are excluded from public political debate (Scott, 1990). The hip-hop arts, for example, are recognized as important sites for sharing counterstories of the experiences of Black and Brown youth in the United States and, increasingly, marginalized young people around the world (Malone & Martinez, 2010; Mitchell, 2002; Rose, 1994). They also serve to connect newer generations to histories of cultural and political resistance (Alridge, 2005). Many educators today use the arts to support young people in developing cultural pride and honing counterstorytelling abilities (e.g. Bell, 2010; Buras, 2009; Flores-Gonzáles, Rodríguez, & Rodríguez-Muñiz, 2006; Jocson, 2006; Lee & López, 2013).

At PHH, the process of uncovering counterstories and developing cultural efficacy begins with the study of history. Its longest-running program is the Civil Rights Tour, a trip through the U.S. South to visit historical sites, meet veterans of the African American civil rights movement, and connect with young civil rights activists. The trip, which has been run on and off since PHH's founding, includes a focus on the ways that the arts—particularly music—were used to develop consciousness and catalyze action during the civil rights struggle. This trip frames young people as inheritors of the civil rights legacy who can carry the torch forward. Over the years, PHH has expanded its historical focus to include African history and the history of hip-hop culture, both of which are presented as parts of the young people's cultural heritage. As Jalen puts it, "here it's like, okay, this is actually teaching me something about *my* race, *my* history, *my* culture."

In addition to the Tour, youth engage with history through lectures, discussions, videos, writing, and theater exercises. Historical learning is reinforced with the introduction of shared cultural practices connected to these histories. For example, at one point staff members introduce a West African call and response as a shared ritual. In discussing the use of West African call and response with Black youth, Ferai explains that the ritual serves as,

> another way to bring the group together and reinvigorate, in some way, that idea that you have a culture that you haven't been that exposed to. Your culture is not slave culture. You, yourself, don't come from slaves; you come from a group of people that was captured and then *en*slaved. But the journey back is hard.

Youth also learn how hip-hop has served as a cultural resource for social change work. They learn about ways that hip-hop artists like Grandmaster Flash, KRS-One, Public Enemy, and Mos Def have used their art to bring marginalized voices and stories into the public sphere, and to address issues of injustice in Communities of Color. The youth, in turn, are asked to carry on this legacy through their cultural organizing—sharing counterstories based in their own lives, their communities, or the histories they have learned. For example, one PHH performance revolves around a counterstory about Rosa Parks. The action, performed on public buses, explains that Parks took her famous action not just because she was tired, but because she was a committed organizer involved in the civil rights movement. As Mariama puts it, "[Parks] wasn't just tired, she was brave, and we need to be brave."

Explaining the importance of such performances, Ashley Cooper—an African American poet and high school senior—embodies the justice-oriented cultural citizen's orientation towards advocating for marginalized cultures and stories.

> Sometimes you need to be reminded of things that are important. It's important to remind people of where they came from, what happened—what happened with colored people, what happened to Black people in general. If we don't remind them, then who will?

As this quote suggests, PHH youth not only feel that it is important to disseminate marginalized stories; they also come to feel a sense of responsibility for being the ones to carry it out.

Responsibility to use the Art towards Justice in the Community

Citizenship is broadly understood as conferring both rights and obligations onto members of a community or nation, although the literature on culture and citizenship has paid much more attention to the former than the later (Stevenson, 2011; Turner, 2001). For the justice-oriented cultural citizen, rights related to cultural freedom and participation come with an attendant obligation to engage in the arts in a way that promotes justice.

This orientation involves understanding that one's artistic choices can affect other people, and ensuring that artistic creations do not perpetuate oppression; for example, avoiding the use of sexist or racist stereotypes. To use a term from media education, the justice-oriented cultural citizen has developed "critical solidarity" (Ferguson, 2001). Critical solidarity involves recognizing that we are not purely autonomous in our engagement with media; rather, we are always "taking sides" within larger social contexts. Therefore, we must understand "the interrelationships and consequences of [our] actions and lifestyles" (Kellner & Share, 2005, p. 381), and ultimately stand in solidarity with others toward an "understanding of justice and exploitation and our democratic rights and responsibilities" (Ferguson, 2001, cited in Jocson, 2013, p. 17).

Based in a sense of critical solidarity, the justice-oriented cultural citizen feels a responsibility to use her artistic practice to actively promote justice and address oppression in her multiple, overlapping communities. Amid long-running debates about the roles and responsibilities of the artist in society (Becker, 1994; Becker & Wiens, 1995; Gaztambide-Fernández, 2008), she conceptualizes the artist as *change agent*. As Goldbard (2006) writes, about the artist-educators in the community arts movement, "without exception, they recognize an obligation to deploy their gifts in the service of larger social aims as well as individual awareness and transformation" (p. 58).

PHH works from what it calls an "African-based vision of art that says that the artist does not simply create his/her own vision but (s)he has the responsibility to chronicle the history of his/her people and articulate a vision for the future" (Strategic Planning Document). Mariama uses the metaphor of the hip-hop cypher to explain the group's goal. A hip-hop cypher is an improvisational practice in which artists take turns performing (e.g. rapping, singing, dancing) while others back them by beating out a rhythm or shouting words of support. The cypher can be a space for individual artists to compete and to increase their reputation, while at the same time serving to build communality and collaboration through musical exchange and interaction (Emdin, 2013). As Mariama puts it,

> We are reclaiming a version of hip-hop that is about the individual connected to the whole, not the individual just as the individual. The individual just as the individual is a capitalist model, but the individual that's part of a collective is part of ancient traditions. Our work is to help young people to aspire to the cypher, where there will be space for them to shine, but they will still be part of a collective.

Building a connection to community begins within the youth membership through ensemble-building exercises, rituals that promote listening and respect, the sharing of personal stories, and the collaborative study of history. Youth are also sent out into the neighborhood to interview and survey community members and elicit stories about community issues, the results of which are used to inform the group's performances. For Mariama, this outreach is a key part of a cultural organizing model. "To do cultural organizing, you have to be in relationship with the people . . . You can do political art, and I think that's a worthy thing. But if you want to do cultural organizing, you have to be with the pulse, you have to produce something that people can grasp."

PHH youth are then charged with creating art that will catalyze individual and collective change in the community. Staff members encourage youth to see themselves as "cultural leaders" whose performances can spark action and reflection in others. One summer, youth decide to address issues of community violence and the need for unity in the neighborhood. Building on what they have been learning about the history of African slavery and its ongoing repercussions, the youth create a piece of street theater that links community violence with the violence of slavery. Through the performance, the youth exhort community members to learn about their own history. Performances like this situate the PHH members not only as students but also as teachers, with an important role to play in the community. As Ashleigh Brown puts it, "[The staff] wanted us to feel like we're learning, but we can teach this too. We're the youth that can bring this to other youth."

Over time, PHH youth may shift how they see themselves and their art. When asked how PHH has affected him, Peedub Welch, a rapper and high school junior with African American and Native roots, explains:

> It's sort of changed the way I rap a little bit. I used to just rap about myself, things that happen in my life. And now I'm rapping about things that happen in the community. So I rap about basically how we need to stop the drugs how we need to stop the violence and things like that.

Importantly, PHH teaches that in order to move from this sense of community responsibility toward real shifts in cultural power, youth must understand that social change work is a collective endeavor.

A Collective Approach to Change

Civic education programs vary in the extent to which they call for individual and/or collective actions from democratic citizens. According to Westheimer and Kahne's (2004) typology, programs promoting personally responsible citizenship encourage students to take individual actions such as obeying laws, recycling, and voting. Programs promoting participatory and justice-oriented citizenship, on the other hand, put a greater emphasis on voluntary organizations, social movements, and other collective endeavors, based in the belief that significant social change cannot be brought about by individuals acting alone.

Similarly, the justice-oriented cultural citizen understands that working for justice requires more than just individual artists making political statements. It requires collaboration, coordination, dialogue, and partnership among artists and other cultural workers, as well as between artists and more traditional organizers. The arts alone are not enough; just as traditional political work alone is not enough. Thus, the justice-oriented cultural citizen sees herself as part of a larger movement using multiple change strategies.

This concept is in line with scholarship on the roles of the arts and culture in social movements. While much attention is given in the press to the political statements made by individual artists, the social movement literature offers a more complex vision of how the arts are implicated in social change efforts. Scholars like McAdam (1994), Reed (2005), and Street (2007) demonstrate how artistic practices can serve as a form of collective cultural work embedded in larger processes of cultural and political change. These authors describe an array of different roles played by artists in the service of movement-building, including enhancing feelings of solidarity, fostering dialogue across lines of difference, framing collective demands, creating space for healing and fun, and inspiring public action.

From day one, youth at PHH are engaged in working collaboratively with peers rather than as individual performers. They learn to merge their various interests and art forms into single, multi-media performances. Moreover, many of their public performances and events are designed to make space for other young people and community members to join in—as part of a cypher, for example, or as a dancer in a flash mob. In addition, PHH develops alliances with other social justice groups in the area. These relationships are held in place by adult staff members, and offer PHH youth a chance to learn and partner with other young activists at rallies, retreats, celebrations, and other events.

PHH does not see itself as a lone organization with full control over a social change process. Rather, it sees itself as bringing a particular artistic and cultural strength to a larger movement for social justice. Staff members speak of being part of the "cultural wing" of the youth organizing movement in Boston, much as the Black Arts Movement served as the "cultural wing" of the Black Liberation Movement (Street, 2007). One of their training frameworks lays out five roles of artists in a social movement. These "5 E's" of cultural organizing include:

- **Educate** the Masses
- **Empower** our Youth and Community
- **Embarrass** and **Expose** Power
- **Envision** a Better World

In 2012, PHH joined a coalition fighting to stop fare hikes and service cuts on Boston's public transportation system. PHH already had long-running relationships with some of the key youth organizing groups leading the effort, and began to strengthen those by bringing youth and staff from the organizations together during meetings and trainings. As the other organizing groups planned public actions, PHH developed two performances based on themes from the campaign—one a flash mob/street theater performance designed to be part of a rally, and the other a song and music video designed to be distributed online and performed at a large music competition. In their performances, PHH youth worked to educate audiences about the campaign; build momentum within the coalition; incite action among outsiders; and connect the short-terms goals of the campaign with broader issues of environmental destruction and economic inequality.

After two years with the organization, Ashley Cooper says that the most important thing she learned from being with PHH was this need for collective action.

> [Before coming to PHH] I knew how to articulate [racism] and I knew how to say how it's bad and how it could be changed. Except I never really knew about how to do organizing. Because it can't be just me doing it, and I didn't realize it at the time ... I thought I knew how to make it happen, except it's not realistic without other people, and I didn't see that part of it.

This commitment to collective action does not imply that Ashley, or other justice-oriented cultural citizens, will necessarily become full-time organizers and activists. It does mean that they will be more likely to see themselves as part of larger struggles for justice, and be open to the kind of collaboration that undergirds successful social change efforts.

Implications and Conclusions

In this article, I have argued that we can usefully reframe the work of arts education by thinking of it as a process of developing cultural citizens. This reframing focuses our attention on how arts education practices relate to questions of participation, belonging, democracy, and social change. If we understand the arts as forms of cultural production—as culturally-situated activities involving "actual people, under real social circumstances, in particular cultural contexts, and within specific material and symbolic relations" (Gaztambide-Fernández, 2013, p. 226)—then we cannot escape the ways that artistic practice is implicated in larger social, economic, and political systems. Unfortunately, many of the frameworks we currently use in arts education are inadequate for addressing the socio-political aspects of our work. I believe that the concept of cultural citizenship can assist in this regard, and have attempted to begin that conversation.

Breaking somewhat from previous literature, I have conceptualized cultural citizenship as multiple and have taken some initial steps in documenting how different types of arts programming encourage youth to become different types of cultural citizens. This typology is not comprehensive, and in reality the lines between the types are blurry. Within each category there will be wide variation, including efforts across the ideological and political spectrum. For example, while PHH approaches social change from what would be considered a leftist or progressive ideology of liberation, one could imagine other programs focused on an idea of justice that is based in traditionally right-of-center political positions. Moreover, some of the best arts education programs will not fit into any one category.

Though I have delved deeper into the concept of the justice-oriented cultural citizen because that is where my research is focused, my goal is not to privilege one type of cultural citizen or to promote one type of arts education. There will always be a need for diverse approaches, and I have attempted to describe the strengths of all three types. Rather, I am calling for increased consciousness and explicitness about how different educational models implicitly or explicitly teach students about their role as members of cultural communities.

At the same time, I do see some reasons for increasing efforts focused on participatory and justice-oriented approaches to cultural citizenship. For example, given the rapid growth of "participatory culture" around the world (Burgess & Green, 2013; Jenkins, 2006, 2009), younger generations may not have the patience for more uni-directional forms of aesthetic education, demanding instead participatory opportunities to be cultural producers and to engage in art forms that directly connect to their lives and interests (La Senna, 2010). Moreover, considering the ongoing trend towards corporate consolidation of mass media by an increasingly narrow group of companies and interests (Turner, 2013), broadening access to cultural participation and representation may take more than encouraging participation through available channels. It may take increased attention to developing justice-oriented cultural citizens who can critically analyze and challenge these ever-evolving cultural hegemonies.

Arts education is not the only, or even the most dominant, force shaping young people's orientations towards engagement in cultural life. Family, pop culture, social networking, and widely-availability computer-based media tools are all extremely influential. Still, arts education represents an important piece of the puzzle, particularly in the context of major advocacy efforts to increase access to arts education for all young people. By putting arts education into conversation with the literatures on civic education and cultural citizenship, we gain a new perspective from which to hone and improve our efforts.

In terms of next steps for scholars interested in this line of inquiry, I suggest conducting case studies of diverse arts education programs with the research question, "What kind of cultural citizenship are these programs encouraging?" Given the complexity of the arts education landscape, I suspect it will not be as simple as a three-part typology. We may even find that some forms of arts education discourage participation in the cultural realm. Whatever the findings, such research would help us to rethink the goals and pedagogies of arts education, as well as the role of arts education in an aspiring democracy.

In addition, this line of thinking suggests that arts educators begin asking themselves important questions, such as: What kinds of cultural citizens are we educating? What are we teaching about who can be an artist, and what the arts are for? How might education in the arts support young people as they seek to be recognized as full citizens? Whether or not such questions lead to changes in practice, they can help educators to be more explicit about and conscious of their influence on young people as members of overlapping local, national, and international communities.

Notes

1. The boundaries of what is and is not art have long been debated, with no agreement in sight. Nelson Goodman (1978) has argued compellingly that the question "what is art" is not even the right question. We should be asking, "when is art?"—a pebble in the street is not art, but when we place it in a museum in such a way that it comes to symbolize hardness, or simplicity, or steadfastness, it can function as art. Art, then, is a social process of meaning making carried out in relation to a cultural product. I do not offer a solution to these debates. Instead I use a pragmatic definition based on what has been popularly recognized as art. The very fact that we carve out particular cultural practices and label them as art makes the category meaningful. At the same time, I am purposefully blurring the lines between the arts and other forms of symbolic creativity.
2. I refer to the settlement house art classes because I believe that they embody the best of the participatory approach to arts education as laid out here, and have inspired many others in this mold. It must be mentioned, however, that these art classes were embedded in a larger vision of social justice and activism. Some of the courses, and certainly many of those *teaching* the courses, would likely fall under the third type of cultural citizen described here. This is another sign that the real world is always a bit more complicated than any typology can capture.
3. For social justice arts education, see Quinn, Ploof, and Hochtritt, (2012); and Hanley, Sheppard, Noblit, and Barone, 2013. For community-based arts, see Knight and Schwarzman (2005). For the participatory action research, see Cahill et al. (2008); and Lykes (2006). For youth media,

88 CULTURAL PRODUCTION AND PARTICIPATORY POLITICS

see Soep and Chávez (2010). For the use of arts in youth organizing, see Clay, 2012; and Flores-Gonzáles, Rodríguez, and Rodríguez-Muñiz (2006). For critical media literacy, see Kellner and Share (2005). For hip-hop education, see Akom (2009). For community cultural development, see Goldbard (2006). For cultural organizing, see Benavente & Richardson, (2011).

4. All names of participants in this article are real. While youth had the opportunity to use a pseudonym, most (and all those quoted here) chose to use their actual names, in line with the public role they were playing as cultural organizers.

References

Akom, A. A. (2009). Critical hip hop pedagogy as a form of liberatory praxis. *Equity & Excellence in Education, 42*, 52–66.

Alridge, D. P. (2005). From civil rights to hip hop: Toward a nexus of ideas. *The Journal of African American History, 9*, 226–252.

Alvermann, D. E., Moon, J. S., & Hagood, M. C. (1999). *Popular culture in the classroom: Teaching and researching critical media literacy.* Newark, DE: International Reading Association.

Arts & Democracy Project. (2011). *Bridge conversations: People who live and work in multiple worlds.* Washington, DC: Author.

Kuttner, P. J. (2014). Youth cultural organizing at Project HIP-HOP: "Because stories have to be told." Unpublished dissertation, Harvard Graduate School of Education, Cambridge, MA.

Becker, C. (Ed.). (1994). *The subversive imagination: Artists, society, and responsibility.* New York: Routledge.

Becker, C., & Wiens, A. (1995). *The artist in society: Roles, rights, and responsibilities.* Chicago: New Art Examiner.

Bell, L. A. (2010). *Storytelling for social justice: Connecting narrative and the arts in antiracist teaching.* New York: Routledge.

Benavente, J., & Richardson, R. L. (2011). *Cultural organizing: Experiences at the intersection of art and activism.* Washington, DC: Animating Democracy. Retrieved from http://animatingdemocracy.org/resource/cultural-organizaing-experiences-intersection-art-and-activism

Boal, A. (1979). *Theatre of the oppressed.* New York: Theatre Communications Group.

Boal, A. (1995). *The rainbow of desire: The Boal method of theatre and therapy.* New York: Routledge.

Boele van Hensbroek, P. (2010). Cultural citizenship as a normative notion for activist practices. *Citizenship Studies, 14*, 317–330.

Bourdieu, P. (1993). *The field of cultural production: Essays on art and literature.* New York: Columbia University Press.

Brown, R. N. (2009). *Black girlhood celebration: Toward a hip-hop feminist pedagogy.* New York: Peter Lang.

Buras, K. L. (2009). 'We have to tell our story': Neo-griots, racial resistance, and schooling in the other south, *Race Ethnicity and Education, 12*, 427–453.

Burgess, J., & Green, J. (2013). *YouTube: Online video and participatory culture*. Hoboken, NJ: John Wiley & Sons.

Cahill, C., Bradley, M., Casteñada, D., Esquivel, L., Mohamed, N., Organista, J., Sandberg, J., Valerio, M., & Winston, K. (2008). "Represent": Reframing risk through participatory video research. In M. Downing & L. J. Tenney (2008), *Video vision: Changing the culture of social science research*. Newcastle: Cambridge Scholars.

Clay, A. (2012). *The hip-hop generation fights back: Youth, activism, and post-civil rights politics*. New York: New York University Press.

Carpini, M. X. D. (1996). *What Americans know about politics and why it matters*. New Haven, CT: Yale University Press.

Cohen-Cruz, J. (2010). *Engaging performance: Theatre as call and response*. New York: Routledge.

Collins, H. P. (2009). *Another kind of public education: Race, schools, the media, and democratic possibilities*. Boston, MA: Beacon Press.

Delgado, M., & Staples, L. (2008). *Youth-led community organizing: Theory and action*. New York: Oxford University Press.

Delgado, R. (1989). Storytelling for oppositionists and others: A plea for narrative. *Michigan Law Review, 87*, 2411–2441.

Denning, M. (1998). *The cultural front: The laboring of American culture in the twentieth century*. London: Verso.

Dewhurst, M. (2010). An inevitable question: Exploring the defining features of social justice art education. *Art Education, 63*, 6–13.

Dixon-Román, E., & Gomez, W. (2013). En mi barrio: Building on Cuban youth culture, hip-hop, and reggaetón. In K. M. Jocson (Ed.), *Cultural transformations: Youth and pedagogies of possibility* (pp. 183–202). Cambridge, MA: Harvard Education Press.

Dolby, N. (2003). Popular culture and democratic practice. *Harvard Educational Review, 73*, 258–284.

Duncan-Andrade, J. (2006). Urban youth, media literacy, and increased critical civic participation. In P. Noguera, S. A. Ginwright, & J. Cammarota, *Beyond Resistance!: Youth activism and community change: new democratic possibilities for practice and policy for America's youth* (pp. 149–170). New York: Routledge.

Efland, A. D. (1990). *A history of art education: Intellectual and social currents in teaching the visual arts*. New York: Teachers College Press.

Eisner, E. W. (1987). The role of discipline-based art education in America's schools. *Art education, 40*, 6–26, 43–45.

Emdin, C. (2013). The rap cypher, the battle, and reality pedagogy: Developing communication and argumentation in urban science education. In M. L. Hill & E. Petchauer (Eds.), *Schooling hip-hop: Expanding hip-hop based education across the curriculum*. New York: Teachers College Press.

Evrard, Y. (1997). Democratizing culture or cultural democracy? *The Journal of Arts Management, Law, and Society, 27*, 167–175.

Ferguson, R. (2001). Media education and the development of critical solidarity. *Media Education Journal*, 37–43.

Flores-Gonzáles, N., Rodríguez, M., & Rodríguez-Muñiz, M. (2006). From hip-hop to humanization: Batey Urbano as a space for Latino youth culture and community action. In P. Noguera, S. A. Ginwright, & J. Cammarota, *Beyond Resistance!: Youth activism and community change: new democratic possibilities for practice and policy for America's youth* (pp. 175–198). New York: Routledge.

Foster, A. W., & Blau, J. R. (Eds.). (1989). *Art and society: Readings in the sociology of the arts*. New York: SUNY Press.

Franquiz, M. E., & Brochin-Ceballos, C. (2006). Cultural citizenship and visual literacy: US-Mexican children constructing cultural identities along the US-Mexico border. *Multicultural Perspectives, 8*, 5–12.

Freire, P. (1970). Pedagogy of the Oppressed. (M. B. Ramos, Trans.). New York: Continuum.

Galston, W. A. (2004). Civic education and political participation. *Political Science and Politics, 37*, 263–266.

Ganz, C., & Strobel, M. (2004). *Pots of promise: Mexicans and pottery at Hull-House, 1920–40.* Urbana, IL: University of Illinois Press with the Jane Addams Hull-House Museum, Chicago.

Gaughan, J. M. (1990). *One hundred years of art appreciation education: A cross comparison of the picture study movement with the discipline-based art education movement.* Unpublished dissertation, University of Massachusetts, Amherst, MA.

Gaztambide-Fernández, R. A. (2013). Why the arts don't do anything: Toward a new vision for cultural production in education. *Harvard Educational Review, 83,* 211–237.

Gaztambide-Fernández, R. A. (2008) The artist in society: Understandings, expectations, and curriculum implications. *Curriculum Inquiry, 38,* 233–265.

Geertz, C. (1973). *The interpretation of cultures: Selected essays.* New Yori: Basic books.

Gibson, C., & Levine, P. (2003). *The civic mission of schools.* Carnegie Corporation of New York. Retrieved from http://carnegie.org/publications/search-publications/pub/135/

Ginwright, S. A. (2006). Hip-Hop generation. In L. R. Sherrod, C. A. Flanagan, R. Kassimir, & A. K. Syvertsen (Eds.), *Youth activism: An international encyclopedia.* Westport, CT: Greenwood Press.

Ginwright, S. A. (2010). *Black youth rising: Activism and radical healing in urban America.* New York: Teachers College Press.

Giroux, H. A. (1988). *Schooling and the struggle for public life: Critical pedagogy in the modern age.* Minneapolis: University of Minnesota Press.

Goldbard, A. (2006). *New creative community: The art of cultural development.* Oakland, CA: New Village Press.

Goodman, N. (1978). *Ways of worldmaking.* Cambridge, MA: Hackett Publishing.

Gramsci, A. (1971). *Selections from the prison notebooks of Antonio Gramsci.* New York: International Publishers.

Gray, B. (2001). My letter to Hip HOP. On *Shades of Gray* [mp3 file]. Bridget Gray Records.

Hanley, M. S., Sheppard, G. L., Noblit, G. W., & Barone, T. (Eds.). (2013). *Culturally relevant arts education for social justice: A way out of no way.* New York: Routledge.

Jenkins, H. (2006). *Fans, bloggers, and gamers: Exploring participatory culture.* New York: New York University Press.

Jenkins, H. (2009). Confronting the Challenges of Participatory Culture: Media Education for the 21st Century. Cambridge, MA: MIT Press.

Jenkins, T. S. (2013). *Culture, leadership, & activism: Translating Fink's Taxonomy of Significant Learning into pedagogical practice.* Unpublished Manuscript, George Mason University, Fairfax, Virginia.

Jocson, K. M. (2006). The best of both worlds: Youth poetry as social critique and form of empowerment. In P. Noguera, S. A. Ginwright, & J. Cammarota, *Beyond Resistance!: Youth activism and community change: new democratic possibilities for practice and policy for America's youth* (pp. 129–147). New York: Routledg.

Jocson, K. (2013). Barely audible: A remix of poetry and video as pedagogical practice. In K. Jocson (Ed.), *Cultural Transformations: Youth and Pedagogies of Possibility* (pp. 13–31). Cambridge, MA: Harvard Education Press.

Kellner, D., & Share, J. (2005). Toward critical media literacy: Core concepts, debates, organizations, and policy. *Discourse: Studies in the Cultural Politics of Education, 26,* 369–386. DOI: 10.1080/01596300500200169

Knight, K., & Schwarzman, M. (2005). *Beginner's guide to community-based arts.* Oakland, CA: New Village Press.

Kohl-Arenas, E., Nateras, M. M., & Taylor, J. (2014). Cultural organizing as critical praxis: Tamejavi builds immigrant voice, belonging, and power. *Journal of Poverty, 18,* 5–24.

Koerin, B. (2003). Settlement house tradition: Current trends and future concerns, *The Journal of Sociology and Social Welfare, 30,* 53–68.

La Senna, D. (2010). Adults, appreciation, and participatory arts education. In Clapp, E. P. (Ed.), *20Under40: Re-inventing the arts and arts education for the 21st century.* AuthorHouse.

Lee, T. S., & López, N. (2013). "It's best to know who you are through your culture": Transformative educational possibilities for Native American youth. In K. Jocson (Ed.), *Cultural Transformations: Youth and Pedagogies of Possibility* (pp. 139–164). Cambridge, MA: Harvard Education Press.

Levinson, M. (2012). *No citizen left behind.* Cambridge, MA: Harvard University Press.

Low, B. E. (2011). *Slam school: Learning through conflict in the hip-hop and spoken word classroom*. Stanford, CA: Stanford University Press.

Lykes, M. B. (2006). Creative arts and photography in participatory action research in Guatemala. *Handbook of Action Research: Concise Paperback Edition* (pp. 269–278). London: Sage.

Maira, S. (2013). *Jil Oslo: Palestinian hip hop, youth culture, and the youth movement*. Washington, DC: Tadween Publishing.

Malone, C., & Martinez, G. J. (2010). The organic globalizer: The political development of hip-hop and the prospects for global transformation. *New Political Science, 32*, 531–545.

Marshall, T. H. (1950). *Citizenship and social class: And other essays*. Cambridge: Cambridge University Press.

McAdam, D. (1994). Culture in social movements. In E. Laraña, H. Johnston & J. R. Gusfield (Eds.) *New social movements: From ideology to identity* (pp. 36–57). Philadelphia: Temple University Press.

McCarthy, K. F., Ondaatje, E. H., Zakaras, L., & Brooks, A. (2004). *Gifts of the muse: Reframing the debate about the benefits of the arts*. Santa Monica, CA: The Rand Corporation.

Mercer, C. (2002). Towards cultural citizenship: Tools for cultural policy and development. Author. *Available at SSRN 2153304*.

Miller, T. (2001). Introducing . . . Cultural citizenship. *Social Text, 19*, 1–5.

Miller, T. (2002). Cultural citizenship. In E. F. Isin & B. S. Turner (Eds.), *Handbook of citizenship studies* (pp. 231–244). London: Sage.

Mitchell, T. (Ed.). (2002). *Global noise: Rap and hip hop outside the USA*. Middletown, CT: Wesleyan University Press.

Murray, N., & Garrido, M. (1995). Violence, nonviolence, and the lessons of history: Project HIP-HOP journeys south. *Harvard Educational Review, 65*, 231–257.

Pakulski, J. (1997) Cultural citizenship. *Citizenship Studies, 1*, 73–86.

Quinn, T., Ploof, J., & Hochtritt, L. (2012). *Art and social justice education: Culture as commons*. New York: Routledge.

Rabkin, N. (2013, July 3). The past and the future of the citizen artist. *Huffington Post*. Retrieved from http://www.huffingtonpost.com/nick-rabkin/the-past-and-the-future-o_b_3540154.html

Reed, T. V. (2005). *The art of protest: Culture and activism from the civil rights movement to the streets of Seattle*. Minneapolis: University of Minnesota Press.

Rosaldo, R. (1994). Cultural citizenship and educational democracy. *Cultural anthropology, 9*, 402–411.

Rosaldo, R. (1997). Cultural citizenship, inequality, and multiculturalism. In W. Flores & R. Benmayor (Eds.), *Latino cultural citizenship: Claiming identity, space, and rights* (pp. 27–38). Boston: Beacon Press.

Rose, T. (1994). *Black noise: Rap music and black culture in contemporary America*. Hanover, NH: Wesleyan University Press.

Schein, E. H. (1990). Organizational culture. *American psychologist, 45*, 109–119.

Scott, J. C. (1990). *Domination and the arts of resistance: Hidden transcripts*. New Haven, CT: Yale University Press.

Seidel, S., Tishman, S., Hetland, L., Palmer, P., & Winner, E. (2008). The qualities of quality: Excellence in arts education and how to achieve it. Cambridge, MA: Project Zero.

Share, J. (2009). Media literacy is elementary. *Teaching youth to critically read and create media*. New York: Lang

Smith, R. A. (2004). Aesthetic education: Questions and issues. In E. W. Eisner & M. D. Day, (Eds.), (*Handbook of research and policy in art education* (pp. 163–186). London: Lawrence Erlbaum Associates.

Soep, E., & Chávez, V. (2010). *Drop that knowledge: Youth radio stories*. Berkeley: University of California Press.

Stake, R. E. (1995). *The art of case study research*. Thousand Oaks, CA: Sage.

Stevenson, N. (1997). Globalization, national cultures and cultural citizenship. *The Sociological Quarterly, 38*, 41–66.

Stevenson, N. (Ed.). (2001). *Culture and citizenship*. London: Sage.

Stevenson, N. (2003). *Cultural citizenship: Cosmopolitan questions*. Maidenhead: Open University Press.

Stevenson, N. (2011). *Education and cultural citizenship*. London: Sage.

Street, J. (2007). *The culture war in the civil rights movement.* Gainesville: University Press of Florida.

The Culture Group. (2014). *Making waves: A guide to cultural strategy.* Author. Retrieved from http://theculturegroup.org/2013/08/31/making-waves/

Turner, B. S. (2001) Outline of a general theory of cultural citizenship. In N. Stevenson (Ed.), *Culture and Citizenship* (pp. 11–32). New York: Sage

Turner, B.S. (1995). Rights and communities: Prolegomenon to a sociology of rights. *Australian and New Zealand Journal of Sociology, 31*, pp. 1–8.

Turner, S. D. (2013). *Cease to resist: How the FCC's failure to enforce its rules created a new wave of media consolidation.* Florence, MA: Free Press.

United Nations General Assembly. (1948). *Universal declaration of human rights.* Paris: Author.

Wang, L. J. (2013). Towards cultural citizenship? Cultural rights and cultural policy in Taiwan. *Citizenship Studies, 17*, 92–110.

Weiss, M. (2003). *Youth rising.* Applied Research Center.

Westheimer, J., & Kahne, J. (2004). What kind of citizen? The politics of educating for democracy. *American educational research journal, 41*, 237–269.

Willis, P. E. (1990). *Common culture: Symbolic work at play in the everyday cultures of the young.* Boulder, CO: Westview Press.

Yosso, T. J. (2005). Whose culture has capital? A critical race theory discussion of community cultural wealth. *Race Ethnicity and Education, 8*, 69–91.

Zakaras, L., & Lowell, J. F. (2008). *Cultivating demand for the arts: Arts learning, arts engagement, and state arts policy.* Santa Monica, CA: RAND Corporation.

5 The art of youth rebellion

Nathalia E. Jaramillo

In this essay, the author examines the art of rebellion in the context of the 2014 Venezuelan student uprising. Utilizing the lens of Latin American decolonial thought and examining the processes of developing popular power among youth, the author looks into the various ways that youth produce art to communicate and enforce the ideas and values that circumscribe their collective identities. It is necessary, the author argues, for educators to consider the historical, economic and political forces that shape youth's cultural production and to engage decolonial thought in art pedagogy.

The intensification of neocolonial-capitalist relations of exploitation, alienation and ecological devastation have ushered an era of unprecedented rebellion. The global financial crisis of 2007 spawned wide-scale discontent with crony capitalism, the demise of social democracy and the pillaging of the environment. Youth have participated centrally in many of these uprisings, and in some cases, were considered the primary protagonists of resistance.

The Arab Spring and the proliferation of Occupy movements around the globe represent a mixed array of protesters, from young to old and poor to middle classes. They stand out, not least in part, for the participation and commitment of millions of young people to organize and for the creative practices and ideas they set forward as examples of individual and collective power. Other popular uprisings are almost entirely driven by youth, as in Chile, where students have waged a prolonged demonstration against the privatization of higher education. Similar student-led protests against neoliberal education have been seen throughout Europe, South Africa, Sri Lanka and Kenya. Most recently, the spotlight of protest has shined on Venezuela, where thousands of youth have denounced the economic and social conditions of the country. In the case of Venezuela the wider international public blindly celebrates the student-led protests, anticipating, perhaps, that the end of the socialist Bolivarian Revolution will be forthcoming. This latter example, as I intend to outline later in this paper, however, is much more complex.

Social critics and observers alike are not only stunned by the level and intensity of youth rebellion, they are also intrigued by the ways that the "lost generation" (Oyole, 2014) has seemingly come back to life. The general sentiment that youth are apathetic, passive consumers in society, is more myth than fact, as young people through acts of resistance show that they are not only concerned with the present and future, they have the capacity to initiate rebellion and teach their observers along the way. Youth teach us about the creative skills and habits of mind they wield to organize and protest, through social media and alternative technologies or what Jeffrey (2011) calls "ecologies of protest." More importantly, youth communicate their understandings of their place in the social hierarchies of neocolonial capitalism.

In this essay, I examine the art practices of youth's rebellion, with a specific focus on Venezuela. Art, I argue, constitutes a communicative network through which youth subcultures enact their political agency and reflect their grasp of the social totality. Within the Western and Eurocentric canon, art is typically understood as a set of practices, a skill set, acquired from observing and learning from works deemed as "art." Art — conceived as an object or product — is evaluated against a set of standards and norms of beauty (aesthetics), that ultimately deem the object under question as art or not. The art of youth rebellion, however, disrupts the hegemony of art and compels us to consider the communicative, political, and relational dimensions that connect to youth identities. This is especially the case when we take a look into the production of art of subaltern youth in rebellion, as the making of art is not concerned with meeting a prescribed aesthetic standard to deem the work artistic but rather, is the means through which critiques, values, beliefs, hopes and aspirations are expressed.

As noted by Lorblanchet (2007), art has the power to represent phenomena and is "the sign of humanization," the "symbol of the transition from animal to human" (see Lorblanchet, 2007, p. 98). Yet, mainstream Eurocentric conceptions of art have evolved in highly ethnocentric ways. Art, considered a manifestation of progress, as the depiction of modern humans, and the expression of rational and aesthetically sophisticated civilizations, has created systems of judgment. In the Kantian sense, feelings of pleasure or disgust reify art as an object, as opposed to the subject of relationships that can mobilize processes of creation and in some instances, visions for social transformation. While art on murals or as a component of rebellion and protest may not classify as art within a Eurocentric gaze, it is a form that communicates a group's identity and perceptions of context and place. In the case of youth, they organize, cohere, and advance social and political projects through art practices. What I refer to in this article as the art of rebellion compels us to question representations of the social from the standpoint of the indignation that afflicts youth. Art, as Adolfo Albán Achinte (2011) asserts, is not solely the production of an object, it also reflects the social processes that creative actors use to communicate and think differently about their realities. In wielding their creative capacities to question and problematize the social order, youth turn art practices into insurgent acts.

Take, for example, the Occupy movement. In addition to the occupation of public spaces, youth performed protest by dressing in costumes, playing the part of the unemployed, the debt-ridden, and the downtrodden. The art of youth rebellion has been discussed in terms of entertainment, conceptualizing protest as "fun" and as a way to broaden the scope of participation regardless of a protester's artistic ability (Everhart, 2012). Protest as entertainment, however, is not necessarily about breaking the monotony or boredom of what Katherine Everhart refers to as "the typical methods of marching in a circle, shouting slogans" (2012, p. 202). The entertaining and creative artistic expression of protest evoke play as the means for youth to connect to their audience, establish bonds, and unleash their creative capacities in spite of their anger and melancholia. It is on this point that I engage art as a way to examine youth's cultural production and identity formation. I pay particular attention to the youth in Venezuela.

Over the last twenty years, Venezuela has undergone a tumultuous social transformation with the election of the late Hugo Chávez and the implementation of the Bolivarian Revolution. As the recent spate of wide scale student protests indicate, it is also a society that continues to confront deep social conflicts. I will address the contradictions of the current youth uprising in this essay, as they hint towards the complexity of social transformation in a society marked by the legacy of severe class inequalities and racial and ethnic antagonisms. However, my aim is to explore in greater depth the principles of popular power that undergird the Bolivarian revolution, and in particular, the emergence of youth art *colectivos*/collectives. My analysis is framed by the notion of youth's evolving use of power as a form of producing culture from the position of alterity. This is further supported using the lens of Latin American decolonial thought, a sociological and philosophical framework that provides a reference point from which to understand youth's evolving identity formation in the context of the coloniality of power. In the first part of this essay I provide a brief overview of the Venezuelan context. I then examine the emergence of artist *colectivos* as the expression of popular power. In the second part of the paper I examine the implications that artist *colectivos* and decolonial thought have for art education.

The Venezuelan Context

The analysis I present here is strongly shaped by my travels to Venezuela that date back to 2004. I have spent days and weeks at a time traveling throughout the country, working with teacher educators and speaking to university students and professors. At times I have found myself in the midst of heightened social conflict and tension. My 2007 visit to the University of Zulia, Maracaibo, for example, coincided with mounting student opposition protests against a constitutional referendum that would have advanced the socialist (and controversial) goals of the Bolivarian revolution. During the upheaval, one student was shot dead, the gunman killed, and a second gunman injured apparently by his own crossfire. On the last day of my lecture the university shut down and university police escorted me off campus. The tension between youth in support of and those opposed to the Bolivarian revolution and its accompanying constitutional referendums had reached a fever pitch.

Venezuela is a country in a constant state of mobilization. Since the 1958 overthrow of the dictatorship, the country has experienced various trends of relative passivity among its citizens and periods of increased social conflict (Maya, Lander & Parker, 2005). Open conflict has developed into an essential element in prevailing social dynamics, especially in light of the Chávez government and the emergence of a political elite attempting to implement an alternative project for the country (Maya, Lander & Parker, 2005). When Hugo Chávez assumed power in 1999, the country was characterized by deep economic and political inequality, largely the result of neoliberal policies supported by the Washington consensus.

The most striking example of the effect that neoliberal policy had on the population was evidenced through the now infamous *Caracazo* incident. On February 27, 1989 hundreds took to the streets in protest across a number of Venezuelan cities (Maya, 2003). Then president Carlos Andrés Pérez had signed an economic agreement with the International Monetary Fund, which demanded severe austerity measures in exchange for economic investment. Overnight the price of petrol increased by 100 percent, resulting in exorbitant transportation costs (Maya, 2003). In the days that followed, bus passengers – especially university students – voiced their discontent, occupied transportation centers, and barricaded roads. The revolt soon swelled with Venezuela's working-class and poor joining the movement (Maya, 2003) and became extremely violent when police and security forces clashed with protesters. Throughout the week the President authorized an ill-prepared army onto the streets to restore order. The army used automatic rifles to shoot indiscriminately into people's homes and the gathering places of protest, literally painting slums and city centers red with blood. Roughly 400 people were killed in a matter of days (Maya, 2003), though the actual number of dead is thought much higher. Witnesses reported seeing bodies thrown into the ocean from army helicopters. Human Rights Watch eventually unearthed one massive grave called *La Peste* (The Stench) in Caracas. Sixty-eight bodies were found, many corpses had their hands, feet and other body parts severed to fit into garbage bags (Maya, 2003).

At the time that Chávez assumed the Presidency (he was democratically elected in 1999, but it should be noted that he attempted a coup d'etat in 1992) nearly 50 percent of the population lived in poverty (Weisbrot, Sandoval & Rosnick, 2006) and only 11 million Venezuelans were registered to vote in a country of 27 million people (Lendman, 2008). The Caracazo was still a bleeding wound. The Bolivarian Revolution initiated under the Chávez presidency was simultaneously an act of redress to gaping economic inequality and a process initiated to redefine the very terms of democracy. The 1999 rewriting of the constitution recognized the universal right to protest, lending the nation to an ongoing and visible stream of "street politics" where social and political actors expressed their support and grievances of the state in public spaces (Maya, Lander & Parker, 2005). An emphasis on popular power through enacting direct democracy (as opposed to representative democracy) redefined the role of the nation-state as one in service of creating the spaces and the opportunities for those historically excluded from political processes to develop active and protagonist citizenship. This was accomplished through a variety of public welfare programs (such as the Misiones/missions) but was also evidenced in the construction of the Citizen's branch of government and the writing of the Organic Law of Popular Power, which together attempted to secure the social, economic and cultural rights of the most disenfranchised sectors of the nation (Lander, 2011).

Youth play a particularly important role in the development of popular power. Since 2007 over two million youth have registered to vote. They represent the emerging class of political actors in a country undergoing a reconfiguration of the relationship between the underclasses of society and the State. The nationalization of industries, a redirection of state revenue to social welfare programs, constitutional amendments that establish frameworks for epistemological, cultural, ethnic, gendered, and economic justice are both the artifacts of popular struggles that preceded the election of Chávez and a new era among countries in Latin America (i.e. Bolivia and Ecuador) in pursuit of a post-capitalist alternative (see Escobar, 2010). Edgardo Lander characterizes these shifts in Venezuela and the Latin American region in general, as the outgrowth of two, "at times separate and at times more interrelated" dimensions aimed towards the struggle for liberation. In Lander's terms, the discussion of civil society is, "contained within the limits of 'modern' western democracy" (2011, p.32). This is where the discourse of inclusion, equality, citizenship and individual rights turns into a contested arena within the formal political spectrum. The other dimension of civil society represents what Lander calls "civilizational confrontations" and "cultural wars" that is, "the historical struggle between the modern/colonial modes of life, and the multiple expressions of both resistance and the practical construction and reconstruction of other cultural alternatives" (2011, p.32). The 1999 Venezuelan constitution reform was thus an effort to transform the vestiges of Spanish colonial occupation and the implementation of Western notions of liberal democracy as the only political model able to usher human progress and development. The focus on popular power and direct participation was intended to loosen the systems in place that reinforced social difference and that denied broad swaths of poor, racial, ethnic and indigenous subjects to live and take part meaningfully in matters of the nation. Attempts to undo the legacy of coloniality and Western notions of democracy remain a work in progress, however, and require an ongoing critique of the practices in place to reconstruct the relationship between a nation and its people.

The process of developing youth's cultural identity predicated on the ethic of direct participation and the undoing of a legacy of economic and social alienation is grounded in a socio-historical model to encourage the development of critical consciousness and protagonist civic agency. It is foregrounded in the ideals of collective popular power as a way to initiate youth in the formal politics of the state. The principles that guide the Bolivarian revolution include a commitment to struggle against racial, sexual, gender, and economic exploitation; a principled and practical opposition to imperialism (both economic and military); a celebration of the rich diversity of global human struggle for a socialism for the 21st century in the pursuit of the expansion of human development for the purpose of creating a culture of freedom (Jaramillo & McLaren, 2008). Venezuelan youth are recognized as the collective outgrowth of a society undergoing political, economic and social transformation, reflecting a new "independent" citizenry released from the confines of imperialist-capitalist exploitation (Lima, 2011).

2014 Student Opposition Protests

On February 12, 2014 tens of thousands of youth took to the streets in more than 100 cities throughout Venezuela. The wide scale protests occurred on the nationally recognized "Day of Youth" in commemoration of youth's participation in the Battle of Victoria, a key event in Venezuela's independence from Spanish colonial rule. To the general public, the emergent wave of youth protest signaled another epoch of resistance to colonial dominance, referred by many international presses as the "authoritarian regime" of Venezuelan president, Nicolas Maduro (Nahon-Serfaty, 2014). The protesters waged a full-throttle assault against President Maduro and the Bolivarian revolution that he inherited from the late Hugo Chávez. The revolution, they surmised, had failed. Its failure, the protesters claimed, was evidenced by the weak economy, an inflation rate over 50 percent, scarcity of basic goods, and high rates of crime throughout the country. Yet the least cited source of protest was the slogan "*SALIDA*" (exit), a call for the removal of President Maduro. The protesting youth draped themselves in the bright red, yellow and blue colors of the Venezuelan flag. Images of youth wearing steely-eyed Guy Fawkes masks – associated with the anarchist hacktivist collective Anonymous – and Venezuelan baseball caps peppered the Internet. Together, the images relayed contempt, rebellion, and the pursuit of an abundant, peaceful and harmonious nation.

While many youth clung to banners and flags, others clutched Molotov cocktails instead. The violence that ensued between the youth and the government resulted in 33 deaths and over 100 arrests (as of March 22, 2014; see Ore & Ellsworth, 2014). Reports of the government's crackdown filled Twitter feeds, Facebook posts, and mainstream media outlets. News headlines reported the "tragedy of Venezuela," published "shocking images of repression in the streets of Caracas" and portrayed youth as "the vanguard of a society no longer willing to tolerate an abusive government with disastrous results to show for its 15-year grip on power" (Naím, 2014, para 5). For many observers, the Arab Spring had finally spread to the South American Winter – four years later. State violence against youth is deplorable under any circumstance. Yet, to read the violence that transpired in Venezuela as parallel to other uprisings fails to consider the intricacies of social conflict among youth in a country that is attempting to break from its political and economic past.

The protesting youth are generally recognized as part of the long-standing opposition to the Bolivarian revolution. From the perspective of the Venezuelan poor, they represent the interests of the upper classes of society, the "*pitiyanqui*" (mini-Yankees in support of US empire) and "*hijita de papá y mamá*" (daughters and sons of mommy and daddy) (Gómez, 2014). The opposition, on the other hand, considers their struggle as one of recuperating the Venezuelan nation from the grip of the socialist values of the Bolivarian revolution. The youth of the opposition also wield racial and class based epithets toward the youth in support of the revolution. To the opposition, youth in support of the Bolivarian revolution are nothing short of "hordes of Chávista monkeys," "terrorists" and "armed bandits" (Ciccariello-Maher, 2014). In the simplest sense, the youth of Venezuela are in a standoff, with no conceivable pathway to transcend the central class-racial-ethnic antagonisms that produce and are actively reproduced in their cultural identities. When these discordant classes of youth see one another, they confront the repressed underside of their collective identity formation. Opposition youth see the savage, dark, and bestial underdeveloped subject that fails to succumb to modernity's empty promise of progress and social and intellectual enlightenment. The youth in support of the Bolivarian revolution, on the other hand, encounter the oppressor within. They see modernity's project of progress and development as the outgrowth of a system of differentiation based on a social-economic ethos of violence and exclusion.

The current polarization of youth is reflected through protest, but also through the acts, practices, and visual representations constructed as part of their political participation; what I refer to in this paper as the art of rebellion. It is to this that I now turn, examining the use of art as the medium of collective identity formation and consciousness. In the section that follows, I briefly examine the opposition youth's artistic expression during the current social crisis. This is important in order to understand the deep forms of neocolonial and neoliberal consciousness embedded within the modes of cultural production that the opposition youth mobilize in their political participation and through which they express cultural identities. I then delve into the colectivos/collectives of art that were formed throughout the course of the Bolivarian revolution. In the latter case, youth engage art as both process and content, revealing a set of values and aims that speak to and against the overriding logic of neocolonial capitalism on their identity formation. It is through the contradictions evidenced between the production of art among opposition youth and that of the *colectivos* that I position an argument for a decolonial rendering of art as a pedagogical practice.

Opposition Art: Zombies for Consumption

Shortly after the initial wave of violent protests in February 2014, opposition youth formed *Protesta Creativa Venezuela*. The youth identify as a heterogeneous group of artists, performers, professionals, student, sons, daughters and parents of the Venezuelan nation. As a counterpoint to violence, they pronounce "Art moves us towards peaceful protest" (Protesta Creativa, 2014). *Protesta Creativa* claims to be a space open to all Venezuelans, irrespective of political affiliation. They consider themselves a cohesive group of resistance and the innovative spirit of Venezuela. Through art, *Protesta Creativa* argues, participants communicate their persistence, creativity, and commitment to move forward and struggle for peace. They caught the attention of mainstream media and the wider public alike, for their spontaneous street performances. They lie on the ground, place their distorted bodies on the pavement to signal "*muertos virtuales*" (the virtually dead) with signs that read "*vine a hacer turismo y me asesinaron delante mi hija*" (I came to be a tourist and I was assassinated in front of my daughter) (Gómez, 2014). In this way, they not only aim to appeal to Venezuelans, but speak directly to an international audience about the perceived insecurity in the country.

Notably, *Protesta Creativa* has wielded the spectral floating signifier of the zombies that has become increasingly emblematic in pop culture over the last decade. In full macabre style, participants discolor their faces in a ghoulish grey, darken the circles around their eyes, and with the rigid movements of a body entering rigor mortis, they walk the aisles of grocery stores and stand in checkout lines with fellow patrons. The Zombies speak through the placards hung around their necks that read, "*sin harina, sin leche, sin mantequilla. . .me toca comer sesos*" (without flour, milk, or butter, I am left to eat brains) and "*llevo diez o veinte y más años haciendo cola por el aceite – o azúcar, café, mantequilla* (I've been waiting in line ten or twenty or more years for oil, sugar, coffee or butter) (Ovalles, 2014, para 4).

Protesta Creativa argues that the art of protest reaches those segments of the population that are "indifferent" to the social upheaval in the country (Ovalles, 2014). With each passing week, they extend their performance and street art, building makeshift altars on busy streets to pay homage to basic household items and boarding busses dressed as newscasters to provide passengers with real and uncensored news. The embodied image of death and zombies in particular may be banal, but it also illustrates the extent to which the social upheaval in Venezuela is a struggle about and over capitalism. The allegory of zombies implies a relationship between society and the implosion of neoliberal capitalism (Comaroff & Comaroff, 2002). Predicated on an ethos of brute commercialization where our collective understanding of species being depends upon our ability to consume objects, zombies come to represent the "embodied, dispirited phantasm widely associated with the production, the possibility and impossibility of. . .new forms of wealth." (p. 782). Consumption, Comaroff and Comaroff argue, is the "moving spirit of the late twentieth century." This claim, they further note:

> captures popular imaginings, and their mass-media representation, from across the planet. It also resonates with the growing Eurocultural truism that the (post)modern person is a subject made by means of object. Nor is this surprising. Consumption, in its ideological guise – as consumerism – refers to a material sensibility actively cultivated, ostensibly for the common good, by Western states and commercial interests, particular since World War II. (p. 780).

Under such conditions, the protesting opposition youth of Venezuela invoke art as a plea to return the state to a model of neocolonial capitalism where their desire to consume freely and unapologetically is protected.

Compared to other forms of zombie politics (such as Zombie mobs in the Occupy Wall Street Movement or the Zombie student protesters against neoliberalism in Chile; see Wallin, 2014), the opposition youth in Venezuela are not engaged in a critique of neoliberal capitalism that yields "unthinking, insatiable consumers" that zombies signify (see Wallin, 2014). The protesting Venezuelan youth double their character of victim and zombie precisely because they perceive the state as limiting their opportunity to consume. Their death-world lacks products.

Protesta Creativa's artistic production conveys the image of the living dead without the recourse of return to a life of abundance and harmony, but this fails to capture the historical conditions that have led to the crisis currently experienced by Venezuelan society. The reduction of the social crisis to one of basic goods serves as a ruse to the deeper social antagonisms among youth in the nation. This is perhaps best captured by examining the counterpoint to *Protesta Creativa*, the youth art *colectivos* that have emerged in the country over the last decade as a means to exercise and put into motion an evolving sociability predicated on the values and ethics of popular power developed by the Bolivarian Revolution. In contrast to *Protesta Creativa*, the *colectivos* produce art as a means to establish social relationships and uphold the ideas and beliefs of popular power that they associate with their struggle for collective humanization. Put simply, the art of the colectivos is an expression of the emerging cultural forms and practices of subaltern groups defying the enduring logic of coloniality and brute capitalist exploitation on their species being.

Urban Art and the Aesthetics of Subversion: *Colectivos* for Social Transformation

The antithesis of the protesters' call for regime change has received less attention from the international public. The other segment of Venezuelan youth ignored in mainstream media are the *colectivos*/collectives of organized youth that also number in the thousands, representative of the poor, darker-skinned Venezuelans for whom the Bolivarian revolution has created the conditions and provided the space for their direct participation in the politics of everyday life. Colectivos — contrary to public opinion — are not a formal political structure within the government. The term is applied loosely and generally to any group of individuals that come together to resolve certain economic, political, and/or social conditions they have in common (see Pearson, 2014). Colectivos have always existed in Venezuelan society, the difference is that the Bolivarian revolution provided the constitutional right of popular power and encouraged new and existing social collectives to develop a common identity, form links with one another, and develop their self-esteem to participate directly in political processes (see Pearson, 2014; Andaluz, 2013).

The colectivos also wield the methods of artistic expression to enact their agency and express their evolving subjectivity in a nation that emphasizes the development of popular power among the dispossessed. For the colectivos, art is a political space that needs to be understood in relation to worldly pressures. Through their collective organization and artistic acts, they demonstrate a sense of the history that has rendered poor communities disposable; they recognize that unfreedom lies next to forgetfulness. Thus, their cultural practices become a means through which to recuperate and produce a new architectonic of memory to aid in social transformation.

In preparation for the 2012 presidential elections, a grassroots art movement called *Otra Beta* formed in support of Hugo Chávez. Beta is an expression used to define a plan of action in everyday life in the working class barrios and shantytowns across Venezuela. (Ortiz, 2012). These youth collectives conceive of the Bolivarian Revolution as another *beta* because it represents the hope and possibility of superseding the logic of capitalist exploitation, which they consider as the principle cause of violence, death and destruction among popular classes (Ortiz, 2012). Chávez was conceived as *otro beta* because he did not punish youth for using urban art to express their rebellion (Ortiz, 2012).

The *Otra beta* campaign was created by *Redada*, a consortium of more than 20 youth colectivos across the country that experiment with art and urban culture to transform their cities into creative laboratories of direct popular participation in the production of *art* (Rosati, 2012). Similar to *Protesta Creativa, Redada* also conceives its objective of concientizing the wider public to the issues afflicting youth outside of traditional political paradigms. In their words, "We wanted to create an image that's Chávista (pro-government), but not so (typical) Chávista . . .we wanted. . .to show you don't have to wear a red shirt, or work for the government to support Chávez" (Rosati, 2012, para 8). These *colectivos* take their art to the street, defying the compartmentalization of art as an object for visual consumption in museums or galleries; they take art to the urban centers. *Ejército Comunicacional de Liberación* (ECL), for example, organizes festivals as urban interventions, where youth are invited to paint murals, graffiti, engage in spontaneous performance art, video projects, and sound installations (Suazo, 2013). The spatial intervention in urban centers functions as a clear and effective promotion of messages that contribute to the processes of social transformation and the redistribution of aesthetic wealth (Suazo, 2013).

The desire among youth for art to approach the immediacy of their lived environments underscores the complex political geography that inspires youth's artistic production. Urban murals reflect the spontaneous codes of urban life, a recuperation of public space as educative acts for generating critical awareness and consciousness among marginalized sectors of society. They also reflect the social cohesion among youth who share a histori- cal memory of oppression and who are committed to a novel rendering of art. More than visualizing and telling a story of their current status in society, these youth use art to imagine what is possible. Youth art colectivos respond to their historical invisibility and the erasure of popular classes' voices on art and aesthetics. They redefine the terms of aesthetic 'value' through murals that depict the unrecognized beauty of the underclasses: the dark-skinned, the poor, and the figures that reflect the ideals and values of popular power in the revolutionary movement. Colectivo art thus functions as a response to the invisibility and erasure of popular classes' voices on art and aesthetics. The city becomes the canvas through which art is explored. Public art of the street combines a new artistic language with a political transformation of reality.

The challenge that the colectivos present to dominant conceptions of aesthetics, reso- nates with what the decolonial philosopher Walter Mignolo refers to as "aestheSis." From a decolonial perspective aesthetics represent a singular and Eurocentric philosophical the- ory of what is beautiful and rational within the artistic domain (Mignolo & Vázquez, 2013). AestheSis, on the other hand, denotes the senses and sensibility that comes from subaltern and colonized subjects that have been considered less or deficient human beings (Mignolo & Vázquez, 2013). As a decolonial philosophical theory, aestheSis challenges the cultural homogeneity and progressive history of human creativity assigned to art (Jimenez del Val, 2013) and proposes that there are multiple ways to perceive, sense, understand and experience 'beauty' to rebuild and change the world (Tlostanova, 2010).

In many ways, the city of Caracas and other popular urban spaces throughout the coun- try have transformed into visually stimulating cultural centers, where the image of the indi- gent, the indigenous, the black woman and peasant man disrupt the copious number of advertisements that historically upheld the image of the white, capitalist-consuming, Euro- pean man and woman as the quintessential object of beauty and development. A mural in downtown Caracas particularly caught my attention during a recent visit (Figure 1). The woman clenches her fists in front of the declaration of independence conveying the image of womanist strength in struggle. Next to her, a man grips the Venezuelan constitution. Here, the past is connected to the present, demonstrating that the Bolivarian revolution sug- gests a movement towards independence, but this time, through the popular classes' direct and active literacy practice of reading the word. Together, the images depict a city of mes- tizas and mestizos, of critical controversies, as the city transforms into the reflection of sub- altern inhabitants in this hybrid urban space (Urdaneta, 2011). The city that adorns itself in street art and graffiti becomes an expression of popular culture through the urban discourse of social upheaval and transformation. In this sense, art generates meaning through its direct relation to the politics of meaning of everyday social struggle, a visual and discursive movement that reorients the act of looking. The artists who created the images on the mural place the underclasses at the center of social transformation. In this sense, the work of the artists defies the logic of the poor and marginalized classes as epiphenomenal effects to a larger project towards progress and development. They − the multi-vocal, multi-ethnic, male and female underclasses − become both the subject and object of liberation. Cultural power is reflected in the recuperation of national history and exemplified through visual art that communicates the memory and struggle for independence. Art as visual politics is supported as a concrete measure to establish a socio-communicative system of interpretation that encourages the public to engage the past through art.

Figure 1. Downtown caracas.

In an ethnographic study of one of the most politically and socially organized colectivos in the shantytowns of Caracas, Caroline Cambre (2009) reflects on the power of imagery to inflect ethical and political togetherness among the community. Colectivo Alexis Vive is named after one of its youth militants (Alexis Gonzales) killed in a countercoup attempt in 2002. Cambre explores the centrality of revolutionary figures, namely Che Guevara, as an organizing principle for youth's artistic production. She writes about the symbolic power of the Che-inspired murals that cover the walls throughout the shantytown, images that embody the relationship that youth ascribe to historical revolutionary figures and their current efforts towards social change. The presence of the mural is more than propagandistic dressing for a community that identifies with the Bolivarian revolutionary project. Rather, it is "a call to action, a call to struggle" (Cambre, 2009, p. 350). In Cambre's words:

> The Colectivo Alexis Vive produces its own images, murals, and scenes, not as reflections of the world, or as remembrances of the past; rather, they act as models of behavior, perception and experience. The images propose action. Indeed, they act in the world by authorizing action. (p. 355)

Murals, in this sense, turn into pedagogical spaces within the colectivos. In addition to Che, Cambre discusses the images of other fallen community members, such as Kley, a twenty-year-old leader who was gunned down in a parking lot by thieves. The youth describe the image of Kley, Che, Alexis and others, not in the sense of memorializing the befallen, but as a means to keep the dead and the legacy of their revolutionary deeds alive. Images turn into the mechanism through which "the imagination defends itself against the linear conception of the world that wants to explain it away" (Flusser as cited in Cambre, 2009 p. 359). In this way, the colectivos establish a collective benefit in artistic production as the figures, images, and words they paint on the community's walls are intended to address their collective wellbeing. Here, the artistic space of the 'mural' is not based on an economic objective, but rather, on the logic of producing knowledge to aid in solving the community's problems and discontent (Garcia and Marco, 2012). As Cambre further details, the youth of Alexis Vive have recovered abandoned public spaces, cleared the urban jungle from trash and debris, dressed public spaces in collectively produced art to make those spaces available to its inhabitants. Youth engage these cultural practices as the means to exercise collective freedom, transfer power to the community, and establish the foundation for continued social action to improve their livelihood.

I had the opportunity to visit the neighborhood of Colectivo Alexis Vive during my most recent trip to Caracas (Figure 2). I went at the invitation of my hosts, academic-activists who worked with various community groups throughout the city. My colleagues warned me that foreigners did not visit these communities, for fear of the violence that they associated with the shantytowns and communal militias. Nearly on the hour, every hour, they would remark, "see, nothing happens here!" I took dozens of photos, of medical centers, newly built playgrounds modeled after McDonald's so that children would want to visit their community park, and admittedly, of the image of Hugo Chávez and other revolutionary icons that adorned a majority of the urban landscape. It was during this visit, which coincided with the passing of Hugo Chávez, that the prevalence of popular art in the city and its urban outskirts left such an impression on me. Mural after mural depicted the various stages of social upheaval in the country, but most — if not all — artistic expression carried a message of social transformation and commitment to liberation. In this city of singular intensities and polarizing dichotomies, I felt invigorated in the spaces where youth and the wider community exercised their collective power through visual art. Engaging the city's underclasses through the codes they leave painted on the wall, forced me to listen carefully to their message. Through popular art, the city's inhabitants occupy the role of teacher, and those of us from the outside turn into their students. That is, if we are able to abandon our prejudices about art as a canon that should be separate from the — oftentimes violent — complexities of everyday life.

Figure 2. Urban art in the communes.

Towards Decolonial Renderings of Youth, Cultural Production and Art Pedagogy

The current 'epoch' of youth activism across the globe has reignited interest in understanding youth as a social group, their ideas, concepts, and strategies for denouncing neocolonial capitalism and the demise of democracy. Currently, the sociology of youth is preoccupied with examining youth's political awareness and cultural production through novel modes of protest as opposed to their passive assimilation and apathy and into existing social orders. The question of whether youth could be effective political agents, or producers of culture at all (see Jeffrey, 2011) has seemingly been put to rest.

Taking our cues from the Venezuelan and Latin American experience, it is important to rethink the very terms through which youth's cultural production is analyzed. This requires recognizing that youth do not represent a homogenous subgroup, but rather they embody unique epistemic and political perspectives from racial/ethnic, gendered, and class locations (Grosfoguel, 2007). Ramon Grosfoguel refers to this as the "body politics of knowledge" that is, the geo-political and body-political location of the subject that speaks.

While the protesting youth of the opposition movement of Venezuela discussed earlier see themselves as the oppressed under the stronghold of a socialist revolution, their experience emanates from a larger historical apparatus where privilege and wealth was distributed on a colonial ethos of social differentiation from which they now feel excluded. Similarly, the youth *colectivos* wage their resistance and artistic expressions based on a rendering of social life that historically positioned them on the fringes of society. The concept of class conflict alone cannot explain the tensions between such opposing fractions of youth. They may physically confront one another on the street, but their open conflict operates at the macro-structure of their subjective formation. Their identities generate meaning through a much more complex interpolation between their class positions and the racial, ethnic, epistemic, gendered, and sexual antagonisms that reside within what the Peruvian sociologist Anibal Quijano (2000) refers to as the coloniality of power.

The coloniality of power underscores the inter-relationship between class antagonisms and the centrality of race in configuring relationships between the world's dominant class and those on the periphery. Importantly, the coloniality of power elucidates the tragic effects of conquest and colonization on the Americas that established the conditions for evolving systems of social differentiation. Christianization, patriarchy, Eurocentric ideas over knowledge and being (epistemology and ontology, respectively), racial constructs, the elimination of indigenous languages and ways of life, and the systems of classification that established acts of inclusion and exclusion (i.e., the civilized versus the savage), set into motion a universal structure of social difference. The racial axis of the global social order has a colonial origin and character, but "it has proven to be more durable and stable than the colonialism in whose matrix it was established" (Quijano, 2000, p. 533). The legacy of this social structure is understood as the coloniality of being (Maldonado-Torres, 2007) referring to the ways that peoples across the globe have internalized colonial hierarchies into their perceptions of 'self' and 'other'.

Culture, as Raymond Williams (1981) reminds us, has always been about the convergence of interests. Understanding culture as a practice that reflects human interests necessitates a consideration of the context and symbolic conditions through which meaning is generated (Gaztambide-Fernández, 2013). The colonial matrix of power adds to our understanding of culture in that it demonstrates the enduring logic of systems of differentiation in neocolonial capitalism. The youth of Venezuela embody this very tension, in the racialized epithets they wield against one another, and in their artistic production during times of social upheaval. Each group perceives their struggle as one for freedom, but the difference lies in the definition they apply to their liberation. The youth of the opposition demonstrate their sympathies towards the Western and Eurocentric model of progress and development associated with neoliberal capitalism. The art-based *colectivos* invoke the image of the revolutionary as emblematic of their commitment to an-other vision of humanity and collectivity. Thus, the artistic production they set forward as an expression of their cultural practices reveals the interests, values, and needs that they associate with their location in the wider social order. Their art becomes the system of signification through which a social order is experienced and communicated.

If we are to take into account the unique and diverse artistic forms that youth use to express their needs, values and grievances, then we are better positioned to examine the complexity that shapes their social existence. The work of critical educators requires that we not only understand the social relations that give rise to the matters affecting youth, we also need to create opportunities for youth to consider pathways that can transcend both the macro structural relations of oppression and the intimate antagonisms among them as a cultural group. Such an effort calls upon educators to have sensitivity to difference but does not require that we rest on differences alone (see DeLissovoy, 2010).

Critical educators have long recognized that traditional frameworks and paradigms of learning are far detached from the lived contingencies of marginalized youth. Scholars of critical pedagogy who embrace art as part of their practice, for example, have developed mechanisms through which educators redesign curriculum and pedagogy to create opportunities for youth to connect education with their lived experiences and to develop the skills and habits of mind to intervene in a world of their own making (e.g. Duncan-Andrade & Morrell, 2008). Through this *critical pedagogy of art*, these critical pedagogues encourage teachers and students to engage their context creatively— through literature, visual art, music — as a means to study everyday culture, develop social critique and importantly, lead to actions for educational justice.

Jeff Duncan-Andrade and Ernest Morrell (2008) have been particularly effective in outlining the relationship between critical pedagogy and art through their focus on hip-hop music and culture. They give centrality to the concrete realities of urban life in the ghettos, allowing youth to bring their street politics into conversation with the official literary canon of school curriculum. This double movement between the official and unofficial school curriculum creates the conditions for dialogue to emerge, creating a psychosocial and emotional relief for youth who confront racial, ethnic, gendered, sexual and class based violence in wider society. By relating the characters of literature to the everyday lives of youth, Duncan-Andrade and Morrell resituate youth culture at the center of educational praxis. Critical educators recognize that unleashing the creative capacities of students is one of the means through which youth connect with one another and with the institution of schooling. Education through the lens of critical pedagogy creates and recreates culture alongside youth, bridging the gaping divide between schooling and the politics of everyday life. The connection between art, culture, and systems of social differentiation in educational praxis transforms the cultural domain into sites of political consciousness (Darts, 2004).

The centrality of art as a pedagogical practice can awaken the unconscious and communicate ideas and emotions otherwise difficult to articulate (Harris, 2013). Art may inspire, offend and enrage audiences, but ultimately, it can be an empowering pedagogical strategy that can move students into spaces of awareness and resistance. It is important for educators not only to consider the power of art in the immediacy of youth's environments, but also to link the particularities of their experiences with global relations of social differentiation. This is what the wide-scale youth-led social uprisings across the world are teaching us. Some youth, such as the *colectivos* in Venezuela, are developing their understanding and awareness of the totality of neocolonial capitalism and the havoc that it has wrought on their collective wellbeing. They wield power in creative and unprecedented ways, illustrating that the art of social transformation builds upon their capacities to cohere, organize, and speak to the concentration of wealth in the hands of the few.

In the case of Venezuela, we are presented with a unique setting where youth disrupt the notion that they represent a homogenous social category or that the culture of resistance among youth can be explained by any one analytical category. The rising tensions and conflicts among Venezuelan youth illustrate the difficulty of putting into motion a wide-scale movement of social transformation and transcendence from neoliberal capitalism's overriding logic and the embodied vestiges of coloniality. Movements towards a world beyond capital are always connected to its very object of critique. In a society where to consume more equates with being more fully human and where asymmetrical relations of power are connected to a historical and colonial ordering of social life, the struggle for social transformation is a continuous and difficult process of unhinging from the seductive (yet misguided) allure of capital.

A decolonial reading of art in pedagogy invites youth to consider the interdependence of societies through the historical lens of the coloniality of power. As educators become more aware of the co-constitutive relations that shape youth dispossession on a global scale, they can be better prepared to wield art as a pedagogical tool that animates youth to think about their relationship to others. In so doing, the use of art as a pedagogical practice can foreground youth's subjugated knowledge(s), counter the Eurocentric gaze that conditions social life, and perhaps, incite youth to think about a world outside of neocolonial capitalist exploitation. Such a move encourages educators to think about the content and value ascribed to art (aesthetics v. aestheSis), but also the process of its production. Establishing the space for youth to learn about themselves through others and emboldening them to exercise their collective power in the production of artistic expression, contributes to youth's critical consciousness and agency. The idea, indeed, the hope, is that encouraging youth to produce art as a decolonial pedagogical practice can catalyze youth to express their embodied understandings and creative capacities to transcend the differences among them. A critical pedagogy of art should also be able to provide youth with the resources to address the problems they encounter in the world. Ultimately, applying a decolonial lens to art in pedagogy is an invitation to imagine an-other society, built upon a set of values, ethics, and relations that can uphold our collective wellbeing.

References

Achinte, A. (2011). *Prácticas culturales basadas en lugar e investigadores locales.* Retrieved from http://www.territoriosonoro.org/marimba/wp-content/uploads/2011/11/Ensayo.-Prácticas-culturales-basadas-en-lugar-e-investigadores-locales.-2013.pdf

Andaluz, J.S. (2013). Entrevista a Marta Harnecker. *Colectivo Prometeo.* Retrieved from http://colectivoprometeo.blogspot.com/2013/07/entrevista-marta-harnecker.html

Cambre, C. (2009). Revolution within revolution: A Caracas collective and the face of Che Guevara. *The Review of Education, Pedagogy and Cultural Studies, 31*, 33–364.

Ciccariello-Maher, G. (2014). Venezuelan Jacobins. *Jacobin/a magazine of culture and polemic.* Retrieved from https://www.jacobinmag.com/2014/03/venezuelan-jacobins/

Comaroff, J., & Comaroff, J. (2002). Alien-nation: Zombies, immigrants, and millennial capitalism. *The South Atlantic Quarterly, 101*(4), 779–805.

Darts, D. (2004). Visual culture jam: Art, pedagogy, and creative resistance. *Studies in Art Education, 45*(4), 313–327.

De Lissovoy, N. (2010). Decolonial pedagogy and the ethics of the global. *Discourse: Studies in the Cultural Politics of Education, 31*(3), 279–293.

Duncan-Andrade, J., & Morrell, E. (2008). *The art of critical pedagogy.* New York, NY: Peter Lang.

Escobar, A. (2010). Latin America at a crossroads. *Cultural Studies, 24*, 1–65.

Everhart, K. (2012). Cultura-Identidad: The use of art in the University of Puerto Rico student movement, 2010. *Humanity & Society, 36*(3), 198–219.

Garcia, T. & Marco, E. (2012). Los colectivos artísticos: microcosmos y motor del procomún de las artes. *Teknokultura, Revista de Cultura Digital y Movimientos Sociales, 10*(1), 49–74.

Gaztambide-Fernández, R. (2013). Why the arts don't do anything: Toward a new vision for cultural production in education. *Harvard Educational Review, 83*(1), 211–233.

Gómez, Á. (2014). Un grupo venezolano protesta desde el arte. *El Universal*, March 13. Retrieved from http://www.eluniversal.com/arte-y-entretenimiento/140313/un-grupo-venezolano-protesta-desde-el-arte

Grosfoguel, R. (2007). The epistemic decolonial turn. *Cultural Studies, 21*(2–3), 211–223.

Jaramillo, N.E. & McLaren, P. (2008). Socialismo nepantla and rethinking critical pedagogy, In N. Denzin, Y. Lincoln, & L. Smith (Eds.) *Qualitative handbook of indigenous methodologies* (pp. 191–210). Thousand Oaks, CA: Sage.

Jeffrey, C. (2011). Geographies of children and youth III: Alchemists of the revolution? *Progress in Human Geography 37*(1), 145–152.

Jiménez del Val, N. (2013). Aesthetics, multiculturalism, and decoloniality. *Revista de Estudios Globales y Arte Contemporáneo, 1*(1), 141–149.

Lander, E. (2011). New state structures in South America, In: J. Heine & R. Thakur (Eds.) *The dark side of globalization* (pp 32–49). United Nations University Press.

Lendman, S. (2008). The media response to Venezuelan elections. *Venezuelanalysis.com.* Retrieved from http://venezuelanalysis.com/print/4005

Lima, B. (2011). La nueva historia oficial en Venezuela y su expresion grafica en espacios urbanos. *Cultura, grafica e ideologia 5*(10), 107–136.

Lorblanchet, M. (2007). The origin of art. *Diogenes, 214*, 98–109.

Maldonado-Torres, N. (2011). Enrique Dussel's liberation thought in the decolonial turn. *Transmodernity: Journal of Peripheral Cultural Production of the Luso-Hispanic World, 1*(1). Retrieved from http://escholarship.org/uc/item/5hg8t7cj

Maya, M.L., (2003). The Venezuelan "Caracazo" of 1989: Popular protest and institutional weakness. *Journal of Latin American Studies, 35*(1), 117–137.

Maya, M.L., Lander, L., & Parker, D. (2005). Popular protest in Venezuela: Novelties and continuities. *Latin American Perspectives, 32*(2), 92–108.

Mignolo, W., & Vázquez, R., (2013). Decolonial aesthesis: Colonial wounds/decolonial healings. *Social Text.* Retrieved from http://socialtextjournal.org/periscope_article/decolonial-aesthesis-colonial-woundsdecolonial-healings/

Nahon-Sefarty, I. (2014, May 23). Networks of international hate will destroy Venezuela. *The Huffington Post.* Retrieved from http://www.huffingtonpost.ca/isaac-nahonserfaty/hate-internatio nal_b_5378232.html

Naím, M. (2014, February 25). The tragedy of Venezuela. *The Atlantic.* Retrieved from http://www.theatlantic.com/international/archive/2014/02/the-tragedy-of-venezuela/284062/

Ore, D., & Ellsworth, B. (2014, March 23). Venezuela death toll rises to 33. *Reuters.* Retrieved from http://www.reuters.com/article/2014/03/22/us-venezuela-protests-idUSBREA2L0LK20140322

Ortiz, J. (2012, July 29). Chávez es otro Beta!!! *Aporrea.* Retrieved from http://www.aporrea.org/actualidad/a148013.html

Ovalles, V. (2014, March 20). Ingenio para despertar de la apatía. *El Universal*, March 20. Retrieved from http://www.eluniversal.com/caracas/140320/ingenio-para-despertar-de-la-apatia

Oyole, A. (2014). Lost and found? Globalised neoliberalism and global youth resistance. *Critical Arts: A South-North Journal of Cultural & Media Studies, 22*(1), 57–68.

Pearson, T. (2014). Demonising the 'Colectivos': Demonising the grassroots. *Venezula Analysis.* Retrived from http://venezuelanalysis.com/analysis/10569

Protesta Creativa (2014). Retrieved from https://www.facebook.com/protestacreativavzla/info? tab=page_info

Quijano, Anibal (2000). Coloniality of power, ethnocentrism, and Latin America. *Nepantla, 1*(3), 533–580.

Rosati, A. (2012). A Venezuelan art group tries to win youth votes for Chávez. *The Christian Science Monitor.* Retrieved from http://www.csmonitor.com/World/Americas/Latin-America-Monitor/2012/1006/A-Venezuelan-art-group-tries-to-win-youth-votes-for-Chavez

Suazo, F. (2013, May 17). Arte urbano: Entre el publico y el "lugar común." *ARTISHOCK*, Retrieved from http://www.artishock.cl/2013/05/arte-urbano-entre-el-publico-y-el-"lugar-comun"/

Tlostanova, M. (2010). La aesthesis trans-moderna en la zona fronteriza Eurasiática y el anti-sublime decolonial. *Calle, 14*(5–6), 13–31.

Urdaneta, B. (2012). Caracas: un museo de arte urbano. *Cuadernos de Vivienda Y Urbanismo, 5*, 88–103.

Wallin, J. (2012). Living…Again: The revolutionary cine-sign of zombie-life, In J. Jagodzinski (Ed). *Psychoanalyzing cinema: a productive encounter with Lacan, Deleuze and Zizek* (pp. 249–270). New York and London: Palgrave.

Weisbrot, M., Sandoval, L., & Rosnik, D. (2006). Poverty rates in Venezuela: Getting the numbers right. *Center for Economic and Policy Research.*

Williams, R. (1981). *The sociology of culture.* New York: Schocken Books.

6 *Shooting back* in the occupied territories
An anti-colonial participatory politics

Chandni Desai

In this article I argue that Palestinians, in particular Palestinian youth engage in forms of cultural resistance such as filming, video production and dissemination in their everyday lives as a way to re-configure place, space, law, knowledge and violence, through a critical race, feminist, anti-colonial theoretical analysis. Recently, interest in forms of youth political engagement has surfaced in scholarly discussions. The concept of "participatory politics" has been used to frame discussions and analysis on youth engagement. I argue that the current conceptualization of participatory politics is limited when applied to colonial and occupation contexts, particular because political participation is premised on the recognition of citizens. I argue that this conceptualization of participatory politics needs to be extended, by taking into consideration the politics of refusal and revolutionary violence. I offer the concept of an anti-colonial participatory politics that considers these aspects as central to politics and political participation by analysing youth testimonies, video's and films produced by B'Tselem volunteers, Youth Against the Settlements and Emad Burnat (director of 5 Broken Cameras). I demonstrate how Palestinians are not merely reduced to bare life, but underscore how they actively resist their colonization. Additionally, drawing on Willis' (1990) notion of symbolic creativity, I suggest that through the symbolic work of shooting back (filming and video production) in their everyday lives, Palestinian youth enact public pedagogy, whereby cultural production becomes a site of teaching, learning and conscientization which could open up possibilities for social change.

On a humid Friday in Bil'in — a Palestinian village — the site of a garden of flowers planted using tear gas grenade canisters captured my attention. The garden was planted in memory of the Palestinian martyr Bassem Abu Rahmeh, who at the age of thirty was shot and killed by a high velocity tear gas grenade fired by Israeli Occupation Forces (IOF) in 2009 during one of the weekly protests. Bil'in has been the scene of weekly protests since 2004, against the ongoing settlement construction and the illegal separation barrier/apartheid wall that cuts the villagers off from a large part of their farmland.[1] While the flower garden marked in the landscape the memory of the colonial violence and death that was produced at that very site, it also symbolized much more. The leaves and flowers that were blooming out of the tear gas canisters told a story of resistance and refusal, that despite the amount of death that Israelis produce through their colonial tactics of violence, life will continue to bloom from the blood drenched soil of those who died fighting for their land. Moreover, the Palestinians that decided to creatively transform the tear gas canister's (colonial weapons of terror) into beautiful flower pots (symbols of life) engaged in what Paul Willis (1990) has called "symbolic creativity," which is central to Palestinian resistance.

Sadly, Baseem Abu Rahmeh was the eighteenth person to die during demonstrations against the separation/apartheid wall since 2004. Abu Rahmeh's death was captured on a video camera by Emad Burnat, a local farmer and resident of Bil'in who decided to take part in the demonstrations with his camera when people in the village decided to resist the construction of the separation wall. The footage of Abu Rahmeh's death circulated globally through a video that was posted on the internet, and was also shown in Emad Burnat's *5 Broken Cameras,* a prize winning and Oscar nominated documentary film that captures and celebrates Palestinian popular resistance against Israeli colonialism and occupation.

One way in which Palestinians, particularly youth, resist is through cultural resistance practices such as Dabkeh, hip hop, spoken word, and graffiti on walls (Desai, in press). With the spread of the internet, social networking sites, and new communication technologies, Palestinians have increasingly started to use these technologies in their struggle. More specifically, in recent years, Palestinians have started to frequently use video cameras to document their daily experiences under occupation and apartheid. This was evident during my most recent visit to the Occupied West Bank, while doing fieldwork for my doctoral dissertation. The field notes that I use later in this article on the importance of the use of video are from participant observation that I conducted during a larger research project on cultural resistance in Occupied Palestine. The dominant media does not represent Palestinians accurately and instead continues to use the same familiar shots, images and footage over and over again (Jhally & Ratzkoff 2004; Said 1979). As such many residents across the Occupied Palestinian Territories (oPt) — West Bank (including East Jerusalem) and Gaza — have started to use video cameras to produce documentation of what takes place in their daily lives, which has been conceptualized by B'Tselem — an Israeli information center for human rights in the Occupied Territories (B'Tselem website) — as "citizen journalism."

In this article, using a critical race and feminist lens, I argue that Palestinians, in particular Palestinian youth, engage in forms of cultural resistance through practices such as filming, video production and dissemination in their everyday lives as a way to re-configure place, space, law, knowledge and violence, and that these practices constitute symbolic work. Recently, interest in forms of youth political engagement has surfaced in scholarly discussions. Scholars such as Joseph Kahne, Ellen Middaugh, and Danielle Allen (2014) among others have used the concept of "participatory politics" to frame discussions and analysis of youth engagement. I argue that the current conceptualization of participatory politics is limited when applied to colonial and occupation contexts, particularly because political participation is conceptualized on the work of citizens and the recognition of citizenship issues. I argue that this conceptualization of participatory politics needs to be extended, by taking into consideration the politics of refusal as an important starting point for politics, as well as a consideration of revolutionary violence (against settler colonialism and imperialism).

As such, I offer a concept of an anti-colonial participatory politics that considers the politics of refusal and revolutionary violence as central to politics and political participation. Specifically, I examine and analyze the cultural practices of filming and video production that Palestinian youth engage by analyzing youth testimonies and videos they have been produced for B'Tselem and Youth Against the Settlements. As well, I explore Emad Burnat's (2011) documentary film *5 Broken Cameras*. Through the analysis of testimonies and videos, I demonstrate how Palestinian life is reduced to "homo sacer" (bare life) by the colonial regime (Agamben, 1998). While most scholars that theorize the state of exception often risk erasing the active agency of the colonized in their analysis, through my theorization of an anti-colonial participatory politics I demonstrate how Palestinians are not merely reduced to bare life, but underscore how they actively resist their colonization.

Drawing on Willis's (1990) notion of symbolic creativity, I argue that their everyday activities and expressions offer insight into the ways in which Palestinian youth engage in resistance. Through filming, producing, and disseminating videos, which I conceptualize as acts of *shooting back*, the colonized produce alternative understandings of what it means to be colonized and Palestinian, against negative, dominant conceptions of Palestine. I argue that Palestinian youth that *shoot back* are involved in symbolic work that is simultaneously pedagogical. I suggest that through their symbolic work, Palestinian youth mobilize public pedagogy, whereby cultural production becomes a site of teaching, learning and conscientization that could open up possibilities for social change.

I write this article as an act of solidarity, as a scholar-activist that has been committed to human rights, social justice movements and de-colonial work on Palestine for the past seven years. As such, I situate this work within a historical understanding of the present politics of Israel-Palestine and of Zionism as a political ideology and a settler colonial regime characterized through the establishment of the state of Israel (Abdo 2011; Davis 2003; Lentin 2010). In 1948, over 750,000 Palestinians became uprooted from their land (s), displaced and expelled by force, now living as refugees in exile all over the world (Masalah, 2012). This catastrophe is known by Palestinians as the Al-Nakba. At the end of the 1948 war, approximately 150,000 Palestinians remained in areas of Palestine that would become Israel. Additionally, Palestinians were also displaced to the West Bank and Gaza and have gone through multiple displacements as a result of the Israeli occupation (Schulz, 2003). After the June 1967 war, what was left of historic Palestine — the West Bank, Gaza and the Golan Heights — became militarily occupied by Israel and continues to be occupied. Though the Oslo Accords were signed in 1993 in which Israel would relinquish control over the oPt, the failure of Oslo further entrenched settler colonial rule and fragmented the Palestinians into ethnic enclaves/Bantustans through policies of racial and ethnic exclusion, or what is better known as apartheid. Spatial enclosures have been put in place by Israel which include Jewish only settlements and the separation wall, which sustain apartheid by encroaching and dominating the land.[2] These are some of the conditions that invoked Palestinian resistance and the particular participatory practices that I examine in this article.

Palestinian Youth Participation

According to *The Status of Youth in Palestine Report* (2009), Palestinian youth are considered amongst the most politicized youth in the world; "every party or faction has a youth organization, student council elections are followed by the political classes as signals of tendencies in the country, youth voting remains high and many young people continue to demonstrate … against Israeli occupation" (Bailey & Murray, 2009). The politics of settler colonialism, occupation and apartheid govern every aspect of the youth's lives, from their freedom of movement to their education. Palestinian youth become politicized at a very young age because they constantly witness or undergo horrific violence as a result of the IOF. For instance, in the months of June and July of 2014 alone, twenty-three Palestinian youth were killed by the IOF in the West Bank. In the month of June, six Palestinian youth were killed and hundreds were arrested when Israel launched its largest military assault on the West Bank, invading refugee camps, villages, cities, and universities after three settler teens were reported missing (Murphey, 2014). In the month of July, following the 2014 Israeli military slaughter of Gaza, sixteen youth were killed in the West Bank. Additionally, on July 2, 2014 in East Jerusalem, 16 year old Mohammed Abu-Khdeir was lynched to death after he was kidnapped, beaten, force-fed gasoline and burned alive by Zionist vigilantes.[3]

Moreover, in most families, one or more members are incarcerated as political prisoners, and therefore Palestinian youth, some of whom are born in prison, are aware of the prison system from a very young age. Many children have also been detained by the IOF; since 2010, 3,000 Palestinian children have been arrested and were subject to threats and torture by Israeli authorities during their investigations (Middle East Monitor, 2014). Palestinian children and youth constantly witness their parents, families, and society at large engaged in resistance towards the occupation in its various forms, and thus are conscious of occupation, political factions, and resistance tactics. In fact, many Palestinians in the oPt begin their resistance in their childhood. For example, on August 12th, 2014 hundreds of Palestinian children in the West Bank marched to the United Nations office in Ramallah, calling for the UN to protect Gaza's children (as 449 children have been slain in the 2014 invasion of Gaza) and all Palestinian children, demanding to live like all other children of the world.

The Arab League of Nations defines youth as those individual's between the ages of 15 and 35, which is the definition the Palestinian Ministry of Youth and Sports adopt and how I define youth in this article (Palestinian National Plan, 2011). Palestinian youth have played a significant role in the development of their struggle. Youth participation in politics reached its peak during the First Intifada, when approximately ninety percent of young males and eighty percent of young females participated in some form of demonstration and activism (Barber, 2000).[4] Only armed with stones, the youth of that generation were able to bring the military power to the negotiating table. However, two decades later, due to the Oslo process, Palestinian youth have become increasingly disillusioned with political life, in particular party politics and factional conflicts (Sharek Youth Study, 2009).

While youth engagement with party politics has declined, Norman (2009) argues that youth are not entirely disillusioned or apathetic; rather 56.6 percent of youth viewed both violence and non-violence as an effective means of resisting the occupation. Similarly, in a Joint Advocacy Initiative (JAI) study 82 percent of the youth agreed to boycotting Israeli products, and 63 percent believed armed resistance was the best way to get rid of the occupation (JAI Study, 2006, cited in Norman, 2009, p. 178-179). Furthermore, in her latest ethnographic study of Palestinian hip hop and the youth movement, Sunaina Maira (2014) underscores how Palestinian youth have "turned to political movements or attempted to engage in political activism outside of established party and factional structures" (p.7). Many youth in the new generation reject the Oslo framework as well as divisive factionalism and elitism. Instead, Wiles (2014) argues that youth,

are working collectively at the grassroots level and calling for a truly representative national leadership that could take the form of a restructured PLO [Palestinian Liberation Organization], or possibly an entirely new framework altogether. Whichever of these approaches are preferred by individual activists, the demand is that the body must be representative of the entire Palestinian people. This includes Palestinians in 1967 occupied lands, those in 1948 Palestine, and all those in international exile. (par. 18)

Participatory Politics Under Settler Colonialism and Occupation in Palestine

In recent years, interest in forms of youth political engagement has surfaced in scholarly discussions. The concept of "participatory politics" has been used to frame discussions and analysis on youth engagement. Youth Studies scholars Joseph Kahne, Ellen Middaugh and Danielle Allen (2014) define participatory politics as:

> Interactive, peer-based acts though which individuals and groups seek to exert both voice and influence on issues of public concern. We propose that participatory politics are rooted in historical struggles for *greater citizen influence* over issues of public concern; and enabled by new media it is becoming an increasingly important form of political participation (p. 2).

Moreover, these scholars suggest that politics includes a variety of activities undertaken by individuals and groups to address issues of public concern and shape how political agendas are set. Activities that would constitute politics include: "electoral activities (such as voting or campaign work), activism (protest, boycotting, and petitions), civic activities (charity or community service), and lifestyle politics (vegetarianism, awareness raising, and boycotting)" (Kahne, Middaugh, & Allen, 2014, p. 6).

Since the Palestinian people are under a settler colonial occupation, their public concerns cannot be negotiated with their colonizer, who doesn't enter negotiations from a place of equality or justice. Rather, Palestinians have been living under the state of exception since the inception of the Israeli state. Achille Mbembe (2003) and Sari Hanafi (2009) have described the way in which the Zionist settler colonial racial state is produced through the exercise of sovereignty over life, by which the sovereign exercises the power to decide who shall live and who shall die. Giorgio Agamben (1998; 2003) draws from Carl Schmitt (2003; 2005) to argue that sovereignty is exercised through exceptions in which "the state remains, whereas the law recedes" (2005, p. 12). Agamben (1998) uses spatial imagery such as the "zone of indistinction" and the "concentration camp" to underscore that those confined to these spaces exist as "bare life" (homo sacer)[5] as no legal status or citizenship rights can protect them. Agamben (1998) argues that the sovereign creates a permanent state of emergency in which the military's authority is extended into the civil sphere, suspending the constitutional norms that protect people's liberties. Razack (2004) argues that "the abandonment of populations, an abandonment configured as emergency, is accomplished as a racial project" as the colour-lined world is governed by the logic of exception (p. 6). In order for the Zionist settler state to maintain its governance in historic Palestine, Palestinians (particularly in the oPt) are cast out of the law.

As such, rather than collectively negotiating with Israel, which suspends the law when dealing with Palestinian concerns, Palestinians partake in collective resistance towards their colonizers. This resistance dates back to the twenties, when Palestinians actively resisted the British colonial administration of Palestine, and has been ongoing both inside historic Palestine as well as from the outside by Palestinians living in exile. Resistance activities have taken various forms over the course of Palestinian history and have included activities such as protesting, boycotting, petitioning, awareness raising, etc, which are constituted within the conceptualization of participatory politics. However, these forms of participatory politics that are outlined by Kahne, Middaugh & Allen (2014) are banned or deemed illegal under Israeli military rule and the state of exception. As Henry Lefebvre (1991) poignantly reminds us "sovereignty implies [. . .] a space established and constituted by violence" (p. 280). For Lefebvre (1974/1991) the ongoing formation of the state depends upon the use of violence to produce the national space. While the notion of participatory politics that Kahne, Middaugh & Allen (2014) provide

114 CULTURAL PRODUCTION AND PARTICIPATORY POLITICS

is partially applicable to the case of Palestine, it is limiting because the definition of participatory politics assumes that all people have achieved their political, economic, and social self-determination and sovereignty.

Furthermore, the notion of participatory politics is centered on the notion of "citizens" and the work "citizens" do to influence issues of public concern within a nation-state. Under settler-colonial military rule, Palestinians – particularly those in the Occupied Territories – are not citizens to any nation, they are stateless and are considered "residents" of a certain territory – a territory under occupation. After the Nakba, Palestinian citizenship ceased to exist (Benko, 2012). 'Palestinian' is a political identity, and although this identity status is recognized internationally, Israel regulates the identity of Palestinians in the oPt by issuing them identity cards. Although the Palestinian Authority issues passports to those living in the oPt with the approval of Israel, these passports are simply travel documents, and they do not equate with citizenship or citizenship status or rights.[6]

In the context of occupation and settler colonialism, the colonized are not only denied from participating in any form of citizen politics, but are severely punished and even put to death if they engage in political participation. In recent years, one way in which Palestinians in the West Bank, youth in particular, engage in participatory politics under settler colonialism and occupation is through popular resistance organized by popular committees in several locations across the region. The popular committees organize at the grassroots level to oppose settler attacks, the construction of the apartheid wall and illegal settlements. Popular committees organize weekly demonstrations, which take place every Friday, though these areas have been ordered by military commanders as a "closed military zone" (entry and presence prohibited during the time of the demonstration), which declares demonstrations as "unlawful" (Naama Baumgarten-Sharon, 2010). The military order that regulates demonstrations in the West Bank is Order No. 101 (from 1967), Order Regarding Prohibition of Incitement and Hostile Propaganda Actions,[7] which "imposes severe restrictions on the right of Palestinians to organize or take part in demonstrations" (Naama Baumgarten-Sharon, 2010)[8]. Such military orders disregard Palestinians freedom to protest and their rights to engage in any form of political activity, which is, by contrast, sanctioned under international law. For example in Bil'in and Ni'lin, the military have used these orders to prohibit demonstrations from taking place before people even gather. Palestinians rarely submit requests (to the military) to hold demonstrations, partly because requests to protest would be rejected by Israel. More importantly, not submitting a request itself "constitutes an act of protest against the occupation and a refusal to recognize its authority" (Naama Baumgarten-Sharon, 2010, p.11). In *Mohawk Interruptus* (2014), Audra Simpson provides some insight on the politics of refusal and the implications for refusal in the context of settler colonialism in Canada. Simpson (2014) explains the centrality of refusal in the context of Mohawk struggles over sovereignty:

> Like many other Iroquois people, the Mohawks of Kahnawa:ke refuse to walk on some beams, and through this gesture they refuse to be Canadian or American. They refuse the gifts of American and Canadian citizenship, they insist upon the integrity of the Haudenosaunee governance. (p.7)

Simpson argues that refusal "comes with the requirement of having one's political sovereignty acknowledged and upheld, and raises the question of legitimacy for those who are usually in the position of recognizing" (p. 11). Drawing from Simpson's work, I conceptualize Palestinian resistance and engagement with politics as a form of refusal. For Palestinians, resistance in the form of refusal involves refusing to recognize the colonizer's power (occupation), in some instances refusal to become citizens of the settler state,[9] and refusal to lay down and die, are some of the ways in which many engage in politics. Additionally, another form of participatory politics under settler colonialism and occupation that youth engage involve economic strikes. More recently in Ramallah, following the killing of Palestinian youth, young people have been enforcing economic strikes in the city (e.g.: the de-shelving and boycott of Israeli products from grocery stores), which was very common during the First Intifada.

Another form of youth participatory politics through which Palestinian youth resist settler colonialism and occupation is citizen/people's journalism. The cultural practice of filming, creating and disseminating videos, and reporting by public citizens (not professional journalists), has been conceptualized as "citizen journalism." For example during the uprisings in Tunisia, Egypt, Morocco and Syria, citizen journalists provided more reliable coverage of what was happening in the streets than media controlled by their governments. These journalists documented police brutality, crackdowns on dissent, and state violence against crowds of demonstrators (Kouddous, 2011).

Courtney Radsch (2013) argues that the term citizen journalism best explains a particular form of "online and digital journalism conducted by amateurs, linking the practice of journalism to its relation with the political and public sphere" (p. 18). However, I strongly suggest using the term a people's journalism instead of citizen journalism, since Palestinians in the Occupied Territories are not considered citizens to a nation. As such, the concept of citizen journalism excludes those not recognized by governments/nation-states such as refugees, undocumented immigrants, and stateless people. Since Palestinians are denied their legitimacy and humanity under the state of exception, I propose using the notion of a people's journalism instead, as this form of journalism doesn't require recognition of identity or national boundaries. Rather, a people's journalists are untrained individuals that document their everyday realities by filming and later distributing footage through online networks. This form of journalism is often collaborative, in service of the community, and seeks to represent the voices and perspectives of those who are often silenced, forgotten, and erased. In the next section, I will discuss how youth in Palestine engage in politics through an anti-colonial framework. In particular, I discuss how a people's journalism is one form of anti-colonial participatory politics deployed in the West Bank.

Anti-Colonial Participatory Politics

Rather than a politics of recognition based on citizenship, an anti-colonial participatory politics would be premised on the politics of refusal. Most Palestinians refuse the settler colonial entity, the system of apartheid, and the occupation. On July 24, 2014, the sixteenth day of the Israeli invasion of Gaza/"Operation Protective Edge," thousands of Palestinians, particularly youth, marched from Al-Amari camp toward Qalandia checkpoint (in Ramallah) in order to refuse Israel's assault on Gaza, extend their solidarity with Gaza, and demonstrate their political steadfastness as Palestinians; this was one of the largest demonstrations in decades. The IOF fired at them with live ammunition. Since September 2014, the IOF has made several attempts to close the Al-Aqsa Mosque[10] in East Jerusalem, which has resulted in clashes, particularly between Palestinian youth and Israeli police and IOF. On October 30th 2014, as extremist right-wing Zionists called on mass intrusion of the Al-Aqsa Mosque and stormed the Mosque compound. Israeli police and troops fired stun grenades at worshippers, and closed the mosque with iron chains barring entry to Palestinian worshippers. Widespread protests and tensions have continued to escalate as Palestinians are refusing to accept the closure of the Al-Aqsa mosque, settlement construction and Israeli encroachment of Jerusalem, and the racist violence enacted upon them by extremist right-wing Zionists/Israelis (Khalek 2014). This leads to the question of whether a Third Intifada is looming or has already arrived. Also the weekly protests that are held across the West Bank are about a politics of refusal, refusing the ongoing construction of settlements, the construction of the wall, the normalization of the occupation, land theft, home demolitions, unlawful administrative detention, restrictions on movement, family separation, the destruction of olive trees, torture, the siege of Gaza, and colonial violence and death.

When colonized peoples individually and collectively refuse to give up their lands and themselves, they refuse to recognize the authority of the colonial power and their presumed lawfulness over them. This includes refusing citizen status as a way to engage in participatory politics. This politics of refusal is primarily a collective process, even though social differences — class, gender, religion, etc — will inform the political viewpoints of individuals and the form of politics in which they may engage. For Palestinians that remain principled and committed to liberation, self determination and decolonization, resistance to colonial power will always be informed by a politics of collective refusal. Refusal is the only way that the colonized can achieve true liberation, self-determination, justice, sovereignty and decolonization.

Furthermore, to extend Kahne, Middaugh & Allen (2014) conceptualization of participatory politics, it is important to consider the activity of revolutionary violence (armed resistance). While activities such as the electoral process, activism, civic activities and lifestyle politics are provided as examples that constitute politics and political activity, in the colonized, Manichean world the problems of decolonization can only be realized through violence (Fanon, 1961/2007). Frantz Fanon (1961/2007) states "colonialism is not a machine capable of thinking, a body endowed with reason. It is naked violence and only gives in when confronted with greater violence" (p. 23). Here Fanon suggests that because colonization is made possible through extreme violence, control, and fear, violence is the only language that a colonial society understands. As such revolutionary violence is one tactic of resistance among many other tactics of struggle that colonized peoples use to refuse their colonizer's power and violence.

For example, in the most recent Israeli invasion of Gaza, the Palestinian armed resistance, which was primarily constituted of fighters from the al-Qassam Brigades (the military wing of Hamas), and the al-Quds Brigades (the military wing of Islamic Jihad) refused the inhumane bombarding of their people and the siege of Gaza by engaging in an armed struggle against the IOF. While the United States and various other nations and media outlets labeled Palestinian armed resistance as "terrorism," within Palestine, particularly in Gaza, there was popular support for the armed resistance, as it is seen as the only source of protection amidst the enormous death and destruction caused by Israeli state terrorism. While Palestinians in the West Bank have primarily used tactics of civil disobedience in their resistance after the Second Intifada,[11] the recent Israeli invasion of Gaza caused the al-Aqsa Martyrs Brigades (the military wing of Fatah) to resurge in the West Bank[12] during Operation Protective Edge.

For the colonized that engage in refusal politics there is much at stake. In the case of demonstrations in the West Bank, soldiers deploy extensive means of crowd control, such as the use of tear gas, stun grenades, foul smelling skunk spray, rubber coated metal bullets, and live ammunition, which has been condemned by the international community. Even though Israeli military orders state explicitly that "live ammunition may not be fired at stone-throwers [...] security forces sometimes do use live fire at demonstrations, usually firing at Palestinians" (Israel's Use of Crowd Control Weapons, 2013). This has lead to several injuries, life altering health conditions, disability and death. On May 15th 2014, two youth – 22 year old Muhammad Audah Abu al-Thahir and 17 year old Nadim Siyam Nuwarah –were shot and killed by Israeli forces with live bullets during a protest rally to mark the 66th anniversary of the Al-Nakba, in the central West Bank. While the Israelis deny using live ammunition, people's journalists that witnessed the shooting released a video and circulated it globally on the internet and social networking sites on May 19th, 2014 capturing the occupation forces' actions.

Furthermore, many Palestinians are arrested, detained, tried and incarcerated for demonstrating or considered to be "inciting violence." Since Palestinians are considered non-citizens, they are tried in the military courts under military law.[13] By contrast, Israelis and foreign nationals who participate in these protests as an act of solidarity are tried in Israeli courts, which recognize the freedom to demonstrate in accordance with the ostensibly democratic standards Israel claims to embrace. As such, in colonial contexts or war zones governed by military law where states of exception are often applied, a conception of anti-colonial participatory politics of resistance must account for the role of refusal along with the use of revolutionary violence as a tactic of participation.

A People's Journalism as a Form of Anti-Colonial Participatory Politics in Palestine

In *Resistance Literature*, Barbara Harlow (1987) explains that the "historical struggle against colonialism and imperialism of such resistance movements as the Palestinian Liberation Organization…is waged at the same time as a struggle over the historical and cultural record" (p. 7). Therefore, while revolutionary violence serves as one form of resistance, cultural resistance is also a central part of the Palestinian struggle. Many cultural studies scholars have theorized the importance of culture as a site of education (see Hall 1997; Freire 1973; Gramsci 1971; Giroux 2004). Cultural studies has provided education scholars a way to explore cultural spaces such as popular culture and public spaces for their pedagogical aspects, by interrogating whether these spaces challenge or reproduce oppressive formations of reality. In particular, Giroux's (2004) work has been central in outlining the way in which culture is a political and pedagogical site where negotiations and struggles over hegemony take place, though they might not always necessarily be won. Giroux (2004) argues that inquiry into culture can provide insight on locating political agency within structures of power. As such Giroux develops the term *public pedagogy* to "urge educators to critically analyze cultural products and processes as important enactments of pedagogy" (Sandlin, O'Malley & Burdick, 2011, p. 8). Here the notion of public pedagogy is premised on the ideas that (a) resistance is possible within the sphere of culture, particularly popular culture; and (b) learning can take place outside of formal educational settings, in multiple sites within the organized social relations of everyday life (Giroux, 2004).

Additionally, Paul Willis (1990) focuses on everyday life, emphasizing that it is in every day activities, expressions, and life that symbolic creativity can be found. For Willis (1990) symbolic creativity in "everyday ordinary culture" is important because it is through the everyday lives of people, not objects and artifacts, that social processes can be understood (p. 5). Since violence is a core practice that settler colonial and occupying states use to maintain their sovereignty, those occupied and oppressed by this violence use creativity to subvert and document processes of violence enacted upon them. In this section I offer a discussion on the symbolic work that is at play for Palestinians, as Palestinian youth *shoot back* through the cultural practice of filming and video making to

118   CULTURAL PRODUCTION AND PARTICIPATORY POLITICS

refuse Israel's state of exception. I will analyze youth testimonies and videos produced for B'Tselem and Youth Against the Settlements, as well as Emad Burnat's *5 Broken Cameras.*

Shooting Violence and Flipping the Script

B'Tselem launched a camera project in 2007 titled *Shooting Back.* The aim of the project was to distribute cameras to residents across the oPt, where tensions and clashes were high and commonplace. Adhering to the notion of citizen journalism, B'Tselem decided that their approach would be to work with the local population, give them cameras, and ask them to film from their "windows, balconies, and roofs as a means of documenting the incidents that occur daily in the Palestinian streets, fields and homes" (B'Tselem Camera Project Website, 2014). Though B'Tselem's field researchers had been collecting written testimonies of human rights violations against Palestinians dating back to the late eighties, getting media and public attention around various issues proved to be very challenging through written reports alone. As such, the organization started giving cameras to Palestinians, to be able to capture violations as they occurred (Shooting Back Interview, 2007).

Oren Yakobovich, Director of the film department at B'Tselem, explains that youth and children often use cameras to capture the violence to which soldiers and settlers subject them, their families, and communities (Shooting Back Interview, 2007). An important video that raised major debates within Israeli society and circulated internationally was filmed by a sixteen year old girl from Hebron. Filming through the barbwire surrounding the windows of her house, the sixteen-year-old girl captured on camera as her sister was being harassed and verbally abused by a settler in Hebron.[14] The video begins with a radical Jewish settler woman yelling at a Palestinian resident of Hebron. The settler tells the Palestinian resident to "get in the house and close the door." The Palestinian resident refuses, and says "I'm not closing the door, I don't want to go inside. . . . It's early in the morning. What do you want from us?" The Israeli settler notices the young sixteen-year-old girl filming and demands that the camera be turned off. Thereafter, the settler starts closing the door of the resident's house while shouting at them. The Palestinian woman asks her to go away. Instead of leaving, the settler comes up against the barbwire of the home and shouts: "Whore. You're a whore (sharmouta).[15] Your daughters, too. Don't you dare open this door!" The Palestinian woman responds, saying: "Don't you dare come here; I'll leave the house as I please!" The settler continues to call her a whore (eight times), while an Israeli soldier captured in the video stands idly watching the settler harass the Palestinian resident without intervening in the matter. The Palestinian resident addresses the soldier and asks: "Don't you see what she's doing?" The solider does nothing while the settler continues to call the Hebron resident a whore.

Under conditions of perpetual war and the state of exception, as Palestinians are denied their existence and rights, activities such as filming/video making are crucial for maintaining political/national identity. One of the symbolic outcomes of shooting back (filming) is humanization, which Willis (1990) outlines as an aspect of symbolic creativity. Despite the harassment and fear that the settlers and IOF try to perpetrate upon Palestinians, such as the sixteen-year-old girl from Hebron and her sister, they refuse their mistreatment by taking the risk of filming in the presence of an Israeli soldier. Symbolic work takes place, through the process of filming the encounter, as the the sixteen-year-old girl from Hebron sustains her identity and story by becoming the protagonist of her own story.

For too long, mainstream Israeli and Western media have told the story about Palestine and Palestinians through racist, Orientalist, Islamaphobic, sexist perspectives that depict Palestinians as "violent" and "backwards." By filming settler violence, the girl from Hebron refuses the image of the "violent Palestinian" by demonstrating through her video who began the violence. By producing and disseminating videos that are made by the colonized themselves about their everyday lives and letting the world witness first-hand the conditions under which they live, Palestinians are able to tell their version of reality, in turn humanizing themselves through symbolic work. By refusing to be afraid and intimidated by settler/solider harassment and violence, young people like this sixteen year old girl film from barb wired windows, roof tops, balconies, and the street to capture their material reality and communicate it through a Palestinian narrative, across and beyond the enclosures of the wall and borders that imprison and confine them to enclosed (racialized) spaces – Bantustans and ghettos.

Filming and video production allows Palestinians who are often spoken about, for, and to, to speak for themselves by sharing their own stories and perspectives. This is not simply a form of empowerment in which a young woman was able to claim her so-called voice. Rather, the sixteen-year-old girl enacts an anti-colonial participatory politics by flipping the dominant script of the "violent" and "backwards" Palestinian, to show how she is a human being that is living under oppressive material conditions. In doing so, she re-creates the images and meanings of whom and what it means to be Palestinian, and who and what it means to be a soldier and settler from her perspective as a person living under colonial occupation.

The re-creation of meanings through symbolic work is evident in the way in which the video was received by Israeli and international audiences. In an interview with Amy Goodman on *Democracy Now*, Oren Yakobovich explains the impact this video footage had both inside Israel and globally. The video was first posted on the internet, and hours later news channels in Israel began to show the video on their networks. Yakobovich says that the video "became a huge issue" (Shooting Back Interview, 2007). The video raised controversy because of the soldier's lack of intervention while the incident took place. Due to the system of enclosures, people in Israeli society are not fully aware of what happens on the other side of the wall, therefore such footage is important in raising knowledge and consciousness about what takes place inside the occupied territories. Often, Israelis turn a blind eye to human rights violations in the oPt, and therefore "a strong video" enables an organization like B'Tselem to demonstrate the reality of occupation. Yet, despite the various reactions these videos might have produced in Israeli society, the conditions of occupation and violence still continue. Eventually this led to comments issued from the Prime Minister and Defense Minister.[16] This led CNN, ABC and European media outlets and networks all around the world to show the video footage shot by the sixteen-year-old Palestinian girl in Hebron.

Furthermore, over the last few years, people's journalists in Palestine have captured hundreds of hours of footage, out of which many videos have been produced. Below I have provided a list of a few titles of the videos that have been created through the *Shooting Back* camera project. The titles below underscore the themes of what Palestinians in the West Bank endure on a daily basis. The bolded words underscore the material reality of racial terror that Palestinians are subjected to by Israeli soldiers, police officers, and settlers.

Soldiers **fire rubber coated metal bullet** from short range at demonstrator in Bil'in (2008)

Soldiers **order Hebron resident to take down** Palestinian flag from his roof
Settlers harass Palestinians and **steal crops** during olive harvest (2009)
Settler shoots at Palestinian demonstrators with soldiers present (2010)
Army **seals Palestinian shops** in Hebron (2010)
Violent dispersal of a demonstration in Nabi Saleh (2011)
Direct **shooting** in Nabi Saleh – collection of footage (2011)
Officer **points loaded weapon** into face of Palestinian (2011)
Hebron: Border Police **officer kicks** Palestinian child (2012)
Detention of Palestinians who complained of trespassing settlers (2013)
Soldiers **detain** five year old child in Hebron (2013)
Officer fires tear gas canister at B'Tselem videographer
Violating orders: **Police pepper spray** non-violent civilians (2013)
Soldiers beat journalists filming demonstration (2013)
Khadrah tells what it's like to film **settler attacks** (2014)

The disturbing footage shown in the videos listed above is not only eye opening to the kinds of inhumane treatment Palestinians go through, but also serves as evidence against all sorts of accusations and allegations Israeli soldiers, settlers and police officers make about Palestinians in order to justify their acts of violence. As such the video footage becomes extremely important; perhaps even a necessity, in the protection of Palestinian life, especially when Palestinians are brought in front of the military court.

During my visit to Hebron's H2 area,[17] youth from the organization Youth Against the Settlements (YAS) shared with me the importance of filming. Hebron is one of the only Palestinian cities where Jewish settlers live within the heart of the city, among and alongside Palestinians. Typically settlements are around or close by to Palestinian areas but not inside them, as in the case of Hebron. As such, the encounters between Israeli settlers and Palestinians are very frequent. Therefore YAS youth film to document settler and military attacks and violations and expose these violations that take place in their areas. In a conversation with one of the shabab (youth), he mentioned the camera serves as an honest witness, because as he explained, they can't fabricate what you see on the video or what is photographed. He continued to explain that they keep these videos and use them especially in the courts as evidence when anyone is arrested, to show accurately what the settlers and soldiers do to them (Fieldnotes, 2013).

In an online video made by YAS, several youth explain that they film and use video footage to share with the world how the army besieges people in their homes, the symbiotic relationship between the settlers and the army, and how the occupation is driving them out of their homes. They explain that they use social media networks – Facebook, Twitter and YouTube – to disseminate their videos and testimony and share their content with activists, advocacy organizations and journalists both local and foreign (YAS Video, 2013). As well, due to the political work that the youth from YAS engage in, such as protests, members in their group have been subject to arrest, and are accused of inciting violence or of being violent. In the online YAS video, one of the youth says, "when people were arrested from YAS, we sent original videos to court, without editing of course. ... They were cases in Tal Rumeida, the Old City, Shuhada Street, and Kiryat Arba when either (members of) our group or foreigners were arrested, and later released because of our videos" (Youth Against Settlements, 2012).

Moreover, in a video testimony Ayat, a young woman who is a member of YAS, explains that she got involved in the organization and in filming because of the issues women particularly face. Under Israeli military occupation, the IOF deploys patriarchal perceptions of honor, purity and sexuality, sanction sexual violence (ie: rape, forced undressing, torture in prisons) upon Palestinian women as a way to defeat, and bring the downfall – *Isqat* – of the Palestinian people and nation (Abdo & Lentin 2002; Shalhoub-Kavorkian, 2009). Women's bodies are controlled and "weaponized" in conflict zones because their reproductive abilities allow for the continuity of the unwanted racial, ethnic or religious group. As such women are constantly harassed and abused by the occupation forces. As a woman, Ayat feels that she has been denied many things; she says "I'm denied my education, freedom of movement, my own life" (Youth against Settlements, 2012). She refuses to obey the military order and accept the denial of her fundamental rights, exercising her agency by partaking in protests and videotaping. Ayat says, "Palestinians aren't allowed to be on the street [referring to Shuhada Street] or aren't allowed to walk for a long distance, if they walked there, they are checked every 500 yards" (Youth against Settlements, 2012).

Ayat enacts an anti-colonial politics that refuses the restriction of movement imposed upon her by walking down the street and attending protests while filming her activities. She knows that there is military presence everywhere in Hebron and she is more vulnerable to harassment. Though the IOF instills fear in the colonized, having a video camera in hand makes it a little bit easier for them to walk down the street, stand outside, partake in protests and confront soldiers, knowing that the colonial encounter is being recorded. Yakobich asserts that settlers will run away when Palestinians take out the camera, or back away because they know they are being filmed (Shooting Back Interview, 2007). The partial elimination of fear to engage in the most banal activity – walking down the street - is part of the humanization process, through which the colonized can remember and recognize their agency among harsh and violent living conditions (especially for women), while simultaneously re-configuring colonial space through the symbolic work of film making.

Authenticity: *5 Broken Cameras*

In response to their colonizer's violence, Palestinians fight by speaking back to soldiers or settlers, or throwing stones to protect themselves, which Israel considers violent activity. Palestinian resistance is constantly fetishized by the colonial power, as their politics of refusal are delinked from the history of Zionism and the formation of the racial, settler colonial state. As such the colonial power ontologizes Palestinians as violent and violent only. Therefore it is not surprising that the authenticity of the raw video footage that Palestinians capture of their everyday reality is denied. Here the state of exception once again is enacted. Because Palestinian life is not deemed worthy, any documentation and evidence that protects their lives such as the raw video footage of the violence that is enacted upon them is automatically discredited or accused of being false or forged.

Israeli soldiers, for example, accused Emad Burnat's film *5 Broken Cameras*, of being fabricated. Emad, a local resident of Bil'in, initially bought a used video camera in 2005 to capture the birth of his son Gibreel. Without any formal training, he began making home videos, then began to capture memories for his neighbors on his camera, and later developed a sense of duty to use the camera as a means to document the popular resistance that was taking place in Bil'in. Burnat took footage that he captured over five years of his life attending weekly protests and developed the footage into a documentary film. The film tells the story of Bil'in through the narrative of the birth of Burnat's son Gibreel, who grew up against the background of the village's struggle. In the film Burnat documents the arrests, beatings, bullets, tear gas, violence, and the death of his cousin Bassem Abu Rahmeh.

One of the most moving scenes takes place at the end of the film when Gibreel (age 4) has the following dialogue with his father, painfully capturing the loss of a Palestinian child's innocence, and the child's confusion and simultaneous desire to refuse and resist the occupation.

> Gibreel: Daddy, why don't you kill the soldiers with a knife?
> Emad Burnat: Because they'd shoot me. Why do you want to hurt them?
> Gibreel: Because they shot my Phil (referring to Baseem Abu Rahmeh). Why did they shoot Phil? What did he do to them? (5 Broken Cameras, 2011).

This film shows some of the fiercest footage of everyday moments of colonial violence. This is most poignantly seen as Burnat's five cameras, which represent various stages of his life, are smashed by bullets and tear gas canisters, a reminder of "life's fragility" (*5 Broken Cameras*, 2011). Though Emad's camera became an Israeli target, and he encounters near death experiences as a result of the IOF's live ammunition, Emad enacts an anticolonial politics by refusing to stop filming. For example, one evening when Emad was filming in the village, the soldiers arrested him and sent him to jail. They took his camera and tape, beat him, and upon release he was placed under house arrest. Once again Emad refused to let the colonizers intimidate and silence him and adopted a politics of refusal by continuing to film the weekly protests to share with the world the realities of Bil'in. The camera serves as a weapon for Palestinians because it acts as an eyewitness technology that is able to capture firsthand accounts of what the Israeli soldiers are doing to them. Israeli soldiers attempt to destroy such eyewitness technologies because under the state of exception this is one of the few weapons Palestinians have to show the world how they are inhumanely treated and the numerous human rights and international law violations that occur under occupation. When the soldiers aren't able to destroy the evidence, they accuse it as being fabricated information.

Notwithstanding the numerous awards and recognition *5 Broken Cameras* has received globally, the film has received two major criticisms. The first major criticism of *5 Broken Cameras* was from soldiers who contested the film and who said "the film editors joined together frames taken at different events to create the false appearance of Israeli soldiers using violence against demonstrators without provocation" (Stotsky, 2013, par. 1). In response to the death of Bassem Abu-Rahmeh, a Zionist film reviewer writes,

> an Israeli military investigation determined that the killing was accidental, although some dispute this finding. But the film misleads its audience. In reality the soldiers operate under well-defined rules of engagement. These rules are announced to the protesters. Not shown in the film. (Stotsky, 2013, par. 5).

Once again it is the "sovereign" that determines whose reality should be incorporated into the political body and whose should not, attempting to erase and invisibilize Palestinian reality. Those with sovereign power defend their acts of violence as "an accident," because ultimately the sovereign holds the power to decide and justify who can live and who cannot, whether its murder or an accident becomes irrelevant.

The second criticism of *5 Broken Cameras* was that because Emad collaborated on the project with an Israeli film-maker (Guy Dividi) to produce the final product, he in effect violated the call for cultural boycott. It is important to recognize the various politics individuals may have on video production/dissemination. Some Palestinians will produce footage and share it with Israeli individuals and organizations regardless of their politics, while others will be very specific, ensuring that they only share their footage with anti-Zionist individuals or organizations (such as B'Tselem or Guy Dividi). Others will refuse to work with any Israeli organization, seeing this collaboration as a way of normalizing the occupation, and will strictly follow the guidelines of the cultural boycott outlined by the Palestinian Academic and Cultural Boycott of Israel (PACBI). The politics of refusal, particularly when pertaining to cultural production, can become a bit messy as people choose what they want to do with their cultural artifacts, and how they want to disseminate their material if they choose to do so.

Despite these challenges and accusations, a people's journalism enables Palestinians in the West Bank to re-configure the space of law (the exception), by challenging the sovereign's accusations, allegations and justifications to kill, through narratives of resistance using reel imagery. The cultural practice of filming and video making becomes a powerful practice, perhaps even a necessity, for the colonized to re-insert and claim their existence against the sovereign's power, in turn re-configuring Palestinians' right to life, from the death worlds, which is symbolic work. Thus enacting an anti-colonial participatory politics that is, as I will argue in the next section, simultaneously pedagogical.

People's Journalism as Public Pedagogy

By engaging with videos produced by the colonized – a people's journalism - an opening may develop for the colonizers to humanize themselves in the process, which is one of the outcomes of symbolic work. This is illustrated when Guy Dividi, the co-director of *5 Broken Cameras,* showed the video to a group of Israeli youth in Tel Aviv in an alternative education space (*5 Broken Cameras* Screened to Israeli Youth, 2012). Upon seeing the film, the Israeli youth had a conversation and expressed shame, disappointment, surprise at what they were seeing, and concern for what to do next, now that they had seen the film and learned about what happens on the "other side." The conversation begins with a boy who says, "I wasn't aware of these things, so this exposure to what is going on there as told through the man's personal story, it gave me the chills, I didn't know what to do, I don't have the words for that." Relating to a scene in which Israeli soldiers arrest children, another boy responds and raises questions:

> We are their age, and if we were living in Bil'in [the soldiers] would knock on our doors at night to tell us we threw stones. So why? Just because I was born a few miles over the other side?

Following his comment, a girl responds with anger, saying:

> the strongest feeling I had during the film was anger towards the soldiers [...] when I saw the soldiers behave like that, it just felt so terrible [...] I really want to show this film at my school [...] because it changes the way we think in one hour.

Her views open up a conversation about the censorship that takes place in Israeli schools. One girl says, "By not showing us anything like it, [the government and ministry of education] take a clear political stand. When they censor films like this one, but other things, they let in," such as films shown in schools by the military. Responding to the issue of censorship, another girl says, "If those [Palestinian] kids are able to see it and cope with it head on, I don't think there's any reason for why a [Israeli] kid our age cannot confront this film."

Showing this film to Israeli youth is important because these youth will be drafted to military service in the future. The responses elicited after watching *5 Broken Cameras* from Israeli youth underscore the way in which meanings —what it means to be Palestinian, Israeli, a solider — are questioned, re-made, re-thought and re-configured. Symbolic work occurs through cultural production as new meanings, knowledge and perspectives are generated about "the enemy," the Israeli government, the education system and the occupation among Israeli society (in particular by the youth). Willis (1990) suggests that symbolic work and creativity place identities in larger wholes. "Identities do not stand alone above history, beyond history. They are related in time, place and things" (p. 209). The symbolic work that occurs through the practice of filming and video making enables Palestinian youth to connect their individual stories of violence to the collective story of Palestine,[18] while Israeli youth and others in Israeli society are challenged to think about their collective identities as Israelis, settlers and colonizers, through their engagement with the videos. When videos such as the one produced by the sixteen-year-old girl in Hebron cause public debate to take place within Israeli society, symbolic work is once again pedagogical. Though these videos might not be able to change law, policy or the political situation in the immediate moment, the symbolic work of communicating new meanings about violence, Palestine, Israel, settler colonialism, the occupation etc., has the possibility of influencing public opinion inside Israel, which is an enactment of public pedagogy. Additionally, at a documentary film festival in New York in 2012, world renowned filmmaker Michael Moore said, "if a copy of the film [*5 Broken Cameras*] was sent to every home in the United States [. . .] within 24 hours, public opinion on this issue would change dramatically" (Michael Moore Introduces 5 Broken Cameras, 2012).

The internet has also been an important platform that has allowed circulation of videos to surpass state borders, enabling dissemination of information globally through the virtual world. Communication via video and film allows the global community to see what Israel is doing to Palestinians inside the Occupied Territories. As more awareness is raised about the ongoing Palestinian tragedy, new alliances are forged between Palestinians and people from the global community. One way in which solidarity with Palestine has been extended is in the form of activist visits to the West Bank. Many international allies from across the world go to the West Bank to partake in protests in solidarity with Palestinians.[19] Though such solidarities are not new, within the past decade more and more activists are going to Bil'in, Nabi Saleh and Hebron to partake in protests (often through collectives such as the International Solidarity Movement). The presence of international allies is at times problematic for several reasons which is beyond the scope of this article, but are eloquently outlined by Gada Mahrouse (2007) and Linda Tabar (Forthcoming), whose critiques should be considered very seriously by international allies who do solidarity work with Palestinians.

Nevertheless, an international presence allows stories about the occupation and colonial violence to circulate across borders, which also has the potential of influencing public opinion globally. Moreover, as more awareness about Israeli settler colonialism and violence is raised, new solidarities are being forged in support of the Palestinian call for boycotts, divestments and sanctions (BDS). Increasingly, intellectuals, cultural workers, students, unions, churches and consumers are joining the global BDS campaign. Shooting back with reel imagery further allows movement building across spatial enclosures and borders. Through cultural practices such as filming, video production and dissemination in their everyday lives, Palestinians are able to partake in an anti-colonial participatory politics of refusal that allows them to re-configure place, space, law, knowledge and violence, while forging new solidarities. Thus a people's journalism in Palestine is effective and necessary. As the Palestinian writer and academic Ghada Karmi poignantly says in an interview,

> Years of writing about this, this whole terrible situation, the Israeli occupation, the theft of Palestinian land, and the way they build these settlements illegally, years, never brought home the message about how awful this was, as well and as successfully as films like [5 Broken Cameras]. This is the way, really, to do it! (5 Broken Cameras PressTV interview, 2012).

Notes

1. The wall is 8 meters high, with electric fences, trenches, surveillance cameras, sensors, military patrols and watchtowers attached to it.
2. Notwithstanding their illegality, 125 Israeli settlements have been established from 1967 until now, with an estimated settler population of approximately 531,000 in the West Bank, of which routinely harass and physically assault Palestinians (B'Tselem Land Appropriation and Settlements, 2014). The wall cuts through most of the West Bank, and has detrimental effects for Palestinians, as families are divided from one another, children from their schools, and farmers from their agricultural lands, which is the primary sector of the Palestinian economy. As well, the construction of the wall has imposed new restrictions on movements limiting access to schools, hospitals, and jobs. This wall is deemed illegal under the July 2004 Advisory Opinion of the International Court of Justice (ICJ).
3. Since July 2014, the IOF have punished Palestinians in East Jerusalem for reacting to the lynching of Abu Khdeir "waging the largest arrest campaign since the second intifada" (Khalek, 2014).
4. The First Palestinian Intifada was a Palestinian uprising against the Israeli Occupation of the oPt, which lasted from 1987 -1993.
5. A Roman concept, *homo sacer* (sacred man) is he who may be killed but not sacrificed.
6. The Palestinian National Authority (PA) is an interim self-government body that "governs" Areas A and B of the West Bank (as of Oslo Accords in 1993).
7. Order No. 101 was commonly used during the first intifada, its use declined after the beginning of the Oslo process. In early 2010, the army once again expanded use of the order, warranting a re-examination of the order and its significance (Btselem - http://www.btselem.org/demonstrations).
8. To see the full details of the order see Naama Baumgarten-Sharon, 2010, p.8
9. Some Palestinians living in East Jerusalem and the Golan Heights have been offered Israeli citizenship. Many refuse, as they don't recognize Israel's claim to sovereignty over them. Instead they are permanent residents.
10. The Al-Aqsa Mosque is considered the third holiest site in Islam located in the Old City of Jerusalem. The mosque sits alongside the Dome of the Rock. In 2000 when Ariel Sharon (the former Prime Minister of Israel) made a trip to the Temple Mount surrounded by hundreds of riot police, Palestinians viewed this gesture as a provocation and the Second (Al-Aqsa) Intifada broke out.
11. The Second Intifada was the second Palestinian uprising against Israeli occupation. It began in September 2000 -2005 and was a period of intensified violence between both Israelis and Palestinians.
12. The al-Aqsa Martyrs Brigades have gone against their official party line by engaging in revolutionary violence, demonstrating their refusal of the killing of Palestinians in the oPt. On July 24th at the mass demonstration at Qalandia checkpoint, after demonstrators were shot at by the IOF, the al-Aqsa Brigades opened fire at the IOF and a prolonged gun fire ensured (Wiles, 2014).

13. "Actions committed by Palestinians are liable to lead to ten years of imprisonment and a fine, where the same actions if committed by Israelis would not be considered as offenses" (Naama Baumgarten-Sharon, 2010, p. 8).
14. Barbwire is put all around the house, particularly around windows, to protect Palestinian homes from settler attacks. It feels like Palestinians in areas like Hebron live in a cage (Field notes, 2013).
15. Abdo (2014) explains that sexual terms like sharmouta or manuouka (whore) or qahba (prostitute or whore) in Arabic are tabooed and "normatively women should refrain from using them in public. [. . .] Such slurs are frequently used by Israeli interrogators against female political detainees" (Abdo, 2014, p. 10).
16. Ehud Olmert said after seeing the video, "he felt ashamed" (Shooting Back Interview, 2007).
17. Hebron is home to 140 000 Palestinians. The city has been divided into two parts, H1 and H2 areas. The H2 area is inhabited by 30 000 Palestinians and 500 Israeli settlers. See map of Hebron's divisions. http://www.ochaopt.org/documents/ocha_opt_the_closure_map_2011_12_21_hebron_old_city.pdf
18. Though differences of class, gender, religion and identity status create different conditions for each Palestinian, the identity as a colonized people, without self determination, is a collective identity and form of collective resistance that is shown through each of the videos – whether the video is one minute or ninety minutes.
19. As a result, the Israeli authorities continue to make it harder and harder for people to enter Israel. Those suspected to be travelling to the West Bank for solidarity activities will almost always be denied entry.

References

5 Broken Cameras. (2012). *Press TV interview with Ghada Karmi*. Retrieved from https://www.you tube.com/watch?v=_qIpO3EDo2Y

Abdo, N. (2011). *Women in Israel: Race, gender and citizenship*. New York: Zed Books.

Abdo, N. (2014). *Captive revolution: Palestinian women's anti-colonial struggle within the Israeli prison system*. London: Pluto Press.

Abdo, N. & Lentin, R. (2002). *Women and the politics of military confrontation: Palestinian and Israeli gendered narratives of dislocation*. New York: Berghahn Books.

Agamben, G. (2005). *State of exception*. Chicago: University of Chicago Press.

Banko, L. (2012). *Citizenship and the new 'State of Palestine'*. Retrieved from http://www.jadaliyya.com/pages/index/8736/citizenship-and-the-new-%E2%80%9Cstate-of-palestine%E2%80%9D-.

Baumgarten-Sharon, N. (2010). *The right to demonstrate in the occupied territories. Position paper, July 2010*. B'Tselem Publication.

B'Tselem Camera project (background). Retrieved from http://www.btselem.org/video/cdp_background.

B'Tselem.: Land expropriation and settlements fact sheet (2011). Retrieved from http://www.btse lem.org/settlements.

B'Tselem: Military law. (2013). Retrieved from http://www.btselem.org/demonstrations/military_law.

B'Tselem. (2013). *Report on crowd control: Israel's use of crowd control weapons in the West Bank*. Retrieved from http://www.btselem.org/settlements.

B'Tselem: Shooting back the Israeli human rights group B'Tselem gives Palestinians video cameras to document life under occupation. Retrieved from http://www.democracynow.org/2007/12/26/shooting_back_the_israeli_human_rights.

Burnat, E. & Davidi, G. (2011). *5 broken cameras*. Kino Lorber.

Davis, U. (2003). *Apartheid Israel: Possibilities for the struggle within*. New York: London Books. Democracy Now Interview. (2007).

Desai, C. (in press). Trackin' the Arab uprisings: battlin' the imperial production of death in the post 9/11 world through Arab hip hop. In A. Ibrahim, N. Ng-A-Fook, & R. Giuliano (Eds.) *Provoking curriculum studies: Strong poetry and the arts of the possible* (pp. 15). Abingdon: Routledge.

End the occupation fact sheet on apartheid policies. Retrieved from http://www.endtheoccupation. org/downloads/AAF%20Fact%20Sheet%20.pdf.

Fanon, F. (1961/2007). *The wretched of the earth*. New York: Grove Press.

Fanon, F. (1967). *Black skin, white masks*. New York: Grove Press.

Freire, P. (1973/2000). *Pedagogy of the oppressed*. New York: Continuum.

Giroux, H. A. (2004). Cultural studies, public pedagogy, and the responsibility of intellectuals. *Communication and Critical/Cultural Studies, 1*, 59–79.

Gramsci, A. (1971). *Selections from the prison notebooks*. New York, NY: International.

Hall, S. (1997). Introduction. In S. Hall (Ed.), *Representation: Cultural representations and signifying practices* (p. 1–12). London: Sage Publications.

Hanafi, S. (2009). Spacio-cide: colonial politics, invisibility and rezoning in Palestinian territory. *Contemporary Arab Affairs, 2*, 106–121.

*Israeli settler violence in the West Bank. (*2011). United National Office for the Coordination of Humanitarian Affairs Occupied Palestinian Territory. Retrieved from http://www. ochaopt.org/documents/ocha_opt_settler_violence_FactSheet_October_2011_english.pdf?utm_ source=Mondoweiss±List&utm_campaign=c46ac6052c-RSS_EMAIL_CAMPAIGN&utm_ medium=email.

Jhally, S. & Ratzkoff, B. (2004). *Peace, propaganda and the promise land*. Media Education Foundation.

Kahne, J., Middaugh, E. & Allen, D. (2014). *Youth new media, and the rise of participatory politics*. YPP Research Network working paper #1, March 2014. Retrieved from http://ypp.dmlcentral. net/sites/default/files/publications/YPP_WorkinPapers_Paper01.pdf

Kahne, J., Middaugh, E. & Allen, D. (in press). Youth new media, and the rise of participatory politics, youth new media and citizenship. In D. Allen & J. Light (Eds.), *Youth new media and citizenship*. Cambridge: MIT Press.

Khalek, R. (2014). *Palestinians struggling survival in Jerusalem. Electronic intifada*. Retrieved from http://electronicintifada.net/blogs/rania-khalek/palestinians-struggling-survival-jerusalem

Lefebvre, H. (1974/1991). *The production of space*. (D. Nicholson Smith, Trans.). Cambridge: Blackwell.

Lentin, R. (2010). Re-thinking Israel-Palestine: Racial state, state of exception. Retrieved from http:// www.ronitlentin.net/2010/12/01/re-thinking-israel-palestine-racial-state-state-of-exception/.

Mahrouse, G. (2007). *Deploying white-western privilege in accompaniment, observer, and human shield transnational solidarity activism: A critical race, feminist analysis*. (Unpublished doctoral thesis). University of Toronto, Canada.

Maira, S. (2013). *Jil Oslo: Palestinian hip hop, youth culture, and the youth movement*. Washington D.C.: Tadween Publishing.

Masalha, N. (2012). *The Palestine nakba : decolonising history, narrating the subaltern, reclaiming memory*. New York: Zed Books.

Mbeme, A. (2003). Necropolitics. *Public culture, 15*, 11–40.

Murphy, M. (2014). *As Israel bombs Gaza, it kills Palestinians in the West Bank too*. Electronic Intifada. Retrieved from http://electronicintifada.net/blogs/maureen-clare-murphy/israel-bombs-gaza-it-kills-palestinians-west-bank-too

Norman, J. (2009). *The Activist and the olive tree: Nonviolent resistance in the second intifada*. (Unpublished doctoral dissertation). American University, Washington, D.C.

Palestinian national plan: Youth cross-cutting strategy. (2011). Retrieved from http://planipolis. iiep.unesco.org/upload/Youth/Palestine/Palestine_Youth_cross_cutting_strategy.pdf.

Pappé, I. (2006). *The ethnic cleansing of Palestine*. Oxford: OneWorld Publishing.

Radsch, C. (2013). *The revolutions will be blogged: Cyberactivism and the 4th Estate in Egypt*. (Unpublished doctoral disseration). American University, Washington, D.C.

Razack, S. (2008). *Casting out the eviction of Muslims from western law and politics*. Toronto: University of Toronto Press.

Report: Israel has detained 3,000 Palestinian children since 2010. (2014). *Middle East Monitor*. Retrieved from https://www.middleeastmonitor.com/news/middle-east/12500-report-israel-detains-3000-palestinian-children-annually

Saïd, E. (1979). *Orientalism*. New York: Vintage Books.

Sandlin, J., Malley, M., & Burdick, J. (2011). Mapping the complexity of public pedagogy scholarship: 1894-2010. *Review of Educational Research, 81*, 338–375.

Shalhoub-Kevorkian, N. (2009). *Militarization and violence against women in conflict zones in the Middle East*. New York: Cambridge University Press.

Sharmuta Video: Settler harassment of Palestinians in Hebron. B'Tselem. Retrieved from http://www.youtube.com/watch?v=KUXSFsJV084

Shresthova, S. (2013). *Between storytelling and surveillance: American Muslim youth negotiate culture, politics and participation*. Retrieved from http://ypp.dmlcentral.net/sites/default/files/publications/Shresthova-Between%20Storytelling%20and%20Surveillance-Working%20Paper%20Report-Sept11-2013.pdf

Simpson, A. (2014). *Mohawk interruptus: Political life across the borders of settler states*. Durham: Duke University Press.

Sliman, N. (2004). *World court's ruling on the wall speaks with utmost clarity, MERIP*. Retrieved from www.merip.org/mero/mero072704.html

Stotsky, S. (2013). Review: 5 Broken Cameras. Retrieved from http://www.camera.org/index.asp?x_context=2&x_outlet=35&x_article=2583.

Taber, L. (in press). From third world internationalism to "the internationals": The domestication of solidarity with Palestine.

The apartheid wall fact sheet: Stop the wall. Retrieved from http://www.stopthewall.org/downloads/pdf/2010wallfactsheet.pdf.

The status of Palestinian youth, Sharek youth study. (2009). Sharek Youth Forum. Retrieved from http://www.youthpolicy.org/national/Palestine_2009_Youth_Study.pdf.

Wiles, R. (2014). Uncovering the roots of Palestinian resistance #GazaUnderAttack. *Middle East Eye*. Retrieved from http://www.middleeasteye.net/essays/uncovering-roots-palestinian-resistance-264145062

Willis, P. (1990). *Common culture: Symbolic work at play in the everyday cultures of the young*. Buckingham: Open University Press.

Youth against the settlements information video. Retrieved from http://www.youtube.com/watch?v=o0nD8opcgIE.

7 Glyphing decolonial love through urban flash mobbing and *Walking with our Sisters*

Karyn Recollet

> This article contributes to understanding multi-plexed Indigenous resistance through examining spatial tags. As symbolic, moving critiques, spatial tagging intervenes normative structures of settler colonialism and provides the space through which radical decolonial love can emerge. This discussion of the production of spatial glyphs has implications for new ways of thinking about the processes of solidarity building, social activism and the generation of new pedagogical practices of resistance. An analysis of Christi Belcourt's walking with our sisters commemorative art installation (2013–2019) and the urban flash mob round dance at the intersection of Yonge and Dundas streets in downtown Toronto, reveals how spatial tagging formulates Indigenous acts of creative solidarity. This article contributes to an analysis of Indigenous resistance strategies through focusing on the interstitial passageways as generative sites of knowledge production and possibilities for new ways of being in the world.

This article contributes a spatial analysis of two distinct forms of spatial tagging, the Idle No More[1] urban flash mob round dance and *Walking with our Sisters* (Belcourt, 2013-2019) commemorative art installation. The approach in this analysis is multi-faceted and explores new geographies of resistance through forms of *petroglyphing* urban landscapes. This discussion of the production of spatial glyphs has implications for new ways of thinking about the processes of solidarity building, social activism, and the generation of new pedagogical practices of resistance. I examine spatial tags created through embodied pathways of Indigenous motion as Indigenous artists (singers and dancers), dancing with non-Indigenous settler allies, produce urban flash mob round dances. I also demonstrate how strategically positioned vamps (the tongues of moccasins) and emergent pathways within the commemorative ceremony *Walking with our Sisters,* illuminate complex Indigeneities where tagging produces glyphs as new geographies of resistance. Spatial tags carry on a legacy of glyph production as a key practice shaping Indigenous resistance, and thereby formulate the central focus of this article, which aims to recontextualize our understandings of Indigenous resistance in Canada.

To that end, in this article I situate the practices of spatial tagging within a larger framework of Indigenous resistance preceding the #Idle No More[2] and #MMIWG2P (missing and murdered Indigenous women, girls and 2 spirited) solidarity movements. Since the arrival of European settlers, Indigenous peoples have been engaged in embodied acts of defiance, producing intervening sovereign acts to challenge encroachments of non-Indigenous development and resource extractions on contested Indigenous territories within the Canadian nation-state. I propose that these embodied Indigenous acts assume the form of the spatial tag, thus contributing to a long-standing glyph-making strategy of resistance. I suggest that the current manifestation of spatial tagging and glyph making are extensions of past glyphs mobilizing Indigenous resistance towards settler-colonialist accumulation of capital through resource extraction on Indigenous land. The larger network of contemporary public acts of Indigenous resistance in Canada precipitating these manifestations of spatially glyphing Indigenous resistance include: the Temagami First Nation blockades of 1988 and 1989 in Ontario to challenge clear cut logging in their traditional territories; the Lubicon Cree struggle against oil and gas development in their traditional territories; and the 1990 defense of the Mohawk territories of Kanehsatake/Oka from settler colonial interests.[3] This 1990 Kanien'kehaka resistance was a major event informing Idle No More public acts in response to the colonial state.

In examining the mechanics of the spatial glyph, I describe the interstitial passageway as an important focal point for understanding the effects of spatial glyphing in shaping patterns of Indigenous resistance and Indigenous futurity. This article also illustrates how a radical pedagogy of decolonial love lies within the details of both the urban flash mob round dance, and in the commemorative act of *Walking with our Sisters*. I share that it is in the interstice, that space of in-betweeness, where practices of solidarity and significant pedagogies of resistance, such as the notion of radical decolonial love can emerge. Radical decolonial love is spatial and generative, made manifest in the glyph-making strategies of "creative solidarity" (Gaztambide-Fernández, 2010). As a relationship building strategy, this form of Indigenous love critiques the conditions of coloniality in the very act of love making (inclusive and beyond acts of sex) - as through living Audre Lorde's (1984) articulation of an erotic life. It produces a self-reflexive space, challenging the conception of love as a space of permanence, or as a strategy of containment. I offer this analysis of spatial tags to convey their nature as complex manifestations of radical decolonial love in working with and through this rupture and impermanence.

Exploring Multi-plexed Geographies of Indigenous Resistance through the Spatial Tag

Amongst the key concepts mobilized within this article are the relationships between spatial tagging and urban glyphing as they produce new geographies of resistance. The notion spatial tagging describes the function of visual and aural symbols actuated within Indigenous hip-hop culture and round dance revolutions. As a practice, spatial tagging is in relationship to the old school practice of petroglyphing, a long-standing act of inscribing Indigenous collective memory on rock surfaces by knowledge holders and artists. In Cree/Métis visual artist, singer/songwriter Cheryl L'Hirondelle's view, tagging is a manifestation of petroglyphing, connecting us to ancient Indigenous travel across the land. As she describes, "the notion of tagging is so old school that it's ancient when one recalls the repeating petroglyphs and pictographs that make their own trail across the land" (L'Hirondelle, cited in Ritter & Willard, 2012, p. 86).

Traditionally achieved through the strategic application of *waabigan* (clay) on rock surfaces, petroglyphing functioned in the following ways: to record a critical occurrence, relationship or alliance; as signifiers describing a futurism; images demarcating a battle; and a modality through which to demarcate a sighting, or home space for sacred beings (I. Murdoch, personal communication, 2013).

Glyphing practices share a history of producing geographies of resistance, achieved through making visible an active Indigenous presence and futurity in otherwise contested

Indigenous territories. I utilize the concept of urban glyphing to accentuate the doing, and the intrinsic Indigenous motion entailed in producing symbols and narratives as forms of cultural production that are inherently political. I perceive how the collective and communal motion expressed within the dance form of the flash mob round dance produces significant spatial glyphs on urban concrete.[4] I acknowledge the relationship between petroglyphing and tagging, as both ascribe to surface an active presence of complex Indigeneities (Vizenor, 1999). At the same time, when actuated in urban spaces, both practices formulate modalities of consciousness dissemination through the creation of Indigenous hub spaces. Indigenous hub spaces, such as the urban flash mob round dances, evoke spatial tags in a consciousness building exercise resulting in the creation of new spatial geographies of resistance.

Hip-hop visual and aural (sonic) culture provides an important framework through which to analyze the significance of flash mob round dances. For example, tagging could be interpreted as a manifestation of an Indigenous futurity through offering what graffiti scholar Anderson (2012) conceptualizes as counter-spaces. In discussing graffiti, Anderson remarks, "resisting this oppressive socio-spatial arrangement, graffiti in turn operates through space. This resistance, this creation of counter-spaces, gives graffiti its true artistic and emotional force" (p. 6). As such, when expressed as flash mobs or commemorative art installations, spatial tagging produces counter-spaces to resist oppressive socio-spatial arrangements of space. One of the outcomes of graffiti's spatial presence is to lift the conceptual ghetto and the identities of its inhabitants from their invisibility, reaffirming the existence of the silenced ghetto residents by making their voices physical and concrete on the urban landscape. The act of visibility carries the potential to transform the street into a visionary space where new futurisms for Indigenous peoples might be possible.

Within hip-hop culture, tags are the displays of a chosen moniker for an artists' graffiti identity and the space from which they come. A form of recognition throughout the city, tags reflect "a possibility for the sons and daughters of adults whose names were rarely mentioned outside the block where they lived" to have visibility (Austin, cited in Anderson, 2012, p.8). According to Anderson, "graffiti conceptually remaps urban spaces through a physical inscription of identity on the very landscape designed to pen in inner-city residents" (p. 8). As such, spatial tagging provides a freedom of motion within hyper-regulated urban spaces where marginalization and segregation are used as containment strategies.

Hip-hop scholar Tricia Rose (1994) explains that graffiti offers "aggressive public displays of counter-presence and voice" (p. 59). Hence tagging accommodates the creation of a counter space where a collective consciousness stemming from unexpected, hidden, furtive Indigenous youth presence, can be visually and sonically experienced. Tagging "inscribes one's identity on an environment that seemed Teflon resistant to its young people of color; an environment that made legitimate avenues for material and social participation inaccessible" (Rose, cited in Anderson, 2012, p. 8). Urban flash mob round dances as tags (with symbolic and narrative functions) not only visibilize, but also intervene in public spaces by creating their own opportunities for material and social participation in contemplating radical difference and as such, can assist in decolonization projects.

An Indigenous act of solidarity, the spatial tag involves collective practices of inscribing embodied motion and creativity in visual, and in some instances, aural form. In the form of a flash mob round dance, tags actuate Indigeneity as a critical site of intervention to address systematic colonizing practices of the nation-state, such as community-rooted practices protesting the over 1000 missing and murdered Indigenous women in Canada.[5] Spatial tag formation involves the creation process as a vehicle to inform an anti-colonial, moving critique of social injustices. For instance, as spatial glyphs of resistance, flash mob round dances have been mobilized as a form of participatory politics to challenge the disappearances of Indigenous women within Canada. These flash mob round dances have been an integral piece of the #MMIW (Missing and Murdered Indigenous women) social media campaign, which has actuated the use of spatial tags as a means of resisting systems and practices constitutive of gender violence.

The concept of spatial tag describes specifically-rooted Indigenous forms of creative solidarity in the sense that it generates fluxual/transformational symbols and narratives of resistance that can be intensely collaborative and communal (Gaztambide-Fernández, 2010). Creative solidarity can be described as an attempt to challenge the inherited coloniality of solidarity discourse as social practice through the production of spatial/symbolic arrangements that mobilize a radical turn towards relationality, difference, and interdependence. As modalities of creative solidarity, the spatial glyph's impermanence and fluidity produce symbolic socio-spatial rearrangements of material and social conditions of oppression. Within the context of the round dance, for instance, as new drummers are drawn to the inner circle and the bodies that pass by enter the round dance, the circuitous, rhizomatic nature of the round dance produces fluid Indigenous acts that transform and challenge boundaries, expressing "solidarity without guarantees" (Gaztambide-Fernández, 2010, p. 90). The spatial tag facilitates the exploration of tensions, contradictions, and the critical examination of how difference is both recognized and negotiated as mobilizing factors in the creation of solidarities. Multiple solidarities are expressed through this process, emergent within the interstices — those spaces between the beats and dancers.[6]

Gaztambide- Fernández (2010) describes creative solidarity as solidarity in constant flux of invention and reinvention. The mobilization of Indigenous spatial tags through the form of the flash mob round dance and *Walking with our Sisters* commemorative art installation embed dis-assemblages and reformations across vast spatial geographies. *Walking with our Sisters* is a touring installation that manifests unique symbologies and forms dependent upon the knowledge holder's vision in each traditional territory it enters. In Thunder Bay (September- October 2014), for instance, the vamps and pathways were assembled to manifest a turtle lodge.

This notion of creative solidarity lends itself to the conversation involving Indigenous futurities, in that it is a persistently dissatisfied form of solidarity, "one that is always imagining things differently, maybe even a bit better" (Gaztambide-Fernández, 2010, p. 90). This notion of creative solidarity allows for us to view glyphing as a modality through which to accentuate difference, including the complexities and tensions, as well as the new spaces of possibilities that this form of resistance provides. Spatial tags of Indigenous resistance are in relationship with a conceptualization of solidarity that "hinges on radical differences and that insist on relationships of incommensurable interdependency" (Gaztambide- Fernández, 2012, p. 46). Contextualized as urban glyphs, tags of Indigenous solidarities on urban spaces are visually archiving traces of actions engaged in the very process of transformation. This is time sensitive, in that they are archiving moments, and happenings of decolonial strategic solidarities. In such instances, the glyph *is* the Indigenous pedagogy.

Considering the shape and form of the flash mob round dance, in relationship to its interstitial/intersectional environment, the concept of multi-plexual describes Indigenous spatial tags in acts of creative solidarity building. Applied to the visual form of the round dance, the notion of multi-plexed informs a key element of the spatial geography of Indigenous resistance. Multi-plexed geographies are actuated through the very form of the flash mob round dance as they create interstitial passageways within urban landscapes and temporarily reshape the main corridors of diasporic movement. Spatial tags visually symbolize the complexities of what it means to be rooted/uprooted in an urban space within a greater Indigenous diasporic community. Spatial tags are quite important as forms of resistance to the erasure of Indigenous presence and territorial sovereignty within urban contact zones such as downtown Toronto, which houses a collective history of Indigenous occupation that has been effaced from the public memory.[7] Multi-plexed Indigenous tagging challenges the multiple layers of occupation and representational practices that produce Toronto as a site of capital accumulation, rather than as an Indigenous territorial homeland and sovereign space.

The concept of multi-plexed describes complex articulations of Indigeneities and represents the contours of Indigenous resistance embodied in spatial tags. Hip-hop artist Daybi-No-Doubt mobilizes the concept of multi-plexed to describe the layered, syncopated nature of the universe. Daybi's song "The Deep End" (First Contact, 2010) references this moment of recognition, "my multi-plexed universe gets very real," he tells us. According to No-Doubt, its categorical use references multiple staging areas for different works, as in a multi-plexed theatre (D. No-Doubt, personal communication, 2014).

Multi-plexed describes the diverse interactions and experiences of the social world (s) in which we live. This positioning informs and produces complex symbologies and spatial formations that help us understand the significance of the urban flash mob round dance. These multiple frequencies are metaphorical threads of diverse experiences of doing Indian identity in the now. When applied to the identity politics of present articulations of Indigeneity, the concept multi-plexed can be mobilized as an intervention, and an "opportunity to finally put the question of essentialism behind us" (Lyons, 2010, p. 59).

The creation of the interstitial passageway is another characteristic of Indigenous resistance through spatial tagging that is articulated through the forms taken on by the round dance and *Walking with our Sisters*. I first encountered this notion in the writings of Homi Bhabha (1994), and through Cheryl L'Hirondelle's (2012) mobilization of the concept to describe the fabric of complex Indigeneities. L'Hirondelle (2012) states, "I inhabit this thin, dotted interstice where colonial and Indigenous overlap as authentically as I can using the language that helps shape and guide my understandings of who I am and where I come from" (cited in Ritter & Willard, 2012, p. 86). As an active space in-between, Bhabha's (1994) conceptual use of interstitial passage between fixed categories can be understood in relationship to a more multi-plexed viewing of Indigeneities. Through accentuating a process of "wedging in" (Deiter-McArthur, 1987), and engaging the interstitial passageways (Bhabha, 1994), multi-plexed geographies of resistance inform fluid, creative solidarities, which focus on the possibilities of different kinds of futurities.

As a central component of the spatial tag, the interstitial passageway illustrates the rupturous nature of in-between spaces, where notions of belonging and home are renegotiated and challenged, and where articulations of various forms of difference come to the forefront. In describing the interstitial spaces of Indigeneity, Martineau and Ritskes (2014) identify the "fugitive spaces of Indigeneity" that are located in the "critical ruptures where normative, colonial categories and binaries break down and are broken open" (p. iii). As I will attempt to illustrate later in this article, practices like the urban flash mob round dance can be viewed as an interstitial articulation of solidarity emerging from converging sites of difference that are generative in their capacity for social transformation.

Having contextualized the spatial tag within a broader framework of Indigenous resistance and highlighted its essential characteristics, in the next two sections I discuss how spatial tags are being mobilized through Indigenous resistance strategies by artists and community activists, beginning with a discussion of Christi Belcourt's *Walking with our Sisters* and then discussing the particular instance of an urban flash mob round dance at the intersection of Toronto's Yonge and Dundas.

Walking with our Sisters Commemorative Art Installation and the Production of Spatial Glyphs

Walking with our Sisters (2014) is a commemorative act of resistance, resurgence, and love comprised of over 1,700 pairs of moccasin vamps, each representing one missing or murdered Indigenous woman. Award winning Métis visual artist and author Christi Belcourt is the lead coordinator for this commemorative exhibit, which has toured thirty-two locations across North America continuing through to the year 2019. The vamps are arranged in a winding path formation on red fabric, and viewers remove their shoes to walk the path alongside the vamps.

Walking with our Sisters can be viewed as a form of spatial tagging, imprinting Indigenous women and girls and the impacts of gendered, racialized violence into dominant consciousness. Amongst the important interventions of violence is the creation of a vocabulary to engage, visibilize, and build connections through our grief and collective resistance (Hunt, 2014). The *Walking with our Sisters* commemorative art installation embodies these elements by spatially mapping the unfinished lives of Indigenous women and girls. It creates a vocabulary of movement and form through which to engage in collective solidarity building by calling on our participation to actuate this walking glyph of resistance. Each vamp enacts a radical pedagogy of love through the very creative process of working with and through rupture, "as the artists created these works, many prayed and put their love into their stitching. Some shared stories of what their work means or who they made their work for" (Walkingwithoursisters.ca).

Spatial tags within the *Walking with our Sisters* commemorative exhibit enact complex representations of home, territoriality, and identity where functional and aesthetic choices in color, symbology, design, and textile actuate geographies of resistance. In some instances, they challenge normative white settler colonial depictions of Indigenous lives through visibilizing racialized, gendered violence within their material forms.[8]

The exhibit's pathway and the forms that the vamps collectively create manifest a spatial tag embodying a lodge. The focus on the pathway calls us to engage the active presence of a collective honoring through the embodiment of ceremony. This active presence gives the spatial tag its relevancy and meaning as a device for Indigenous self-determination, through a decolonial aesthetic whereby elders as ceremonialists and curators determine the form and protocol of the commemorative piece. The September, 2014 *Walking with our Sisters* commemorative art installation in Thunderbay, Ontario, has been described as a sacred bundle that was accompanied by community events such as a community bead and read, teach-ins unpacking settler colonialism, and art and decolonization, self-defense classes and other acts of resistance. Through such attention to physicality, *Walking with our Sisters* actuates a moving glyph focusing on the embodied sovereignty of Indigenous women. This particular glyphing practice actuates embodiment as an intervention, a means of disrupting the marking of Indigenous women's bodies through various forms of violent actions.

Amongst an array of meaningful interventions, artistic contributions create spatial tags to visually map and delineate specific sites as cartographies of violence. *Walking with our Sisters* includes graffiti tagged vamps and vamps that map out the stroll and other sites of colonial, racialized, and gendered violence. For example, one pair of vamps created by artist Miranda Huron utilizes ribbon and beadwork to materially reproduce a road and the sign that hangs over the Balmoral Hotel in East Vancouver, a racialized/ spatial geography marked by dispossession, neglect, and violence against Indigenous women (Razack, 2002). The artist describes her intentions that "more and more women find their way home from such beacons" (Huron, 2014 cited in walkingwithoursisters.ca). Functioning as a signifier, the Balmoral hotel signage physically maps out a stroll as a racialized geography of gender violence. Actuating an urban pathway, the stroll physicalizes the interstitial spaces where settler colonialism, heteropatriarchy, racism, sexism and Indigeneity come into contestation to produce cartographies of violence. Consequently, the intersection has been mobilized within Indigenous solidarity glyphing forms such as the urban round dance, as argued in the next section.

Creating a spatial tag, artist Erin Konsmo's birch bark vamps map out the Eastside of Vancouver in juxtaposition with a mountainous British Columbian landscape. Again, the images of streets and pathways are used to represent the city, one such street formulated out of a white line leading down the curve of a street light, with a possible reference to red light districts as strategies of urban containment, ghettoization, and trafficking, shaping the complex lives and realities of many Indigenous women and girls.[9] Further these images elevate the conversation to focus on the structures, systems, and their role in producing marginalization and poverty that make Indigenous women victims of colonial, gendered, and racialized violence.

The commemorative vamps in *Walking with our Sisters* are manifestations of complex Indigeneities and the spaces they inhabit. Many of the works represent floral designs reflecting fluidity and a generative capacity for resiliency and motion as ways to map Indigenous futurity. The urban glyph created through *Walking with our Sisters* uses embodiment in the process of envisioning a world(s) transformed and looks forward as a way to recall our past. Resembling lodges, the formation of the vamps (as spatial tags) symbolically and literally, transform the landscape of gendered, racialized violence against women through making visible unfinished lives. Evoking processes of reclamation, *Walking with our Sisters* and the urban flash mob round dance illustrate various forms of spatial tagging to mark contested spaces. Embodying new ways of theorizing political protest and struggle, the glyph as a new geography of resistance, creates a vocabulary to speak new worlds into being − lending itself to the creation of Indigenous futurisms.

Urban Flash Mob Round Dances as Geographies of Resistance

As a Cree adoptee, I returned to my community in 1993, during which time my birth mother brought me to a series of round dances as a way to get to know each other through dance and enjoy the company of a collective Cree community. Since I had experienced cultural and symbolic displacement as a Cree adoptee, it was important that I engage in a practice embodying a round dance to find connection to place and to access collective memory. I perceive the embodiment of a round dance as a spatial tag of resistance and am intrigued by the affect it produces in spaces I now choose to call home, such as Toronto, and other parts of southern Ontario. The round dance has been conceptualized as

136 CULTURAL PRODUCTION AND PARTICIPATORY POLITICS

Piciciwin, the moving slowly, or crooked legged dance[10]; *pīhci-cihcīyī,* which translates to "reach your hands in," to describe the process of "people reaching into the circle to grab onto life and blessings"[11]; and *wasakamesimowin* to describe the round dance ceremony (Deiter- McArthur, 1987).

Plains Cree scholar Patricia Deiter-McArthur (1987), describes the round dance as originating with Stoney people. Hosted by different societies, round dances were held in times of sickness, but today are hosted by families and communities in celebration for graduations, anniversaries, and marriages. As well, they take shape as memorials for deceased loved ones and for fundraising initiatives for families and communities. There was certainly a ceremonial element to the round dances that I attended with my mother as we participated in protocols that I sensed spanned generations. Hand drummers formulate the center of the concentric circles, singing songs whose rhythmic structure follows a double beat and four push-ups led by a lead singer. The dancers shape concentric circles, holding hands, and dance in a shuffle-step movement accentuated by the down beat.

According to Deiter-McArthur (1987), the round dance included a practice of relationship or alliance building expressed as *kiskipocikek* (which translates into the English verb, to "wedge in"), an idiom, which means to dance with a woman who is not a relative or a cross-cousin. This would have taken the shape of one who enters the space between two dancers holding hands with the purpose of relationship building. In this way, engaging the interstice through "wedging in" has a history in the structure of the round dance, representing the interstitial passageway, which, I would argue, increases the range of possibilities for an Indigenous futurity. *Kiskipocikek* can be viewed as an important process within alliance and relationship building as it encompasses one of the foundational elements of spatial tagging expressing a form of Indigenous resistance.

Within the context of decolonization, *kiskipocikek* — to "wedge in" and to fill a between space — can be perceived as a form of syncopation produced as an act of love. This is manifest in the reverb that is produced between the drum-beats (the hand drummers act of using their finger to produce a vibration on the hides of the hand drum). Shaping the aural kinesthetic of the space (Kai Johnson, 2009), circuitous motion enacts a radical pedagogy of love through the singing of love songs, which effectively embed between spaces for the wedging in of dancers, thoughts, reconceptualizations, and renegotiations of space. Being an Indigenous adoptee, my own pathway has been informed through this wedging in movement, as I was raised within a family not inherently my own. Indigenous round dances that produce spatial tags are symbologies of Indigenous motion. As such, they become tremendously meaningful as filling rupturous spaces with love.

The power of the round dance can be mobilized in the context of public protest. For instance, the Idle No More round dance situated at the intersection of Yonge and Dundas streets in downtown Toronto expresses a symbolic dissidence towards colonial capital and accumulation. The urban flash mob round dance at Yonge and Dundas challenged settler colonialisms claim over Mississauga and Huron-Wendat territorial jurisdiction. Along with marches taking place on main highways and streets in downtown cores to protest violence against Indigenous women and girls, the Idle No More urban round dance flash mob on the intersection of Yonge St. and Dundas St. in downtown Toronto was one of many locales for strategic actions of solidarity.

Within the context of the Idle No More Movement, the round dance has been mobilized as one way of symbolically *tagging* the contours of Indigenous acts of resistance

Figure 1. Idle No More round dance at Yonge and Dundas in Toronto.
(Photo courtesy of Hayden King).

and displaying solidarity between Indigenous nations and the colonial nation-state. Dene scholar Glen Coulthard (2012) differentiates Idle No More from other forms of political protest, such as the Kanien'kehaka resistance of 1990 and Temagami blockades, citing the absence of widespread economic disruption by Indigenous direct action during the movement.[12] Yet, according to Coulthard, Idle No More has provoked clashes between Indigenous activism and non-Indigenous settler colonialism that have fostered Indigenous acts of resistance strategically enacted in the "thoroughfares of colonial capital" (2012). These include blockades on several major Canadian transportation corridors, including highways and railways, where spatial tags function as Indigenous acts that formulate a resistance specifically engaged in efforts to challenge and "un-settle settler-colonialisms sovereign claim over Indigenous peoples and our lands" (Coulthard, 2012). The urban flash mob round dance intervenes colonial capital by symbolically tagging communal collective action on main thoroughfares that are symbolic of globalization.

Urban flash mob round dances are central to the activities that are part of Idle No More, which include teach-ins, marches, rallies, blockades, and other forms of strategic protest. The flash mob round dance, mobilized in urban malls, intersections, and other public spaces, is shaped by the aural kinesthetic of the dance form (Kai Johnson, 2009). This means that the sonic production and physicality exercised through the dance creates the affect of the spatial tag of resistance. The urban flash mob round dance encompasses a public gathering in which dancers and singers perform and embody an *in the moment* Indigenous act. This act evades permanency and will be followed by dispersal.

Interventionist-pictographing or urban glyph-making is achieved through the creation of spatial tags, which imprint urban thoughts through circuitous song and motion. As acts of multi-plexed Indigenous resistance, their spatial formations are layered modalities capable of reconfiguring power. Spatial tagging becomes an expression of defiant Indigeneity through which artists "perform a configuration of Indigeneity that constantly deconstructs, resists, and recodifies itself against and through state logics" (Teves, 2011, p.77). The urban flash mob round dance can also be viewed as a socially/culturally constructed space with potential alliance building capacity for settler peoples, and provides opportunities for settlers to reflect upon their own difference and the privileges afforded to them within society. Yet, this raises the question: can we deconstruct whiteness at the same time as we enact, perform, and embody the dance form?

I return to hip-hop culture to illuminate the form of resistance that this particular form of spatial tagging takes on. In expressing hip-hop's principles for social change, Tricia Rose (1994) articulates that social change is actuated within hip-hop culture through the building of sustaining narratives, layering these narratives through repetition and the embellishment of these stories. We can apply these same layers to the spatial mechanics of the urban flash mob round dance: with hand drum singers formulating the inner most cypher/circle; layered with double beat drum soundscape; syncopated with the reverb interstice (created through a technique hand drummers use to aurally accentuate the interstice, or space between the beats); layered with hand embraces, love songs, and a stride-and-shuffle to the left. This formula within the Indigenous dance is an important element for creating a geography of resistance. The form of the round dance highlights layers through generatively expressing the interstices in acts of reclamation of urban Indigenous space. The layering and syncopation achieved via the concentric circularity of the round dance carries the potential to unmark bodies of difference and instead, to inscribe multi-plexed Indigeneities as a product of the reverb interstice created through the drum. As ethical spaces these interstitial spaces formulate a reconfiguration and dislocation of power (Ermine, 2007).

The urban flash mob round dance offers a geography of resistance that maps out the intersectional nature of the social discourses and practices within a heteropatriarchal system that reproduces and normalizes racialized and gendered violence. The urban flash mob round dance does this through its concentric circularity, layering, and creation of interstitial spaces. Critique and analysis are embedded within the very form of the urban flash mob round dance. Basically, the structure provides the *spaces between* within which self-reflective anti-colonial critique can manifest.[13] The round dance actuates a consciousness that is always in flux, representing an important pedagogical moment of self-reflexivity and temporal repositioning wherein the past is in the future. Pausing to reflect, challenges us to consider how the past is being negotiated and constructed, while also asking: whose past?; and how are we implicated in the past? These questions are essential to thinking through the spatial mechanics of the round dance as a tag.

The intersections and interstices house the conditions for the most profound solidarity acts that carry transformative potential. It is important to be attentive to the multi-layered strata of such conditions. A spatial positioning in various interstices of difference requires a constant self-reflexivity that carries the potential of problematizing ones own location as part of the cypher. In a process of conscientization (Freire, 1970/2005) through one's embodied action within the dance, one is also engaged in a "paradoxical continuity of self mapping, and transforming" (Mohanty, 2003, p. 122). Consequently, resistance is generated within an interstitial space located at the convergence point of various articulations of difference. A *beyond-the-border* consciousness begins to formulate through the embodiment of the urban flash mob round dance (embedded in the concentric circularity of the dance form), whereby we may be flung into the now as a result of a temporal and spatial shift. Through this act of solidarity exists the possibility that we may exceed the boundaries of our encased Indian identities and be propelled into the beyond as a new generation of "post-Indian" protestors (Vizenor, 1994).

CULTURAL PRODUCTION AND PARTICIPATORY POLITICS 139

Reading the spatial tag as an act of creative solidarity allows for a freedom of motion whereby resistance itself evades being located completely in one space, and at one time, thus challenging overly simplistic categories and conditions of resistance. Interpreting the urban flash mob round dance as a spatial tag reflecting the in-flux nature of a creative solidarity reminds us of the possibilities for new ways of being in the world and provides opportunities for us to reflect upon our differences within an impermanent spatial geography. The round dance eventually distills as participants continue to walk the urban space, or move to another intersection to manifest another spatial glyph. *I reflect upon the conditions that we are apt to change ... this moment is apt to change, and we can reconfigure the spaces between these differences as we honor them through the dance.*

The urban flash mob round dance is characterized as shifting and temporal in enacting its own refusal to be white-washed, and painted over by municipal authorities and state law enforcement anti-graffiti campaigns. The tag articulates a difference that is constantly changing, forcing us to reconsider who is our community. What does community look like in the urban Indigenous diaspora, in downtown Toronto? We can witness the in-flux nature of creative solidarity in spatial tagging itself as this particular form of tagging is literally taking circuitous, ever-changing form in the intersecting lines of the Yonge and Dundas urban space. The spatial tag as an act of creative solidarity is dissatisfied, in the sense that it is constantly changing and challenging form, causing us to reflect upon the compulsion for sameness in shaping solidarity (Gaztambide-Fernández, 2010, 2012).

It might be important to consider how the symbology of the spatial tag can be appropriated to drive certain interests that undermine Idle No More's scope and direction, thereby limiting the possibility of solidarity. Flash mobbing a round dance also generates potential for settler peoples to reflect upon their own constructions and assumptions of Indigeneity. Consequently, some of the tensions might lay in the possibility that these same constructions become reproduced through this act of solidarity. Creative solidarity honours the generative capacity of difference (Gaztambide-Fernández, 2010).[14] As Gaztambide-Fernández (2012) describes, "most relevant to projects of decolonization, yet more rare and complicated to theorize, is a conception of solidarity that hinges on radical differences, and that insists on relationships of incommensurable interdependency" (p. 46). As a practice of creative solidarity, the urban flash mob round dance, can be mobilized to generate critique and evoke critical participation in a movement that looks for transformation within the interstices of those differences. What processes do we employ in our resistance struggles to bravely build upon differences? Tensions may arise through uncritically claiming perceived common experiences as the main driving force determining the nature of the solidarity. However, it is important to also acknowledge the political power derivative from such solidarities built upon common experiences.

Urban flash mob round dances, as manifestations of creative solidarity are attempts to shift socio-spatial symbolic arrangements of inequality. However, symbolically positioned in a nexus of colonial power and capitalistic accumulation, the Yonge and Dundas round dance reveals that spatial tags are actuated as "extensions and manifestations of larger social, economic, political, as well as cultural arrangements" (Gaztambide-Fernández, 2012, p. 57). In these instances, the mobilization of *Kiskipocikek* produces a generative transitional space. For instance, Pile (1997) describes the interstice as an important site invoked through the round dance in creating geographies of resistance. He notes, "material effects of power are everywhere ... but wherever we look power is open to gaps, tears, inconsistencies, ambivalences, possibilities for inversion, mimicry parody, and so on; open that is to more than one geography of resistance" (p. 27). As a practice related to cultural production, mimicry can also create tensions that need to be explored in order to negotiate, and locate, Indigenous resistance.

Potential pitfalls of this form of spatial tagging include the appropriation of Indigenous ceremony, as well as undesirable claims to authenticity in an over-determining practice of cultural fundamentalism. Creating new socio-spatial possibilities, creative solidarity insists upon a more complex and accurate conception of culture that challenges multiculturalism's desire to contain cultural difference, and reinscribe colonial essentialisms. For instance, as Gaztambide-Fernández (2012) explains, creative solidarity embraces multi-plexed approaches to culture and identity "countering the versions of 'culture' and 'identity' that are imposed by the colonial project of modernity" (p. 57). In mobilizing this form of spatial tagging, we run the risk of impeding our solidarity through reproducing narrowly essentialist Indigenous identities. Can we create alternative articulations of Indigenous protest that challenge such expectations?

Round dance revolutions may be perceived as a process of enacting a collectively inspired radical pedagogy of love onto urban spaces through embodied motion. This embodied motion offers a critique of the conditions of coloniality, while simultaneously challenging the colonial practice of using love as a strategy of containment and permanence. However, we should be mindful of potential tensions evoked through a form of cultural revitalization that "encourages Aboriginal people to seek out and *perform* [my emphasis] cultural authenticity as a compensation for exploitation and oppression" (St. Denis, 2007, p. 1080). Within the context of the Idle No More round dance revolution it becomes important to acknowledge the counter-narratives that perceive its practice as an appropriative act that challenges traditional protocol. For example, Cree hand drum singer Marc Longjohn, of Sturgeon Lake First Nation, Saskatchewan shares the view that round dances have their own set of teachings and protocols that activists may not be honoring. As Longjohn suggests, "some are opposed to Indians using hand drums and round dance music for this purpose." He further states, "the round dance is a ceremony with specific purposes. They never had Idle No More flash mob round dances twenty years ago" (M. Longjohn, personal communication, 2014).

Although flash mob round dances function to include non−Indigenous peoples into the concept of relationality, Sherman cautions that it could have unintended consequences if people do not consider the cultural and spiritual implications of displacing its purpose and context (P. Sherman, personal communication, 2014). These shared perspectives illustrate tensions involved in the practice of evoking ceremony as a form of political protest.[15] How, for instance, does performativity function in relationship to urban flash mob round dances; and what are some of the implications of evoking ceremony in spatially tagging resistance?

Perhaps what is being made visible is an alliance in solidarity with multi-plexed Indigeneities including broader, more complex recognitions of Indigenous peoplehood. This visibility can also be problematized in a spatial reading of urban flash mob round dances, when we consider what is and who are made visible through this process; how, for instance, are drums, skirts, and dancing being interpreted within a broader context?; is this form of protest an appropriation of an Indigenous cultural aesthetic?; and how does this particular form of visual/aurally compelling Indigenous protest aesthetic function as a tag, inscribing identity, and as a form of recognition throughout the city? Perhaps it is important to consider the implication of the shifting temporal and spatial nature of the tag as a practice of Indigenous/settler solidarity. The very texture of the tag as a creation of Indigenous motion propels our reading of the flash mob as a forging in multiple directions evading permanency and therefore intervening authenticity discourses.

CULTURAL PRODUCTION AND PARTICIPATORY POLITICS 141

Spatially Tagging Radical Decolonial Love

You are the breath over the ice on the lake. You are the one the grandmothers sing to through the rapids. You are the saved seeds of allies. You are the space between embraces … you are rebellion, resistance, re-imagination (Simpson, 2013, p. 21).

As multi-plexual sites of Indigenous creative resistance, spatial tags like the urban flash mob and the *Walking with our Sisters* commemorative installation contribute a critical praxis, which can be implemented in urban Indigenous life to achieve social justice. In this concluding section, I would like to illuminate some observances or practices that might shape urban protocols for spatial tagging. Reflecting the notion of creative solidarity, these observances inform practices that would need to be interpreted as fluid, impermanent, and apt to change (Gaztambide-Fernández, 2010; 2012). These practices emerge from within the creases of the spatial tags themselves and reflect strategies useful to relationship building.

The first strategy is to *create the space for multi-plexed Indigeneities within the vocabularies that we use to frame and build solidarity.* The visual and sonic interpellative pathways produced in *Walking with our Sisters*, and the Yonge and Dundas round dance provide symbolic textual metaphors for a multi-plexed/intersectional reading of resistance and create the interstitial passageways to mobilize difference as a decolonial strategy. Shaping cartographies of resistance, spatial tags mobilize difference as a way to be creative about the immense possibilities for the future. The enactment of spatial tags allows us to critique whiteness as a construction that continues to affect our spatial relationships within a settler colonial condition.

Another practice stemming from an analysis of spatially tagging Indigenous resistance, is to *enact a radical pedagogy of decolonial love within the context of the everyday in order to assure a freedom of motion; to imbue the streets with love, and enact this as a radical form of everyday protest.* Tahltan artist Peter Morin posited the question, "where do you carry your sacredness when you have been exiled?" (Indigenous Acts: Arts and Activism Gathering, Vancouver, B.C., 2014). In this sense, radical decolonial love requires a shift from conceiving of love as a holding space of permanence, or a vehicle of containment; towards an embrace of it's molten lava-like properties, as it flows within and through our bodies to connect with others. The glyph can be useful as a way to kiss the urban space, imprinting a form of radical decolonial love that presents itself in all of its flaws, inconsistencies, imperfections, ruptures, and pauses. [16] This is a form of love that is unfinished and indeterminate, attributes that resonate with creative solidarity. In its surfaces and surges it finds strength and solitude within its own impermanence. The spatial tag's impermanent nature strengthens an Indigenous futurity through radically asserting that our past is in our future.

To extend the conversation, I would also suggest that we *circle as we would cypher-it's all about flow; and to acknowledge rupture in our solidarity building. We can work with, and through rupture to create Indigenous futurisms.* Glyphing Indigenous solidarity relies on the formation of intimate relationships with rupture and impermanence. These two conditions inform Indigenous motion necessary for radical decolonial love and are mobilized through acts of *kiskipocikek* (wedging in), or rupturous movement. Like hip-hop, the creation of spatial glyphs accommodates rupture in its very aural/sonic form. In short, this kind of creative solidarity relies on rupture as a generative practice. The urban spatial tag propels decolonial love where it is possible to "love one's broken-by-the colo-niality of power self through holding the hand and walking with another broken-by-the-coloniality-of-power person" (Diaz, cited in Simpson, 2013, p. 7). Working within and through the ruptures, the new spatial geographies produced through the urban flash mob round dance and *Walking with our Sisters* offer alternative world(s) through the act of infusing pathways, intersections and other spaces with this very specific form of love. Spatial tagging uses wedging in a generative capacity to shift, unsettle and generate new futurisms for Indigenous peoples. Both *Walking with our Sisters* and the urban flash mob round dance invite our own body narrative as part of the solidarity creation. As Leanne Simpson writes in the above spoken word poem, *you are the space between embraces*, you become that space between the honoring of the missing and murdered women as you are invited to walk with our sisters; you are the one that mobilizes the interstices of solidarity through wedging in at a round dance.

Finally, the practice of spatial tagging reminds us to *pay attention to Indigenous futurisms embedded in the vocabularies and the praxis of our next generation of visionaries.* Youth engagement in Indigenous participatory politics has been a crucial thread of the Idle No More movement, where youth develop a critical consciousness through the creation of new media and the use of technology to mobilize. Flash mobbing is typically organized via social media. Idle No More has impacted settler-colonial consciousness and "now encompasses a broad range of conversations calling for recognition of treaty rights, revitalization of Indigenous cultures, and an end to legislation imposed without meaningful consultation" (Kinew, 2014, p. 96). The mobilization required for interventionist forms of urban pictoglyphing are contingent upon social media and youth organizing. As a consequence of the movement, youth are producing Indigenous new media hub spaces to actuate reclamation and generate complex reassertions of urban territoriality. We need to pay attention to these youth visionaries as they spatially map their own forms of resistance with vibrancy, brilliance, and much love. They are the next generation of glyph makers.

As this article makes explicit, the concepts of spatial tagging and urban glyphing describe the generative production of Indigenous solidarity through forms and practices such as *Walking with our Sisters* and the urban flash mob round dance. Evoked through the spatial tag, creative solidarity challenges the influence of multiculturalism's narrowly defined Indigeneity, and offer up geographies of resistance which manifest in relationship with traditional caretakers of the land -within distinctive Indigenous urban spaces. This form of spatial tagging posits an extension of Belcourt's ethical practice of changing the form of the *Walking with our Sisters* commemorative pathway to reflect local Indigenous pedagogy in the now; it situates this process as an urban protocol. This mobilization would be inclusive of Indigenous urban identified youth and grassroots organizations such as the Native Youth Sexual Health Network,[17] and Indigenous hip-hop collectivities with whom to ascertain the appropriate abstraction through which to codify Indigenous protest rooted within a particular spatial geography.

This form of creative solidarity offers new possibilities for Indigenous resistance, and the creation of spatial tags through shifting the focus away from the performance of cultural appropriation. In stating this, effective solidarity building disrupts comfortable notions of Indigeneity and Indigenous protest while maintaining a radical pedagogy of decolonial love through acknowledging multi-plexed Indigeneities stemming from rich and complex interstitial urban Indigenous pathways.

Notes

1. Founded in December 2012, Idle No More has been a sustained, coordinated, strategic national-now global movement originally led by Sheelah McLean, Jessica Gordon, and Slyvia

CULTURAL PRODUCTION AND PARTICIPATORY POLITICS 143

McAdam in Saskatoon, Saskatchewan. Idle No More began as a voice to oppose Bill C-45, omnibus legislation, which would significantly impact water and land rights under the Canadian Indian Act.

2. The hash tag formulates an Indigenized digital spatial glyph, and informs a significant mobilizing force within contemporary Indigenous solidarity movements. Within the Idle No More movement, the hashtag has been an integral component of what has been described as a #RoundDanceRevolution. According to spoken word artist, performer, and radio producer Jamaias DaCosta, "Social media networks, prove that Indigenous resistance and resurgence is alive and well, and continues to flourish and express itself in dynamic ways, most of which can be followed via a hashtag revolution" (#HASHTAG #REVOLUTION, Muskrat Magazine, March 14, 2014).

3. The Kanien'kehaka resistance involving a 78-day armed standoff between the Mohawk nation of Kanesatake Quebec, the Quebec provincial police (SQ) and the Canadian armed forces near the town of Oka, Quebec. This standoff, informing the shape and form of Indigenous resistance, was an effort to defend Indigenous sacred lands from resource development on land that the Mohawk nation had been struggling to have recognized for almost 300 years. The land, known as the pines, was slated for the expansion of a golf course. This act was part of a decade of Indigenous resistance leading to the federally sanctioned Royal Commission on Aboriginal People (RCAP), which produced 440 recommendations calling for a renewed relationship based on the core principles of "mutual recognition, mutual respect, sharing and mutual responsibility." RCAP was the most expensive public inquiry in the nation's history intended to pacify the decade of Indigenous protest. For brief descriptions of these Indigenous acts of resistance, and a how they fit within a contextual history of IdleNoMore please see Glen Coulthard's (2012) #IdleNoMore in Historical Context (http://decolonization.wordpress.com/2012/12/24/idlenomore-in-historical-context/).

4. I would like to extend this conversation through future research to include the context of visual tagging through graffiti and mural creation on urban street spaces as part of this larger decolonization project of spatially tagging Indigenous resistance.

5. A 2014 R.C.M.P (Royal Canadian Mounted Police) report on missing and murdered Aboriginal women in Canada reported that 1,181 Indigenous women and girls have gone missing over the past 30 years.

6. Participants of urban flash mob round dances represent a variety of perspectives and interests that may include those embracing an Indigenous feminist, and/or environmental justice, reproductive justice ethic, non-governmental organizations and those who oppose legislation threatening resources and livelihoods, as well as community allies and people of color advocating for social justice for Indigenous peoples.

7. Previous to the 1793 British occupation at York (which was to become the city of Toronto in 1847), for instance, the Mississauga (Anishinaabek/ Ojibway) of the New Credit River, and the Wendat Haudenosaunee nations had territorial jurisdiction within the area. The Toronto Purchase expropriated approximately 250,880 acres of land from the Mississauga's in 1805.

8. Herein, I utilize the term white settler in its function as it "evokes a nexus of racial and colonial power" (Morgenson, 2014; see also Razack, 2002).

9. We need a careful consideration of the historical context of colonization and the tensions in settler –Indigenous relations that contribute to practices of state-sanctioned racialized and gendered violences. Additionally, please see Hunt and Kaye's (2014, Sept. 24) discussion of the misunderstood stigmatisms towards sex work that are cast in the broad category of trafficking.

10. Description provided by Cree storyteller, musician, language speaker Joseph Naytowhow (Sturgeon Lake First Nation, Saskatchewan).

11. Translation provided by Cree musician, language speaker Jason Chamakese (Chitek Lake First Nation, Saskatchewan) in conversation with a knowledge holder from Ocean Man First Nation, Saskatchewan.

12. Coulthard (2012) strategically claims, "if history has shown us anything, it is this: if you want those in power to respond swiftly to Indigenous peoples' political efforts, start by placing Native bodies (with a few logs and tires thrown in for good measure) between settlers and their money, which in colonial contexts is generated by the ongoing theft and exploitation of our land and resource base. If this is true, then the long term efficacy of the #IdleNoMore movement would appear to hinge on its protest actions being distributed more evenly between the

144 CULTURAL PRODUCTION AND PARTICIPATORY POLITICS

malls and front lawns of legislatures on the one hand, and the logging roads, thoroughfares, and railways that control to the accumulation of colonial capitol on the other."

13. Anzaldúa (1987/2012) conceptualization of the borderlands is quite meaningful to this exploration of the temporality of the space between the break beats.

14. A focus on similarities rather than difference could stifle an otherwise emergent critique of the conditions of oppression. Is it possible that some of these problematic positionings of Indigeneity get reaffirmed as settler peoples bask in the glow- and peer through the hand drums to connect with other settlers-holding hands in circuitous motions, as if, in solidarity.

15. In preparation for the Yonge & Dundas urban flash mob round dance Anishinaabe artist, activist, and curator Wanda Nanabush, and Cree/Métis coordinator for Idle No More Toronto Charm Logan sought permission to host round dances within Idle No More demonstrations. In consultation, Cree elders supported the dance as a public performance, given that it was not intended to be ceremonial. Outside of it's ceremonial context, this urban flash mob round dance was understood as a public performance of political unity, maintaining its meanings of unity and mourning towards missing and murdered Indigenous women (W. Nanabush & C. Logan, personal communication, 2014).

16. New spatial geographies created out of radical decolonial love are also expressed through the aural/visual/narrative glyph manifest in Leanne Simpson's Islands of decolonial love (2013).

17. The Native Youth Sexual Health Network (NYSHN) is an organization by and for Indigenous youth that works across issues of sexual and reproductive health, rights and justice throughout Canada and the United States.

References

Anderson, C.L. (2012). Going 'all city' : The spatial politics of graffiti. *Graduate Journal of Visual and Material Culture, 5*, 1–23.

Anzaldúa, G. (1987/2012). *Borderlands/ La frontera: The new mestiza* (4th ed.). San Francisco, CA.: Aunt Lute Books.

Bhabha, H. (1994). *The location of culture*. New York: Routledge.

Carter, J. (2008). Chocolate woman visions an organic dramaturgy: Blocking-notation for the Indigenous soul. *Canadian Women Studies, 26*, 169.

Coulthard, G. (2012). #IdleNoMore in historical context. *Decolonization: Indigeneity, Education & Society* (Dec. 24, 2012). Retrieved from: http://decolonization.wordpress.com/2012/12/24/idle nomore-in-historical-context/

Daybi No Doubt. (2010). The deep end. *First Contact*. Bombay Records.

Deiter-McArthur, P., Cuthand, S. & Federation of Saskatchewan Indian Nations. (1987). In S. Cuthand (Ed.), *Dances of the northern plains*. Saskatchewan Indian Cultural Centre.

Ermine, W. (2007). Ethical space of engagement. *Indigenous Law Journal, 6*, 192–203.

Friere, P. (1970/2005). *Pedagogy of the oppressed*. New York: Continuum.

Gaztambide-Fernández, R. (2010). Toward creative solidarity in the "next" moment of curriculum work. In E. Malewski, (Ed.), *Curriculum studies handbook—Next moments* (pp.78–100). New York: Routledge.

Gaztambide-Fernández, R. (2012). Decolonization and the pedagogy of solidarity. *Decolonization: Indigeneity, Education & Society, 1*, 41–67.

Haraway, D. (1988). Situated knowledges: the science question in feminism and the privilege of partial perspective. *Feminist Studies, 14*, 575–599.

Her Majesty the Queen in Right of Canada as Represented by the Royal Canadian Mounted Police (2014). *Missing and murdered Aboriginal women: A national operational overview*. Retrieved from http://www.rcmp-grc.gc.ca/pubs/mmaw-faapd-eng.pdf

Hunt, S., & Kaye, J. (2014). *Human trafficking research reveals Canada's role in violence against Aboriginal women.* Retrieved from http://rabble.ca/news/2014/09/human-trafficking-research-reveals-canadas-role-violence-against-aboriginal-women

Huron, M. (2014). *Artist description.* Retrieved from http://walkingwithoursisters.ca/art/miranda-huron/

Kai Johnson, I. (2009). *Dark matter in b-boying cyphers: Race and global connection in hip hop.* (Unpublished doctoral dissertation).

Kinew, W. (2014). Idle no more is not just an 'Indian thing.' In Kino-nda-miimi collective (Eds.), *The winter we danced: Voices from the past, the future, and the Idle no more movement* (pp.95–98). Winnipeg, MB: Arp Books.

L'Hirondelle, C. (2012). Cheryl L'Hirondelle. Ritter, K., & Willard, T., (Co-curators). *Beat nation: Art, hip hop and Aboriginal culture,* 86. Vancouver: B.C.: Vancouver art gallery and grunt gallery.

Lorde, A. (1984) Uses of the erotic: The erotic as power. In A. Lorde (Ed.), *Sister outsider: Essays and speeches* (pp. 53–59). Trumansburg, N.Y: Crossing Press.

Lyons, S.R. (2010). *X-marks: Native signatures of assent.* Minneapolis: University of Minnesota Press.

Martineau, J. & Ritskes, E. (2014). Fugitive indigeneity: Reclaiming the terrain of decolonial struggle through Indigenous art. *Decolonization: Indigeneity, Education, & Society, 3,* i–xii.

McLean, S. (2014). Idle no more: Re-storying Canada. In Kino-nda-niimi collective (Ed.), *The winter we danced: Voices from the past, the future, and the Idle no more movement* (pp.92–95). Winnipeg, MB: Arp Books.

Mohanty, C.T. (2003). *Feminism without borders: Decolonizing theory, practicing solidarity.* Durham & London: Duke University Press.

Morgensen, S. (2014). White settlers and Indigenous solidarity: Confronting white supremacy, answering decolonial alliances. *Decolonization: Indigeneity, Education and Society.*

Pile, S. (1997). Introduction: Opposition, political identities and spaces of resistance. In S. Pile & M. Keith (Eds.), *Geographies of resistance* (1–32) London & New York: Routledge.

Razack, S. (Ed.). (2002). *Race, space and the law: Unmapping a white settler society.* Toronto: Between the lines.

Rose, T. (1994). *Black noise: Rap music and black culture in contemporary America.* Hanover: Wesleyan University Press.

Simpson, L. (2013). *Islands of decolonial love.* Winnipeg, MB: Arp Books.

St. Denis, V. (2007). Aboriginal education and anti-racist education: Building alliances across cultural and racial identity. *Canadian Journal of Education, 30,* 1068–1092.

Teves, S.N. (2011). 'Bloodline is all I need': Defiant Indigeneity and Hawaiian hip-hop. *American Indian Culture and Research Journal, 35,* 77.

Vizenor, G. (1999). *Manifest manners: Narratives on postindian survivance.* Lincoln, NE.: University of Nebraska Press.

Walking with our sisters (2014). *A commemorative art installation for the missing and murdered Indigenous women of Canada and the United States.* Retrieved from http://www.walkingwithoursisters.ca

Index

5 Broken Cameras (Burnat, Emad) 110, 121–3; internet distribution of 124; Israeli youth, and film viewings by 123–4; Moore, Michael, introduction by (2012) 124

Abu Rahmeh, Baseem 109, 110
aestheSis theory 101
affinity networks and 'spaces': and building shared practice 19–20; and youth political engagement 14–15, 17
Agamben, Giorgio 113
America: arts education, and standards of 76; black men, and police brutality against 1
Anderson, C. L. 131
Anyon, Jean 8
arts education: aesthetic education and art appreciation 75; civic goals of 74; and critical media literacy 79; and cultural citizenship 69, 70–71, 73–6; definition of 71; Discipline Based Arts Education (DBAE) movement 76

Beach, King 14
Belcourt, Christi 134; *Walking with our Sisters* 6, 129, 132, 133, 134–5
Biesta, Gert 64
blogging 33–4
Brown, Ashleigh 80–81, 84
Brown, Michael 1, 2
B'Tselem, 110; *Shooting Back* 118–20
Burnat, Emad 110; *5 Broken Cameras* 110, 121–3

Cambre, Caroline 102–3
Canada: Idle No More movement 1, 2, 6, 129, 136–8, *137*, 142; Indigenous resistance strategies 129–34; Indigenous women, murder and disappearance of, 1, 131–2; Kanien'kehaka resistance (1990) 130, 143n3; Lubicon Cree protest 130; Temagami First Nation Blockades (Ontario, 1988 & 1989) 130; *Walking with our Sisters* (Belcourt, Christi) 6, 129, 132, 133, 134–5
Center for Investigative Reporting (California) 18–19
Chávez, Hugo 96

citizen journalism: *5 Broken Cameras* (Burnat, Emad) 110, 121–3; B'Tselem, and *Shooting Back* camera project 110, 118–20; concept of 115; in participatory politics 110, 115, 118–19; and public pedagogy, 123–5
Comaroff J. & J. 99
'connected civics' 4, 8, *15*, 25–6: building shared practice 19–23; causes supported by, and reasons for 22; and consequential connections 26; and 'participatory culture civics' 17; youth political engagement 10–11, 13–14, 15–16
Connected Learning Research Network (CLRN) 16
Cooper, Ashley 83, 86
Coulthard, Glen 137, 143n12
cultural citizenship: active participation in 72–3, 76; and arts education 5, 69, 70–71, 73–6; civic engagement and education 69–70; and critical solidarity 83; cultural exclusion and expression 72; cultural organizing, and social change 77; cultural 'rights' and efficacy 72, 81–2; definition of 71, 72; informed cultural citizenship 75–6; justice-oriented cultural citizenship 76–8, 79, 83–4; marginalization and diversity 81–3; personal responsibility and individual actions, impact on 84–5; power in the cultural domain 79–81; Project HIP-HOP 69, 77–8; social movements, in arts and culture 85; types of 74–5
Curriculum Inquiry (journal) 8

Daybi-No-Doubt 133
DeGeorge, Paul 24
Deiter-McArthur, Patricia 136
Desai, Chandni 2
Developing Relief and Education for Alien Minors Act (DREAM) 17; 'coming out' narratives, and sharing of 22–3; DREAM activists, campaigns of and motivation for 22; DREAMactivist.org, and activities of 23–4; 'illegal immigrant crossing' road sign, artwork relating to 19; T-shirt designs in support of 19

INDEX

Discipline Based Arts Education (DBAE) movement 76
Dividi, Guy 122, 123
Dolby, N. 73
Dong Bang Sin Gi 22

Electra, Dorian 19
Electrical Industry and Irrigation Workers Union (Puerto Rico) 58

Fanon, Frantz 116
Fortuño, Luis 52, 55

Galston, W.A. 69–70
Gamber-Thompson, Liana 19
gaming communities: 'collab channels,' and activity of vloggers 21–2; Little Big Planet 20; Star-Craft II 20, *21*
Garner, Eric 1, 2
Gee, Jim 14
Giroux, H. A. 117
glyph production practices (Canada) 129–34; Indigenous resistance strategies 130–34; petroglyphing and pictographs, and history of 130–31; as a radical pedagogy of decolonial love 141
graffiti and spatial tagging practices (Canada) 129–34; #Idle No More 129; #MMIWG2P 129; as creative solidarity 132, 139–40; as Indigenous pedagogy 132; Indigenous resistance strategies 130–34; as a radical pedagogy of decolonial love 141–2; tag formation 132; visual nature of 131, 133; *Walking with our Sisters* (Belcourt, Christi), and examples of 135
Gray, Bridget 80
Green, John and Hank: Harry Potter Alliance (HPA), and fundraising collaborations with 20–21; Nerdfighters 17
Grosfoguel, Ramon 104
Guadeloupe, Ana 52

Harlow, Barbara 117
Harper, Stephen 1
Harry Potter Alliance (HPA) 16–17; Body Bind Horcrux campaign 20; campaigns of 18, 20, 24; Green, John and Hank, and fundraising collaborations with 20–21; Helping Haiti Heal campaign 20; HPA chapters 24; Imagine Better Project 18; Nerdfighters, and fundraising collaborations with 21, 24; study of 18; 'Superman was an Immigrant' campaign 18; Wrock the Vote Campaign 24
Here Comes Everybody (Shirky, Clay) 23
Hull House (Chicago) 76
Huron, Miranda 135

hybrid content worlds: affinity networks, and social media connections 17–18; and narrative connections 17–19

Idle No More movement (Canada) 1, 2, 6, 129, *137*; impact of and reaction to 136–8, 142; preparations for 144n15
Indigenous resistance strategies (Canada) 129; glyph production 129–34; graffiti and spatial tagging practices 129–34; hip-hop culture, and graffiti related to 131, 138; Idle No More movement 1, 2, 6, 129, 136–8, *137*, 142; Indigenous hub spaces 131; Kanien'kehaka resistance (1990) 130, 143n3; Lubicon Cree protest 130; petroglyphing and pictographs, and history of 130; Temagami First Nation Blockades (Ontario, 1988 & 1989) 130; urban flash mob round dances 131–3; *Walking with our Sisters* (Belcourt, Christi) 6, 129, 132, 133, 134–5
Israel: Al-Aqsa mosque (East Jerusalem) 115–16; anti-colonial movements and political protest 2, 5, 109; formation of 111; incarceration of Palestinian political prisoners 112; Olso Accords (1993) 111; state violence, and evidence for in Palestine 2, 111–12, 115–17

Jenkins, Henry 16, 18

Karmi, Ghada 125
Kligler-Vilenchik N., 14; collab channels, activity of vloggers and study of 21–2; Harry Potter Alliance (HPA), study of 17, 18; Nerdfighters, study of 17, 18
Konsmo, Erin 135
Korea, 'Candlelight Protests' 22

Lander, Edgardo 96
Lefebvre, Henry 113
Levinson, M. 69
libertarian youth movement 19
Little Big Planet gaming community 20
Longjohn, Marc 140
Lugo, Israel 57

MacArthur Foundation 11; connecting learning: in-school/out-of-school relationships, and research into 16
Maduro, Nicolas 97
Miller, T. 71
Mohawk Interruptus (Simpson, Audra) 114
Moore, Michael 124
Morin, Peter 141
My Letter to Hip-Hop (Gray, Bridget) 80

Nerdfighters 17; Foundation to Decrease World Suck, and activities of 24; Harry

148 INDEX

Potter Alliance (HPA), and fundraising collaborations with 21, 24; study of 18; YouTube, videos posted by 24

Netanyahu, Benjamin 1

new media literacies: alternative and activist new media 36–7; blogging 33–4; definition of 32–3; digital story projects 36; experiential learning 34–6; genres of participation 34; group presentations 34; participatory culture, and role in 33; social action student projects, and digital media 42–8, 44t–5t; and social media platforms 4, 32–33; student courses, student information and participation 37–42, 38t, 40t–41t; 'technology-rich' environments, and poster projects 34–36, 35

Occupy movement 94

Ok, HyeRyoung 22

O'Leary, Ellin 24

Otra Beta art movement (Venezuela) 100

Palestine: 5 Broken Cameras (Burnat, Emad) 110, 121–3; Al-Nakba 111; anti-colonial movements and political protest 2, 5, 109, 113–15; 'bare life' existence 109, 111, 113; Bil'in, flower garden at and protests held in 109–10, 121–2; citizens, and status of 114; cultural resistance practices 110–11, 117; First Intifada 112; incarceration of political prisoners 112; Israeli state violence, and evidence for 2, 111–12, 115–17; Joint Advocacy Initiative 112; Olso Accords (1993) 111; resistance activities, and history of 113; right to protest, and restrictions of 114–15; Shooting Back camera project (B'Tselem) 118–20; Status of Youth in Palestine Report (2009) 111; video documentation of state violence, youth protest and political participation 2, 5, 6, 110, 111, 115, 118–21; women, treatment of by occupying forces 120–21; Youth Against the Settlements organization 110, 120–21; youth political engagement 110, 111–12

Pantaleo, Daniel 1

participatory politics 3–4; in anti-colonial and occupation contexts 109, 110, 113–17; citizen journalism, as form of 110, 115, 118–19; definition of 113; digital age, and impact on 23; glyph production 129–34; graffiti and spatial tagging practices 129–34; Palestinian youth, and forms of engagement 109, 111, 112; pedagogy, as central to 30–31; and politics of refusal 114–15, 116–17, 123; social media, and influence of 3; and youth political engagement 3, 4, 23

pedagogy: critical pedagogy of art, and youth engagement 105; design-based action research projects, and limitations of 31–2, 48–9; ethics and social movements 65; instructor/researcher participation 37–42; new media literacies, and teaching of 32–7; participatory politics, and centrality of 30–31; and public engagement and events 38–9, 39, 54–6, 64–5; public pedagogy, and popular culture 117, 123–125; social action projects, and digital media 42–8, 44t–5t; social change and public influence 64–6

Pile, S. 139

Project HIP-HOP 5, 69, 77–8; case study (2011-12) 77–8; Civil Rights Tour program 82; development of 77; and justice-oriented cultural citizenship 83; political education, and analysis of 79; and power in the cultural domain 79–81; social movements, role in and impact on 85–6

protest space 57–60

Protesta Creativa Venezuela 98–9

Puerto Rico see also student strike (2010, University of Puerto Rico); countrywide challenges, and connections to student strike (2010) 54–5; Política de no Confrontacíon (No-Confrontation Policy) 57; political action in the public sphere, and history of 52–3

Rancière, J. 55, 61

Rebollo Gil, Guillermo 59

Redada, youth colectivos consortium (Venezuela) 100–01

Rojas, Lena 80

Rose, Tricia 131, 138

Shirky, Clay 23

Simpson, Audra 114

Simpson, Leanne 142

Slack, Andrew 18

social media 4, 32–3 see also new media literacies; and 24/7 connectivity 20

Solá, Aura Colón 61

Star-Craft II gaming community 20; Doctors Without Borders, and money-raising activities 20, 21

state violence 1–2; anti-colonial movements and political protest 2, 5, 109; Israel, and evidence for 2, 5, 111–12, 115–17; and police brutality 1

Stevenson, N. 73, 81

student strike (2010, University of Puerto Rico) 4–5, 52–4; background to 52; clown police (los payasos policías), role in 57–8; countrywide challenges, and connections to 54–5; creative strategies for 53–4; de luto por el fallecimiento de la educación pública (street performance) 61–2, 62; death of the university, trope of and allegorical references to 60–64; el Comité de Acció de Humandiades (Humanities Action

Committee) 54; Electrical Industry and Irrigation Workers Union, role in 58; flowers, and deployment of 61–4, *63*; 'letter to the country' 54; open mic sessions 58–60; protest space, and reconfiguring of 57–60; and public pedagogy 55–6; *Rojo Gallito* (student journalist collective) 61

'survivance,' as form of resistance 2

Theatre of the Oppressed (Boal, Augusto) 79, 80–81

'This is how we shoot back' flash mob event (Times Square, New York) 2

University of California 18

University of Puerto Rico: *Política de no Confrontación* (No-Confrontation Policy) 57; political action in the public sphere, and history of 52–3; student strike 4–5, 52–4

urban flash mob round dances (Canada) 139; as geographies of resistance 135–40; Idle No More movement 1, 2, 6, 129, 136–8, *137*; participants of 143n6; as political protest, spiritual and cultural implications of 140; round dance ceremonies, and origins of 135–6, 138

Venezuela: Bolivarian revolution, support for and opposition to 95, 96, 97; *Caracazo* incident 95–6; Colectivo Alexis Vive 102–3, *103*; *colectivos*, and cultural productions of 5, 7–8, 95, 99–103, *102–3*, 104; colonization, and decolonial thought 93, 95, 101, 104–6; constitutional reform (1999) 96–7; Organic Law of Popular Power, and youth involvement 96; *Otra Beta* art movement 100; *Protesta Creativa Venezuela* 98–9; *Redada*, youth *colectivos* consortium 100–01; Student Opposition Protests, 2014 (Day of Youth) 97–8; unrest and social transformation in 94–5; youth cultural identity in, and development of 96–7; and youth political engagement 5, 93

video documentation, and political participation 115, 120–21

Vizenor, Gerald 2

Walking with our Sisters (Belcourt, Christi) 6, 129, 132, 133, 134–5; Thunderbay (Ontario), installation of 134; vamps, as spatial tags 135

Watts, Daniel J. 2

Welch, Peedub 84

White-Hammond, Mariama 80, 83–4

Wiles, R. 112

Williams, D. Ferai 81, 82

Williams, Jalen 80

Willis, Paul 2, 117, 124

Yakobovich, Oren 118, 119, 121

Youth Against the Settlements organization 110; video documentation of state violence, and political participation (Palestine) 120–21

Youth and Participatory Politics Research Networks (YPP) 16; Media, Activism, and Participatory Politics (MAPP) project 16

youth political engagement 3; affinity networks and 'spaces' 14–15, 17, 23; alternative and activist new media 36–37; in anti-colonial and occupation contexts 110, 111–112; and 'connected civics' 4, 8, 10–11, 13–14, 15–16, *15*; connecting learning, and in-school/out-of-school relationships 13; 'consequential transitions,' and mechanisms of 14; gaming communities, and social connections relating to 20; 'hashtag activism' 13; hybrid content worlds, and narrative connections 17–19; and identity formation 4, 5; networked technologies and 'ecosystems' 4, 10–11; new media literacies 4; new media literacies, and role in 32–33; Palestine, and forms of 109; and participatory politics 3, 4; shared practice, and building of 19–23; social media platforms and 24/7 connectivity 20; and the sociology of youth 5; in Venezuela 5

Youth Radio (Oakland, California) 24–25; and adult collaborations 25; Double Charged project 25; investigative unit of 25; Youth Desk (National Public Radio) 24

youth rebellion *see also* youth political engagement; art practices of 94; background to 93–94

Youth Speaks: Brave New Voices network 18; Center for Investigative Reporting (California), collaboration with 18–19; University of California, collaborative projects with 18

Zimmerman, Arely, 17

'zombie' politics and performance 99

Zuckerman, Ethan 17–18